# Adobe Flash Professional CC: A Tutorial Approach

**CADCIM Technologies**

*525 St. Andrews Drive*
*Schererville, IN 46375, USA*
*(www.cadcim.com)*

*Contributing Author*

**Sham Tickoo**

*Professor*
*Purdue University Calumet*
*Hammond, Indiana, USA*

**CADCIM Technologies**

**Adobe Flash Professional CC: A Tutorial Approach**
**Sham Tickoo**

ISBN  978-1-936646-62-3

www.cadcim.com

## DEDICATION

*To teachers, who make it possible to disseminate knowledge
to enlighten the young and curious minds
of our future generations*

*To students, who are dedicated to learning new technologies
and making the world a better place to live in*

## THANKS

*To employees of CADCIM Technologies for their valuable help*

# Online Training Program Offered by CADCIM Technologies

*CADCIM Technologies provides effective and affordable virtual online training on various software packages including Computer Aided Design and Manufacturing (CAD/CAM), computer programming languages, animation and visual effects, architecture, and GIS. The training is delivered 'live' via Internet at any time, any place, and at any pace to individuals as well as the students of colleges, universities, and CAD/CAM training centers. The main features of this program are:*

## Training for Students and Companies in a Classroom Setting

*Highly experienced instructors and qualified Engineers at CADCIM Technologies conduct the classes under the guidance of Prof. Sham Tickoo of Purdue University Calumet, USA. This team has authored several textbooks that are rated "one of the best" in their categories and are used in various colleges, universities, and training centers in North America, Europe, and in other parts of the world.*

## Training for Individuals

*CADCIM Technologies with its cost effective and time saving initiative strives to deliver the training in the comfort of your home or work place, thereby relieving you from the hassles of traveling to training centers.*

## Training Offered on Software Packages

*CADCIM provides basic and advanced training on the following software packages:*

***CAD/CAM/CAE***: *CATIA, Pro/ENGINEER Wildfire, SolidWorks, Autodesk Inventor, Solid Edge, NX, AutoCAD, AutoCAD LT, Customizing AutoCAD, EdgeCAM, Creo Parametric, ANSYS, and Autodesk Simulation Mechanical*

***Computer Programming***: *C++, VB.NET, Oracle, AJAX, and Java*

***Animation and Styling***: *Autodesk 3ds Max, Autodesk 3ds Max Design, Autodesk Maya, eyeon Fusion, Adobe Flash, and Autodesk Alias Design*

***Architecture, Civil, and GIS***: *Autodesk Revit Architecture, AutoCAD Civil 3D, Autodesk Revit Structure, AutoCAD Map 3D, STAAD Pro, and Revit MEP*

*For more information, please visit the following link:*

*www.cadcim.com*

---

**Note**

If you are a faculty member, you can register by clicking on the following link to access the teaching resources: ***http://www.cadcim.com/Registration.aspx***. The student resources are available at ***www.cadcim.com***. We also provide **Live Virtual Online Training** on various software packages. For more information, write us at ***sales@cadcim.com***.

# Table of Contents

## Project 2

## Index                                                    I-1

# Preface

## Adobe Flash Professional CC

**Adobe Flash Professional CC** is a multimedia platform for creating digital animation, rich web applications, websites, movies as well as content for mobile phones, and other embedded devices. It is frequently used for creating advertisements and games. Some of the most popular games made in Flash are Minesweeper, Pac Man, Tetris, and Bejewelled. Flash has also been used to create many popular movies and series such as Off-Mikes, Gotham Girls, CrimeTime, and Homestar Runner.

**Adobe Flash Professional CC: A Tutorial Approach** textbook introduces the readers to the Adobe Flash Professional CC, one of the world's leading 2D graphics, animation, and web design and development software. This textbook covers all the features of Adobe Flash Professional CC. In this textbook, the author emphasizes on the 2D drawings, animation, web page design and development, Android App development, ActionScript 3.0, sound and videos, and exporting and publishing for web.

This textbook will help you unleash your creativity, thus enabling you to transform your imagination into reality with ease. The textbook caters to the needs of both novice and advanced users of the software. Written with the tutorial point-of-view and learn-by-doing theme, this textbook is ideally suited for learning at your convenience and pace.

The salient features of this textbook are as follows:

- **Tutorial Approach**
  The author has adopted tutorial point-of-view and learn-by-doing approach throughout the textbook. This approach helps the users learn the concepts and techniques quickly and easily.

- **Tips and Notes**
  Additional information related to various topics is provided to the users in the form of tips and notes.

- **Learning Objectives**
  The first page of every chapter summarizes the topics that will be covered in that chapter. This will help the users to easily refer to a topic.

• **Self-Evaluation Test, Review Questions, and Exercises**

Every chapter ends with a Self-Evaluation Test so that the users can assess their knowledge of the chapter. The answers to the Self-Evaluation Test are given at the end of the chapter. Also, Review Questions and Exercises are given at the end of each chapter and they can be used by the Instructors as test questions and exercises.

• **Screen Captures**

About 600 screen captures are given throughout the textbook to facilitate the understanding of various concepts.

## Conventions Used in this Textbook

### Tip

Special information and techniques are provided in the form of tips that helps in increasing the efficiency of the users.

### Note

The author has provided additional information to the users about the topic being discussed in the form of notes.

## Formatting Conventions Used in the Text

Please refer to the following list for the formatting conventions used in this textbook.

| | |
|---|---|
| • Names of tools, buttons, options, areas, panels, button, and tabs are written in boldface. | Example: The **Selection Tool**, the **Position and Size** area, the **Properties** panel, the **Library** panel, the **Publish Settings** button, and so on. |
| • Names of dialog boxes, windows, drop-down lists, text boxes, edit boxes, areas, check boxes, radio buttons, and hexadecimal value of colors are written in boldface. | Example: The **Document Settings** dialog box, the **Family** drop-down list, the **Size** edit box in the **Character** area, the **Align** area, the **Auto-Save** check box, the **Default** radio button, and so on. |
| • Values entered in edit boxes and names typed in text boxes are in boldface. | Example: Enter the value **0.2** in the **Stroke** edit box. |
| • The methods of invoking a tool/option from the menubar. | Example: Choose **Modify > Transform > Flip Horizontal** from the menubar. |

# Naming Conventions Used in the Text

Please refer to the following list for the naming conventions used in this textbook.

## Tool

If you click on an item in the **Tools** panel and a command is invoked to create/edit an object or perform some action then that item is termed as **Tool**.

For example:
**Selection Tool, Subselection Tool, Gradient Transform Tool , Lasso Tool, Text Tool, Pen Tool, Line Tool**

## Button

The item in a dialog box and panel that is rectangular in shape like a button is termed as **Button**. For example, **OK** button, **Cancel** button, **Save** button, and so on. If the item in a dialog box or window is used to exit a tool or a mode, it is also termed as **Button**. For example, **OK** button, **Close** button, **Yes** button, and so on, refer to Figure 1.

*Figure 1  Choosing the **OK** button in the **Tool Settings** dialog box*

## Dialog Box

In this textbook, different terms are used to indicate various options of a dialog box. Refer to Figure 2 for different terminologies used in a dialog box.

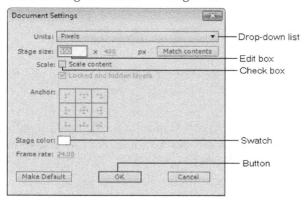

*Figure 2  Different terminologies used in a dialog box*

## Drop-down List

A drop-down list is one in which a set of options are grouped together. You can set various parameters using these options. You can identify a drop-down list with a down arrow on it. For example, **Target** drop-down list, **Script** drop-down list, and so on, refer to Figure 3.

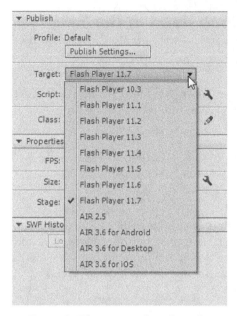

*Figure 3*   *The* ***Target*** *drop-down list*

## Options

Options are the items that are available in shortcut menus, drop-down lists, dialog boxes, and so on, refer to Figure 4.

*Figure 4*   *Choosing the* ***Marker Range 2*** *option from the flyout*

## Flyouts

A flyout is the one in which a set of common tools are grouped together. You can identify a flyout with a black triangle displayed next to a tool. A flyout is given a name based on the tools grouped in them, refer to Figure 5.

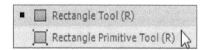

*Figure 5*   *Choosing the* ***Rectangle Primitive Tool***
*from the flyout*

# Free Companion Website

It has been our constant endeavor to provide you the best textbooks and services at affordable price. In this endeavor, we have come out with a free companion website that will facilitate the process of teaching and learning of **Adobe Flash Professional CC**. If you purchase **Adobe Flash Professional CC: A Tutorial Approach** textbook from our website (*www.cadcim.com*), you will get access to the files on the companion website.

The following resources are available for the faculty and students in this website:

## Faculty Resources

- **Technical Support**

  You can get online technical support by contacting *techsupport@cadcim.com*.

- **Instructor Guide**

  Solutions to all review questions in the textbook are provided in this guide to help the faculty members test the skills of the students.

- **PowerPoint Presentations**

  The contents of the book are arranged in PowerPoint slides that can be used by the faculty for their lectures.

- **Flash Files**

  Flash files created in tutorials are available for free download.

- **Exercise Files**

  Solution to exercises are available for free download.

- **Rendered Images and Media Files**

  The media files used in the tutorials and rendered images of all tutorials are provided in the CADCIM website. You can use these images to compare the with your rendered images.

- **Additional Resources**

  You can access additional learning resources by visiting http://adobeflashexperts.blogspot.com.

- **Colored Images**

  You can download the PDF file containing color images of the screenshots used in this textbook from the CADCIM website.

## Student Resources

- **Technical Support**

  You can get online technical support by contacting *techsupport@cadcim.com*.

- **Flash Files**

  Flash files created in the tutorials are available for free download.

- **Rendered Images and Media Files**
    The media files used in the tutorials and rendered images of all the tutorials are provided in the CADCIM website. You can use these images to compare them with your rendered images.

- **Additional Resources**
    You can access additional learning resources by visiting http://adobeflashexperts.blogspot.com.

- **Colored Images**
    You can download the PDF file containing color images of the screenshots used in this textbook from the CADCIM website.

## Stay Connected

You can now stay connected with us through Facebook, Linkedin, Pinterest, and Twitter to get the latest information about our textbooks, videos, and teaching/learning resources. To stay informed of such updates, follow us on Facebook *(www.facebook.com/cadcim)*, Linkedin *(http://in.linkedin.com/in/Cadcim)*, Pinterest *(www.pinterest.com/cadcimtech)*, and Twitter *(@cadcimtech)*. You can also subscribe to our YouTube channel *(www.youtube.com/cadcimtech)* to get the information about our latest video tutorials.

If you face any problem in accessing these files, please contact the publisher at *sales@cadcim.com* or the author at *stickoo@purduecal.edu* or *tickoo525@gmail.com*.

# Chapter *1*

# *Introduction to Adobe Flash Professional CC*

## Learning Objectives

**After completing this chapter, you will be able to:**
- *Understand the Adobe Flash Professional CC interface*
- *Work with various panels in Adobe Flash Professional CC*
- *Import images and sounds*
- *Undo and redo steps in Adobe Flash Professional CC*
- *Save and preview the artwork*
- *Find online resources for Adobe Flash Professional CC*

# INTRODUCTION

Adobe Flash Professional CC is a part of the Adobe Creative Cloud. With the help of Creative Cloud, you can access all the Adobe creative tools and services. It also has a library of video tutorials to enhance the learning process. Moreover, you can access the Sync services, 20GB of online storage, the behance community hub, and updates (the moment they are released) to all programs.

The Flash Professional CC allows you to share your artwork within the application and sync across multiple devices. This application, however, runs from your desktop, not in the browser or in the cloud. It is re-engineered with 64-bit architecture and a new streamlined user interface. The modular architecture of the software allows you to work on multiple large files and publish them faster.

The Flash Professional CC also enables you export the content in full high-definition videos and audios. The HTML5 support in Flash Professional CC has been enhanced. You can use the updated **Toolkit for CreateJS** option available in the **Window** menu to create better HTML5 content. You can also manage large backgrounds or elements using the unlimited pasteboard size supported in Flash Professional CC.

In this chapter, you will learn to start Adobe Flash Professional CC, create a new Flash CC document, and get familiar with Adobe Flash Professional CC interface. You will also learn to work with various panels.

# STARTING Adobe Flash Professional CC

To start Adobe Flash Professional CC, choose the **Start** button on the taskbar; the **Start** menu will be displayed. Next, choose **All Programs > Adobe Flash Professional CC** from the **Start** menu, as shown in Figure 1-1; the **Adobe Flash Professional CC** welcome screen will be displayed, as shown in Figure 1-2.

To create a new Flash CC document, choose **ActionScript 3.0** from the **Create New** area of the welcome screen. Alternatively, choose **File > New** from the menubar; the **New Document** dialog box will be displayed, as shown in Figure 1-3. In this dialog box, choose **ActionScript 3.0** from the **General** tab and then choose the **OK** button; a new flash file will be created.

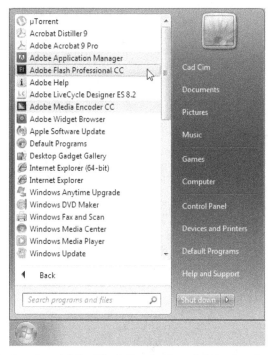

*Figure 1-1* *Starting **Adobe Flash Professional CC** using the **Start** menu*

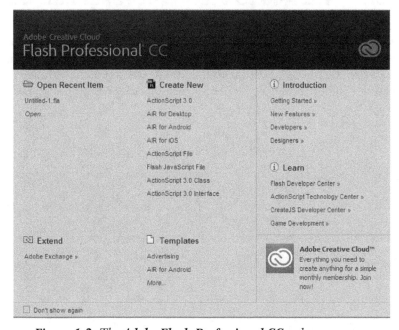

*Figure 1-2* *The **Adobe Flash Professional CC** welcome screen*

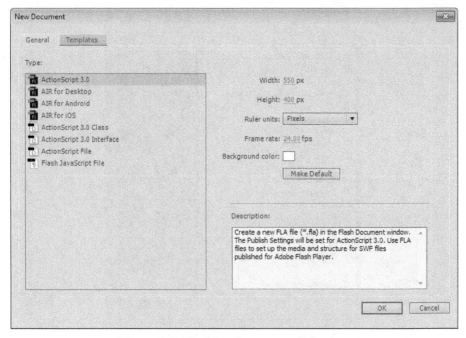

*Figure 1-3*  *The **New Document** dialog box*

# EXPLORING THE Adobe Flash Professional CC INTERFACE

The interface of Flash CC consists of a Stage, **Tools** panel, **Timeline** panel, **Properties** panel, menubar, and application bar, as shown in Figure 1-4. Using the tools in this interface, you can create interactive websites and digital animations as well as edit and add elements to your movie. You can also import files from Adobe Illustrator, Adobe Photoshop, and Adobe After Effects in Flash CC.

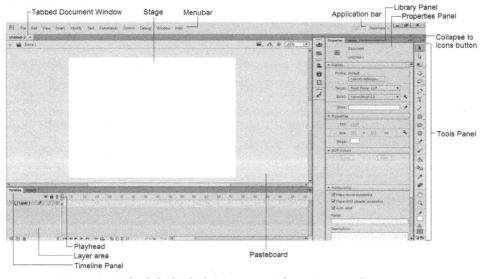

*Figure 1-4*  *The default Flash CC screen with various panels*

## Workspace

In Flash CC, the main screen is called the Application screen. In Flash CC, there are several workspace profile presets, which allow you to change the layout and arrangement of the panels based on your primary usage. You can also arrange panels based on your requirement and save the current interface as your workspace. To save the current arrangement of panels as your workspace, choose the Workspace switcher button from the application bar; a flyout will be displayed. In this flyout, choose the **New Workspace** option, as shown in Figure 1-5. The **New Workspace** dialog box will be displayed. Next, type the name of the workspace in the **Name** text box and then choose the **OK** button; the current arrangement of panels will be saved with the name that you specified in the dialog box and it becomes the active workspace. You can also choose the preset workspace from the workspace flyout. Various components of the Flash CC interface are discussed next.

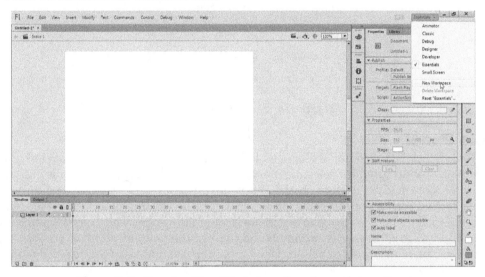

*Figure 1-5  Choosing **New Workspace** from the workspace flyout*

## Stage

The Stage is an area where all activities are performed that the viewers see when a movie is being played. The gray area surrounding the Stage is called Pasteboard. Anything in the Pasteboard is not visible in the final output. You can change the color and size of the Stage by using the options in the **New Document** dialog box and the **Properties** panel, refer to Figures 1-3 and 1-6.

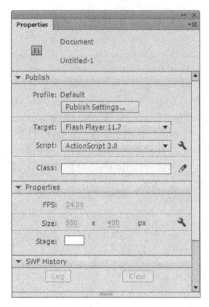

*Figure 1-6  The **Properties** panel*

## Tools Panel

The **Tools** panel is divided into six sections, refer to Figure 1-7. The Selection section consists of the tools that are used for selecting an object or part of an object. The Drawing section consists of tools that are used to create objects, text, shapes, and decorative patterns. The Editing section consists of tools that are used to edit the existing object. The View section consists of tools that are used to pan and zoom in/out in the Stage. The Color section consists of tools that are used to specify or modify the color of the border and fill of an object. The Options section of the **Tools** panel displays the options and modes of the selected tool.

In Flash, the outline of an object is called stroke and the color filled inside an object is called fill. The black triangle next to a tool indicates that there are some more hidden tools in the respective tool category. These tools are called hidden tools. To display the hidden tools, press and hold the left mouse button on that tool; a flyout will be displayed with all the hidden tools. The various tools in the **Tools** panel are discussed next.

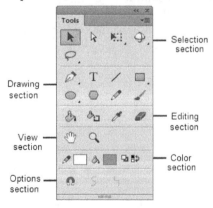

*Figure 1-7  The **Tools** panel*

## Selection Tool

 The **Selection Tool** is used to select an object, group of objects, strokes, and fills. To select an object, choose **Selection Tool** and then click on the object. Alternatively, invoke the tool and marquee select the object. The options displayed in the Options section of the **Tools** panel on invoking the **Selection Tool** are discussed next.

### Snap to Objects

 On choosing the **Snap to Objects** option, the objects that you move in the Stage jump to the edge of the nearest object.

### Smooth

 The **Smooth** option is used to smoothen the edges of the selected object.

### Straighten

 The **Straighten** option is used to sharpen the edges of the selected object.

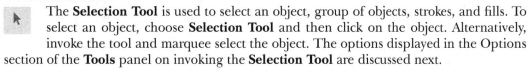 **Note**
*When you invoke a tool, the properties of that tool are displayed in the **Properties** panel.*

## Subselection Tool

 The **Subselection Tool** is used to change the shape of an object.

## Free Transform Tool

 The **Free Transform Tool** is used to rotate, move, skew, and distort an object. The options displayed in the Options section of the **Tools** panel on invoking the **Free Transform Tool** are discussed next.

### Rotate and Skew

 The **Rotate and Skew** option is used to rotate and give an oblique direction to the selected object.

### Scale

 The **Scale** option is used to scale the selected object.

### Distort

 The **Distort** option is used to deform the shape of an object by dragging individual transform points. On invoking this option, each transform point can be moved individually in all directions.

### Envelope

The **Envelope** option is used to manipulate the shape of an object. It creates an envelope of transform points around the object. Each transform point can move independently with respect to other transform points.

## Gradient Transform Tool

 The **Gradient Transform Tool** is used to scale, rotate, and change the direction of the gradient fill in an object. This tool is located in the flyout that is displayed when you press and hold the left mouse button on **Free Transform Tool**.

## 3D Rotation Tool

 The **3D Rotation Tool** is used to create an impression of 3D in Flash CC. With the help of this tool, you can position the object at an angle and rotate it about any axis, refer to Figure 1-8.

## 3D Translation Tool

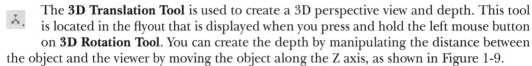 The **3D Translation Tool** is used to create a 3D perspective view and depth. This tool is located in the flyout that is displayed when you press and hold the left mouse button on **3D Rotation Tool**. You can create the depth by manipulating the distance between the object and the viewer by moving the object along the Z axis, as shown in Figure 1-9.

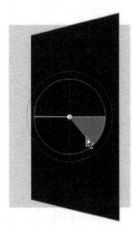
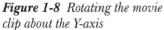

*Figure 1-8* Rotating the movie clip about the Y-axis

*Figure 1-9* Translating the movie clip along the Z-axis

## Lasso Tool

 The **Lasso Tool** is used to select an object or a part of it by creating outlines. When you press and hold the left mouse button on this tool, a flyout will be displayed containing the **Magic Wand** tool and the **Polygon Tool**.

## Magic Wand

 The **Magic Wand** tool is used to select the areas that contain similar colors.

## Polygon Tool

 The **Polygon Tool** is used to select an object or an area by creating linear and interconnected lines.

## Pen Tool

 The **Pen Tool** is used to draw shapes and paths. All the path and shape objects are built from a series of anchor points. You can modify the path by clicking on it and then manipulating the anchor points. When you press and hold the left mouse button on this tool, a flyout will be displayed containing the tools **Add Anchor Point Tool**, **Delete Anchor Point Tool**, and **Convert Anchor Point Tool**.

## Add Anchor Point Tool

 The **Add Anchor Point Tool** is used to add an anchor point to the path. For adding a new anchor point on a path, select the path and then choose **Add Anchor Point Tool**. Next, click on the point in the path where you want to add a new anchor point.

## Delete Anchor Point Tool

 The **Delete Anchor Point Tool** is used to delete anchor points. To delete an anchor point, choose **Delete Anchor Point Tool** and then click on the anchor point that you want to delete.

## Convert Anchor Point Tool

 The **Convert Anchor Point Tool** is used to break the handle of an anchor point into two handles that can be moved independently with respect to each other. To do so, choose **Convert Anchor Point Tool**. Next, select the anchor point and then click on the endpoint of the handle to convert it into two independent handles.

## Object Drawing

The **Object Drawing** button is a toggle button. By default, this button is not chosen. When a drawing tool is in the **Object Drawing** mode, the stroke and fill of an object are not separate elements and the shapes that overlap in the same layer do not alter one another if you move them apart, reposition, or rearrange.

## Text Tool

 The **Text Tool** is used to write text as a vector object. To create a text object, choose **Text Tool** and then drag the cursor in the Stage; a text box will be displayed in the Stage. Now, you can write the text in the text box.

## Line Tool

 The **Line Tool** is used to draw a straight line segment. To create a line, choose **Line Tool**, press and hold the left mouse button, and drag the cursor in the Stage; a straight line segment will be created in the Stage.

## Rectangle Tool

 The **Rectangle Tool** is used to draw a rectangular shape. To draw a rectangular shape, choose **Rectangle Tool**, press and hold the left mouse button, and then drag the cursor in the Stage; a rectangle will be created in the Stage.

## Rectangle Primitive Tool

 This tool is located in the flyout which is displayed when you press and hold the left mouse button on the **Rectangle Tool.** Similar to the **Rectangle Tool**, the **Rectangle Primitive Tool** is also used to draw a rectangular shape with the only difference that the corner radius of the rectangular shape drawn by this tool is modifiable. To draw a rectangle, choose **Rectangle Primitive Tool**. Next, press and hold the left mouse button and then drag the cursor in the Stage; a rectangular shape will be created in the Stage. You can change its corner radius by specifying values in the **Rectangle Options** area of the **Properties** panel, as shown in Figure 1-10.

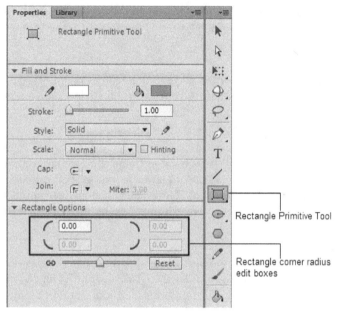

*Figure 1-10 The* ***Rectangle Options*** *area of the* ***Rectangle Primitive Tool***

## Oval Tool

The **Oval Tool** is used to draw an oval shape. To draw an oval shape, choose **Oval Tool**, press and hold the left mouse button, and then drag the cursor in the Stage; an oval shape will be created in the Stage.

## Oval Primitive Tool

This tool is located in the flyout that is displayed when you press and hold the left mouse button on the **Oval Tool.** Similar to the **Oval Tool**, the **Oval Primitive Tool**, is also used to create an oval shape with the only difference that you can change the start angle, end angle, and inner radius of the oval shape by specifying the options in the **Oval Options** area of the **Properties** panel.

## PolyStar Tool

The **PolyStar Tool** is used to draw the polygon and star shaped objects. On invoking this tool, the **Options** button is displayed in the **Properties** panel. On choosing the **Options** button, the **Tool Settings** dialog box will be displayed, refer to Figure 1-11. Using the options in this dialog box, you can change the style, number of sides, and star point size of the polygon and star shaped objects.

*Figure 1-11  The Tool Settings dialog box*

## Pencil Tool

The **Pencil Tool** is used to draw lines and shapes. The options displayed in the Options section on invoking the **Pencil Tool** are discussed next.

### Straighten

The **Straighten** mode is used to draw straight lines.

### Smooth

The **Smooth** mode is used to draw smooth curved lines.

### Ink

The **Ink** mode is used to draw freehand lines.

## Brush Tool

The **Brush Tool** is used to draw brush-like strokes. The options displayed on invoking the **Brush Tool** are **Brush Mode**, **Brush Size**, and **Brush Shape**. You can change the mode, size, and shape of the brush by using these options, refer to Figure 1-12.

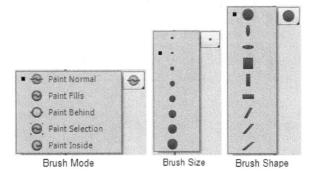

*Figure 1-12  The Brush Tool options*

## Paint Bucket Tool

 The **Paint Bucket Tool** is used to apply the fill (solid, gradient, or bitmap) to a closed path or area.

## Ink Bottle Tool

 The **Ink Bottle Tool** is used to change the color, width, and style of the stroke.

## Eyedropper Tool

 The **Eyedropper Tool** is used to pick the fill and stroke hexadecimal values.

## Eraser Tool

 The **Eraser Tool** is used to erase a section of the artwork in the Stage. There are several options of the **Eraser Tool**, refer to Figure 1-13.

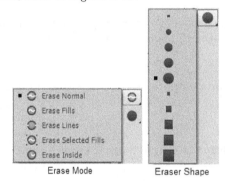

*Figure 1-13  The **Eraser Tool** options*

 **Note**
*When the **Faucet** (⚲) option of the **Eraser Tool** is selected, on clicking even on a part of the stroke or fill, the entire stroke or fill is erased. Therefore, make sure the **Faucet** option is not selected unless you want to delete entire fill or stroke.*

## Hand Tool

 The **Hand Tool** is used to move the Stage in all the directions without affecting the magnification. This tool allows you to pan the Stage along the X and Y axes.

## Zoom Tool

 The **Zoom Tool** is used to magnify (zoom in) and demagnify (zoom out) the Stage. The options displayed on invoking the **Zoom Tool** are discussed next.

### Enlarge

 The **Enlarge** option is used to zoom in the Stage.

### Reduce

 The **Reduce** option is used to zoom out the Stage.

## Stroke Color

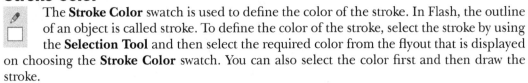 The **Stroke Color** swatch is used to define the color of the stroke. In Flash, the outline of an object is called stroke. To define the color of the stroke, select the stroke by using the **Selection Tool** and then select the required color from the flyout that is displayed on choosing the **Stroke Color** swatch. You can also select the color first and then draw the stroke.

## Fill Color

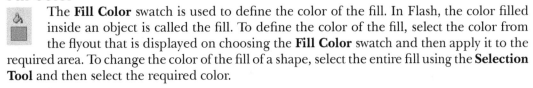 The **Fill Color** swatch is used to define the color of the fill. In Flash, the color filled inside an object is called the fill. To define the color of the fill, select the color from the flyout that is displayed on choosing the **Fill Color** swatch and then apply it to the required area. To change the color of the fill of a shape, select the entire fill using the **Selection Tool** and then select the required color.

## Black and white

 The **Black and white** button is used to redefine the stroke color as black and the fill color as white.

## Swap colors

 The **Swap colors** button is used to swap the stroke color to fill the color and vice-versa.

# Timeline Panel

The animations and drawings in the Stage or Pasteboard are reflected automatically in the Timeline. The **Timeline** panel consists of layers, frames, Playhead, and few other components, as shown in Figure 1-14. The Timeline Header in the **Timeline** panel displays the frame numbers and the Playhead indicates the current frame displayed in the Stage. Various options in the **Timeline** panel are discussed next.

## New Layer

The **New Layer** button is used to create a new layer.

## New Folder

The **New Folder** button is used to create a new folder that can be used to organize layers.

## Delete

The **Delete** button is used to delete the selected layer.

## Go to first frame

The **Go to first frame** button is used to place the Playhead on frame **1** in the **Timeline** panel.

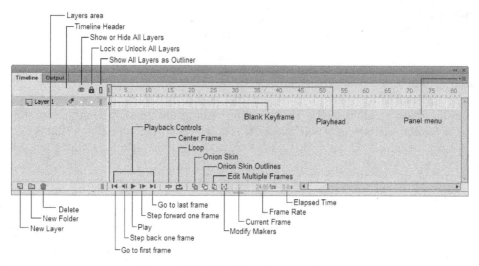

*Figure 1-14* *The* **Timeline** *panel*

## Step back one frame

The **Step back one frame** button is used to move the Playhead backward by one frame from the current frame.

## Play

The **Play** button is used to play the animation in the Stage.

## Step forward one frame

The **Step forward one frame** button is used to move the Playhead forward by one frame from the current frame.

## Go to last frame

The **Go to last frame** button is used to place the Playhead on last frame of the animation in the **Timeline** panel.

## Center Frame

The **Center Frame** option is used to center the Timeline on the current frame.

## Loop

The **Loop** button is used to specify a range of frames to play repeatedly during animation.

## Onion Skin

In traditional animation method, light desks or light tables were used that let you see through multiple layers of paper due to transparencies and the ink lines standing out clearly laid on top of one another.

Flash has an equivalent option of the light table known as onion-skinning. The **Onion Skin** button allows you to view a range of frames both before and after the current frame, progressively fading them out as if they are layered on translucent paper on top of each other. By dragging the edges of the grayed block in the Timeline (Start Onion Skin and End Onion Skin markers) you can expand or reduce the number of frames displayed in the onion-skin mode, refer to Figure 1-15.

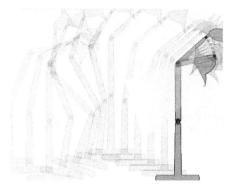

*Figure 1-15* *The frames in the onion skin mode*

## Onion Skin Outlines

The **Onion Skin Outlines** button is used to display the objects on the frames between Start Onion Skin and End Onion Skin markers as outlines, refer to Figure 1-16. The onion skin outlines mode is used for long and detailed animations.

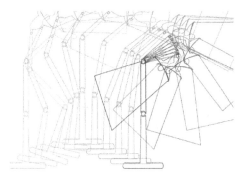

*Figure 1-16* *The frames in the onion skin outlines mode*

## Edit Multiple Frames

The **Edit Multiple Frames** button is used to enable editing of all frames between Onion Skin markers.

## Modify Markers

The **Modify Markers** button is a part of the Onion Skin. It is used to control the number of frames before and after the current frame that will be displayed in Onion Skin overlay. On choosing this button, a flyout is displayed, as shown in Figure 1-17. In this flyout, choose the required range of markers. The options in this flyout are discussed next.

*Figure 1-17   The Modify*
*Markers flyout*

### Always Show Markers

The **Always Show Markers** option is used to display the Onion Skin markers whether or not the **Onion Skin** is on.

### Anchor Markers

The **Anchor Markers** option is used to lock the Onion Skin markers to their current position in the Timeline Header.

### Shift Marker Range

The **Shift Marker Range** option is used to move the loop markers to different positions.

### Marker Range 2

The **Marker Range 2** option is used to apply markers on two frames on either side of the current frame.

### Marker Range 5

The **Marker Range 5** option is used to apply markers on five frames on either side of the current frame.

### Marker Range All

The **Marker Range All** option is used to apply markers to all frames.

### Get Loop Playback Range

The **Get Loop Playback Range** option is used to reset the range of loop markers to its default state.

## Current Frame

The **Current Frame** option displays the frame on which the Playhead is placed. You can also scrub the Current Frame value to place the Playhead on the required frame.

## Frame Rate

The **Frame Rate** option is used to specify the speed at which the movie will be played. By default, the frame rate is set to 24 frames per second. You can change the frame rate from the **Properties** panel, the **Timeline** panel or the **New Document** dialog box.

## Elapsed Time

The **Elapsed Time** option is used to display the time that has elapsed in your animation at the frame that you have selected.

### Show or Hide All Layers

The **Show or Hide All Layers** button is used to display or hide the contents of the layers.

### Lock or Unlock All Layers

The **Lock or Unlock All Layers** button is used to freeze or defreeze the layers.

 **Note**

*If a layer is frozen in the **Timeline** panel, no changes can be made in that layer.*

### Show All Layers as Outlines

The **Show All Layers as Outlines** button is used to display only the outline of the contents of the layers. You can also change the layer properties using the **Layer Properties** dialog box, refer to Figure 1-18. To invoke the **Layer Properties** dialog box, double-click on the layer icon (🗐) located on the left of the layer name in the Layer area of the **Timeline** panel.

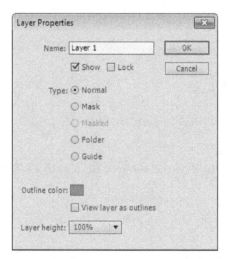

*Figure 1-18  The **Layer Properties** dialog box*

## Working with Library

The library in Flash stores all the media files, such as bitmaps, graphics, sound files, and video clips that you import and symbols that you create in a Flash document. You can organize items in the library in folders and sort them by their type. You can also open the library of the other Flash documents in the current document to make the library items available from that file.

## Library Panel

By default, the **Library** panel is located next to the **Properties** panel in the **Essentials** workspace.

 **Note**

*In Flash CC, every workspace has its own setting of panels.*

To display the **Library** panel, choose **Window > Library** from the menubar. The various parts of the **Library** panel, as shown in Figure 1-19, are discussed next.

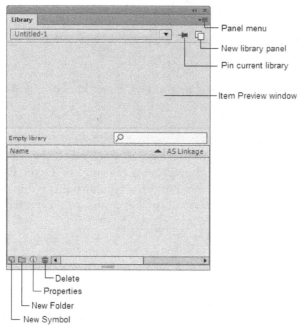

*Figure 1-19  The **Library** panel*

## Item Preview window

The **Item Preview window** displays the selected item in the **Library** panel.

## Pin current library

The **Pin current library** button is used to pin the **Library** panel to make it stay active across multiple Flash documents.

## New library panel

The **New library panel** button is used to create a new **Library** panel that will stay across multiple Flash documents but is active only in the document in which it is created.

## New Symbol

The **New Symbol** button displays the **Create New Symbol** dialog box that is used to create a new symbol.

## New Folder

The **New Folder** button is used to create a new folder in the **Library** panel.

## Properties

The **Properties** button displays the **Symbol Properties** dialog box of the selected symbol.

### Delete

The **Delete** button is used to delete the selected symbol or folder.

## Toolkit for CreateJS

In Adobe Flash Professional, the Toolkit for CreateJS is an extension for Flash Professional CC, refer to Figure 1-20. This extension is used to create assets for HTML5 projects using the open source CreateJS JavaScript libraries. The extension supports most of the features of Flash Professional, such as vectors, bitmaps, classic tweens, sounds, and JavaScript timeline scripting. The **Toolkit for CreateJS** exports the contents on the stage and in the library as JavaScript that can be previewed in the browser. You will learn more about this panel in the later chapters.

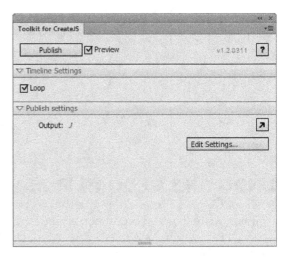

*Figure 1-20  The **Toolkit for CreateJS** panel*

**Note**

*To display this panel in the Flash document, choose **Window > Toolkit for CreateJS** from the menubar.*

# IMPORTING IMAGES

You can import images of different formats such as PNG, GIF, JPG, JPEG, and so on in Flash CC. To import an image to the Stage, choose **File > Import > Import to Stage** from the menubar; the **Import** dialog box will be displayed. In this dialog box, browse and select the required image and then choose the **Open** button. If you choose **File > Import > Import to Library** from the menubar, the image will be saved in the **Library** panel. You can drag and drop images from the **Library** panel to the Stage.

# IMPORTING SOUND

To import sound in Flash CC, choose **File > Import > Import to Library** from the menubar; the **Import to Library** dialog box will be displayed. Browse and select the sound and choose the **Open** button. To add a sound to the Timeline, choose **Insert > Timeline > Layer** from the menubar, as shown in Figure 1-21; a new layer is added in the **Timeline** panel to import sound. Drag and drop the sound from the **Library** panel in the Stage; the sound will be added to the current layer.  The sound formats that Flash CC supports are ASND, WAV, mp3, AIFF, Sun AU.

**Note**

*The ASND (Adobe Sound Document) is the built-in sound format of Adobe Soundbooth.*

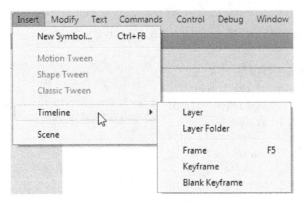

*Figure 1-21*   The **Timeline** submenu

# UNDO AND REDO IN FLASH CC

In Flash CC, you can undo and redo the actions performed by using the **Undo** and **Redo** commands. To undo an action performed earlier, choose **Edit > Undo** from the menubar or press CTRL+Z. Similarly to redo an action, choose **Edit > Redo** from the menubar or press CTRL+Y. You can also use the **History** panel to undo multiple steps. To display the **History** panel, choose **Window > History** from the menubar, refer to Figure 1-22. You can set the number of maximum undo commands based on your requirement. To do so, choose **Edit > Preferences** from the menubar; the **Preferences** dialog box will be displayed. You can set the undo levels from 2 to 300 in the **levels** edit box of the **Undo** area. Next, choose the **OK** button.

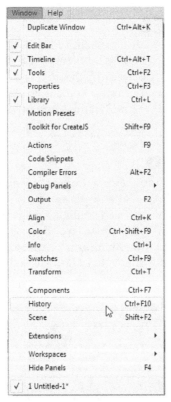

*Figure 1-22*   *Choosing the **History** panel from the window menu*

# SAVING FLASH DOCUMENT

To save a **Flash file**, choose **File > Save or Save as from the menubar**; the **Save As** dialog box will be displayed. Next, specify the name for the file and choose the **Save button**, refer to Figure 1-23. The default format for saving a flash file is FLA. However, you can change it to the XFL format.

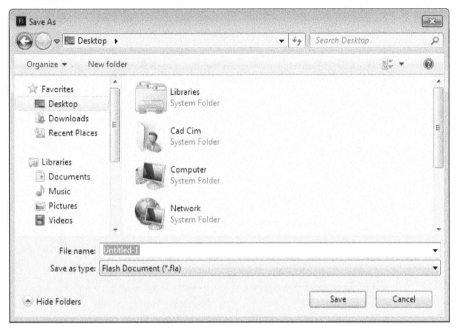

*Figure 1-23  The **Save As** dialog box*

**Note**
*The XFL file format is used to represent a Flash document as an XML document. You can open and work on an XFL file in Flash CC. After working on XFL file in Flash Professional CC, you can save it in the FLA or XFL file format.*

You can also save a Flash file by using the **Save as Template** option. To do so, choose **File > Save as Template** from the menubar; the **Save As Template Warning** message box will be displayed with a message that the SWF history data will be cleared if the file is saved as template, refer to Figure 1-24. In this message box, choose the **Save as Template** button; the **Save as Template** dialog box will be displayed, as shown in Figure 1-25. The **Save as Template** option is useful when you have created a file such as a website that you want to use later. It does not save the undo/change history of a file. As a result, the size of the file saved on your system is reduced.

Flash lets you save the file as a template that can be used later in other Flash documents. In the **Save as Template** dialog box, specify a name for the file and select the category. You can select the preset categories or create your own category. Next, give the description of the category (optional) and then choose the **Save** button.

*Figure 1-24  The **Save As Template Warning** message box*

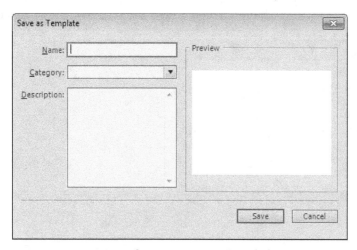

*Figure 1-25   The **Save as Template** dialog box*

# PREVIEWING YOUR WORK

You can preview your work in Flash CC to check whether you are getting the required output. To see how the final output will appear to viewers, choose **Control > Test Movie > In Flash Professional** from the menubar or press CTRL+ENTER; the **Untitled-#** preview window will be displayed, refer to Figure 1-26. The **Untitled-1** file has the .swf extension and is the rendered output of the Flash document. When you press CTRL+ENTER, Flash creates a SWF file from the FLA file. You can view the sizes of all the SWF files created from the current FLA file in the **Properties** panel.

**Note**

*For complete information about using Flash CC, make sure that you have access to the internet and then choose **Help > Flash Help** from the menubar, refer to Figure 1-27, or press the F1 key. On doing so, you will be connected to Adobe Community Help. With Adobe Community Help, you can search Flash Help and support documents.*

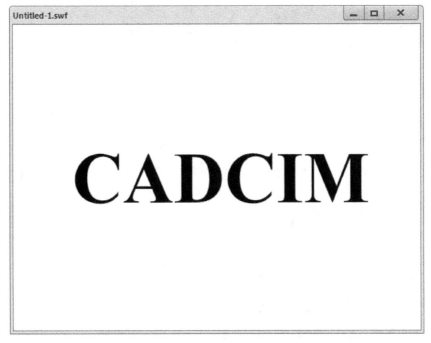

*Figure 1-26* The **Untitled-1** *preview window*

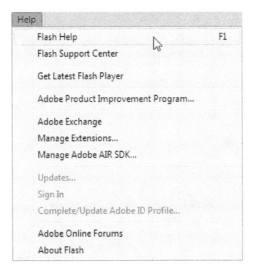

*Figure 1-27* Invoking the **Help** menu from the menubar

## Self-Evaluation Test

**Answer the following questions and then compare them to those given at the end of this chapter:**

1.  Which of the following tools is used to change the shape of an object?

    (a) **Selection Tool**              (b) **Subselection Tool**
    (c) **Line Tool**                   (d) All of these

2.  The _____ is used to scale, rotate, and change the direction of gradient fill in an object.

3.  The gray area surrounding the Stage is called _____.

4.  _____ is the keyboard shortcut for previewing the work.

5.  The _____ is the native sound format of Adobe Soundbooth.

6.  The **Zoom Tool** is used to pan the Stage along the X and Y coordinates. (T/F)

7.  The color filled inside an object is called stroke. (T/F)

8.  The Color tools that are used to change the color of the stroke and the fill of an object. (T/F)

9.  The **Ink Bottle Tool** is used to pick the attributes of the fill and the stroke from an object to apply on another object. (T/F)

10. The **Add Anchor Point Tool** is used to add an anchor point to the path. (T/F)

## Review Questions

**Answer the following questions:**

1.  Which of the following tools is used to select the areas that contain similar colors?

    (a) **Magic Wand**                  (b) **Lasso Tool**
    (c) **Polygon Tool**                (d) All of these

2.  _____ is used to draw a rectangular shape in which you can change the corner radius.

3.  The _____ key is the keyboard shortcut for accessing Flash help.

4.  The _____ displays the frame numbers.

5.  The _____ window displays the selected item in the **Library** panel.

6.  The _____ option in the **Timeline** panel displays the current frame number.

7.  The **Eyedropper Tool** is used to fill color inside an object. (T/F)

8.  The **Pen Tool** is used to draw shapes and paths. (T/F)

9.  The **Subselection Tool** is used to change the shape of an object. (T/F)

10. The **Pin current library** button is used to pin the **Library** panel to make it stay active across multiple Flash documents. (T/F)

**Answers to Self-Evaluation Test**
**1. b, 2. Gradient Transform Tool, 3.** Pasteboard, **4.** CTRL+ENTER, **5.** ASND, **6.** F, **7.** F,
**8.** T, **9.** F, **10.** T

# Chapter 2

# Working with Graphics and Text

## Learning Objectives

**After completing this chapter, you will be able to:**
- *Create vector graphics using drawing tools*
- *Modify the shape and size of the selected objects*
- *Adjust contours in a graphic*
- *Add layers to the Timeline*
- *Apply color to an object*
- *Create and edit curves*
- *Create and edit text*

# INTRODUCTION

Graphics is a representation of a two-dimensional image in binary format as a sequence of ones and zeros. It includes both vector and raster images. Vector graphics are the images produced by using geometrical primitives such as points, lines, curves, and shapes. These graphics are produced on the basis of mathematical equations, such as a circle that includes the information of radius. You can create and animate vector graphics in Flash. Vector graphics have two advantages. The first advantage is that the file size is small and it is downloaded faster and less hard drive space is utilized to save the file. The second advantage is that the image can be scaled to any size without affecting the image quality. In Flash, you can create and animate vector graphics. The other type of graphics is raster graphics. Raster graphics are the images produced by an array of pixels. Each pixel carries Color information, therefore, they are relatively large files.

# TUTORIALS

Before you start the tutorials, you need to download the *c02_flash_cc_tut.zip* file from *www.cadcim.com*. The path of the file is as follows: *Textbooks > Animation and Visual Effects > Flash > The Adobe Flash Professional CC: A Tutorial Approach*.

Next, navigate to the *Documents* folder and create a new folder with the name *Flash_Projects* and then extract the contents of the zip file to *\Documents\Flash_Projects*.

**Note**
*The tutorial zip file that you have downloaded from the CADCIM website contains a folder* **Resources**. *This folder contains all resources related to this chapter.*

## Tutorial 1

In this tutorial, you will create the vector graphic of a honey bee using the drawing tools in Flash CC, as shown in Figure 2-1.                    **(Expected time: 30 min)**

**Figure 2-1** *The vector graphic of a honey bee*

The following steps are required to complete this tutorial:

a.   Create a new Flash document.
b.   Create the face of honey bee.
c.   Create the body of honey bee.
d.   Create the wings of honey bee.
e.   Create the antennae of honey bee.

## Creating a New Flash Document

In this section, you will create a new Flash document.

1.   Choose **File > New** from the menubar; the **New Document** dialog box is displayed.

2.   In the **New Document** dialog box, choose **ActionScript 3.0** from the **General** tab and then choose the **OK** button; a new Flash document is displayed. By default, the **Essentials** workspace is active in the Flash document.

## Creating the Face of Honey Bee

In this section, you will create the face of the honey bee using **Oval Tool** and other editing tools from the **Tools** panel.

1.   Choose **Oval Tool** from the **Tools** panel; the properties of this tool are displayed in the **Properties** panel.

2.   In the **Fill and Stroke** area of the **Properties** panel, choose the **Stroke color** swatch; a flyout is displayed. In this flyout, enter **#000000** in the Hexadecimal edit box and press the ENTER key.

3.   Choose the **Fill color** swatch; a flyout is displayed. In this flyout, enter **#FFFF00** in the Hexadecimal edit box and press the ENTER key. Next, enter **3** in the **Stroke** edit box.

**Note**
*1. In this textbook, colors will be referred by their hexadecimal values.*
*2. The Hexadecimal edit box is also called Hex edit box.*

**Tip:** *You can choose the desired colors for the stroke and fill from the **Stroke color** and **Fill color** swatches in the **Tools** panel. Alternatively, in the **Properties** panel, expand the **Fill and Stroke** area, and then use the **Stroke color** and **Fill color** swatches to choose the colors. In these panels, select the required color by using the color picker or enter the color value manually in the Hexadecimal edit box, refer to Figure 2-2. You can also use the **Color** and **Swatches** panels to apply color, refer to Figure 2-3. To display the **Color** panel, choose **Window > Color** from the menubar or press CTRL+SHIFT+F9. To display the **Swatches** panel, choose **Window > Swatches** from the menubar or press CTRL+F9.*

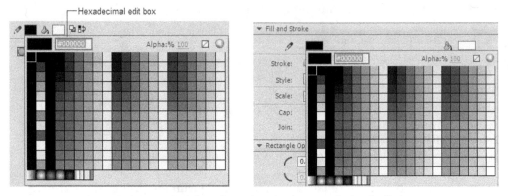

*Figure 2-2  Entering the color values in the Hexadecimal edit box*

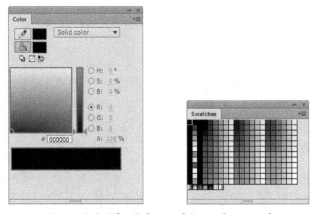

*Figure 2-3  The **Color** and **Swatches** panels*

**Note**
*The fill and stroke are independent of each other, therefore, you can modify or delete either of them without affecting the other.*

4.  Make sure the **Object Drawing** option in the Options section of the **Tools** panel is disabled. Press and hold the SHIFT key and drag the cursor to draw a circle.

**Note**
*When a drawing tool is in the **Object Drawing** mode, the stroke and fill of an object are not separate elements and the shapes that overlap in the same layer do not alter one another if you move them apart, reposition, or rearrange them, refer to Figures 2-4 and 2-5.*

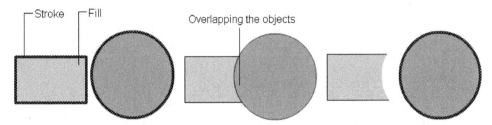

*Figure 2-4* *The behavior of the objects when the **Object Drawing** mode is disabled*

*Figure 2-5* *The behavior of the objects when the **Object Drawing** mode is enabled*

5.  Choose **Selection Tool** and double-click on the circle to select it. In the **Position and Size** area of the **Properties** panel, set the value of **X** to **225** and the value of **Y** to **38**. Next, set the **W** (width) and **H** (height) values to **100**; the circle is positioned and resized in the Stage.

    **X** and **Y** are the coordinates that define the position of an object in the Stage. Next, you will create eyes of honey bee.

 **Note**
*By double-clicking on the fill of an object, you can modify both fill and stroke, whereas by single click, you can modify only the fill of the object.*

6.  Choose **Oval Tool** from the **Tools** panel; the properties of this tool are displayed in the **Properties** panel. In the **Fill and Stroke** area of the **Properties** panel, choose the **Stroke color** swatch; a flyout is displayed. In this flyout, make sure **#000000** is entered in the Hex edit box and then press the ENTER key.

7.  Choose the **Fill color** swatch; a flyout is displayed. In this flyout, enter **#330033** in the Hex edit box. Now, create a small vertical oval in the blank area of the Stage. Choose **Selection Tool** and double-click on the oval to select it. In the **Properties** panel, set the **W** (width) and **H** (height) values to **10** and **26**, respectively.

 **Note**
*To set the value of a particular parameter, click in the respective edit box and then enter the required value. Alternatively, move the cursor over the default value; the shape of the cursor will change into a hand icon called the scrubber. Now, drag the cursor to change the value.*

8.  Make sure the **Selection Tool** is chosen in the **Tools** panel and the oval is selected in the stage. Next, press and hold the ALT key and drag the oval; a copy of the oval is created, refer to Figure 2-6.

**Note**
*To create a copy of an object in Flash, select the object using **Selection Tool**. Next, press and hold the ALT key and drag the object. Alternatively, select the object and choose **Edit > Copy** from the menubar. Next, choose **Edit > Paste in Center** from the menubar.*

9.  Marquee select both the ovals using **Selection Tool** and position them inside the circle as the eyes of the honey bee, as shown in Figure 2-7.

*Figure 2-6  Copy of the oval*

*Figure 2-7  The eyes placed on the face of honey bee*

Next, you will create the cheeks of the honey bee.

10. Choose **Oval Tool** from the **Tools** panel. In the **Fill and Stroke** area of the **Properties** panel, choose the **Stroke color** swatch; a flyout is displayed. In this flyout, choose the No Color button located on the upper right side of this flyout.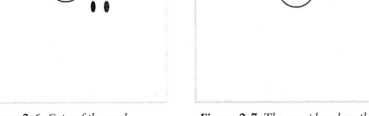

11. Choose the **Fill color** swatch; a flyout is displayed. In this flyout, enter **#FF9999** in the Hex edit box and press the ENTER key.

12. Create a small horizontal oval in the blank area of the Stage and then select it using **Selection Tool**. In the **Position and Size** area of the **Properties** panel, set the **W** (width) and **H** (height) values of the oval to **21** and **7**, respectively.

13. Create a copy of the oval using the ALT key.

14. Using **Selection Tool**, position the ovals on the face as the cheeks of honey bee, as shown in Figure 2-8.

***Figure 2-8*** *The face of Honey Bee with cheeks*

Next, you will create the mouth of honey bee.

15. Choose **Oval Tool** from the **Tools** panel; the properties of this tool are displayed in the **Properties** panel. In the **Fill and Stroke** area of the **Properties** panel, choose the **Stroke color** swatch; a flyout is displayed. In this flyout, make sure the No Color button is chosen.

16. Choose the **Fill color** swatch; a flyout is displayed. In this flyout, make sure **#000000** is entered in the Hex edit box and press the ENTER key. Create a horizontal oval. Next, you need to change the shape of the oval to make it appear like mouth. In Flash, **Selection Tool** can also be used to push and pull the lines and corners of a shape to refine its contours.

17. Choose **Selection Tool** and then move the cursor to the upper edge of the oval; a small curve is displayed below the cursor indicating that the curvature can be changed, refer to Figure 2-9.

18. Click on the curvature and drag it inward; the curvature of the shape bends inward, thereby turning into mouth shape. Now, select the mouth using **Selection Tool** and place it below the cheeks, as shown in Figure 2-10.

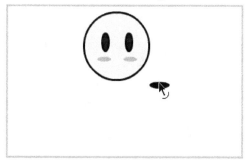

***Figure 2-9*** *The cursor with the curve*

***Figure 2-10*** *The face of honey bee after placing the mouth*

## Creating the Body of Honey Bee

In this section, you will create the body of honey bee using **Line Tool** and **Paint Bucket Tool**.

1.  Choose **Line Tool** from the **Tools** panel; the properties of this tool are displayed in the **Properties** panel. In the **Fill and Stroke** area of the **Properties** panel, choose the **Stroke color** swatch; a flyout is displayed. In this flyout, enter **#000000** in the Hex edit box and press the ENTER key.

2.  In the **Fill and Stroke** area of the **Properties** panel, make sure **3** is entered in the **Stroke** edit box. Next, press and hold the SHIFT key and draw a vertical line segment (stroke) in the blank area of the Stage. The outline of an object is called stroke.

3.  Choose **Selection Tool**. Next, place the cursor over the stroke and drag it to the left; the curvature bends outward, as shown in Figure 2-11.

4.  Select the line segment using **Selection Tool** and create a copy of the line segment using the ALT key. Next, select the copy of the line segment and choose **Modify > Transform > Flip Horizontal** from the menubar; the copied line segment is flipped horizontally and placed.

*Figure 2-11 Changing the curvature of the stroke*

5.  Marquee select the upper portion of the line segments using **Selection Tool** and delete it by pressing the DEL key, refer to Figure 2-12.

6.  Marquee select both the line segments and position them appropriately below the face using **Selection Tool**, as shown in Figure 2-13.

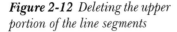

*Figure 2-12 Deleting the upper portion of the line segments*      *Figure 2-13 The honey bee after placing the line segments*

7.  Choose **Line Tool** from the **Tools** panel; the properties of this tool are displayed in the **Properties** panel. In the **Fill and Stroke** area of the **Properties** panel, make sure **3** is entered in the **Stroke** edit box.

8.  Draw four horizontal line segments on the body of honey bee, as shown in Figure 2-14. Next, change the curvature of the line segments using **Selection Tool**, refer to Figure 2-15.

***Figure 2-14*** *The horizontal line segments*      ***Figure 2-15*** *Changing the curvature of horizontal line segments*

9. Choose **Paint Bucket Tool** from the **Tools** panel; the properties of this tool are displayed in the **Properties** panel and the options are displayed in the Options section of the **Tools** panel.

10. In the **Properties** panel, choose the **Fill color** swatch; a flyout is displayed. In this flyout, enter **#330033** in the Hex edit box and press the ENTER key.

11. In the Options section of the **Tools** panel, choose the **Gap Size** button; a flyout is displayed, as shown in Figure 2-16. In this flyout, choose the **Close Large Gaps** option, refer to Figure 2-17.

 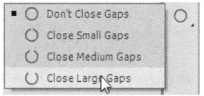

***Figure 2-16*** *Choosing the **Gap Size** button in the Options section of the **Tools** panel*      ***Figure 2-17*** *Choosing the **Close Large Gaps** option*

12. Click in the first horizontal section of the body; the color is filled in this section. Choose the **Fill color** swatch; a flyout is displayed. In this flyout, enter **#FFFF00** in the Hex edit box and press the ENTER key. Next, apply the color in the second horizontal section. Make sure there are no open areas left between the intersection points of one or more line segments as the fill can only be applied in the enclosed areas.

13. Apply the color in the remaining sections as discussed in Steps 9 and 10, refer to Figure 2-18.

***Figure 2-18*** *Filling the color in sections using **Paint Bucket Tool***

## Creating the Wings of Honey Bee

In this section, you will create the wings of honey bee in a new layer.

1.  Choose the **New Layer** button in the **Timeline** panel; a new layer is created. Next, double-click on the default layer name and rename it as **wings**, as shown in Figure 2-19. Next, rename **Layer 1** as **face and body**.

2.  Choose **Oval Tool** from the **Tools** panel; the properties of this tool are displayed in the **Properties** panel. In the **Fill and Stroke** area of the **Properties** panel, choose the **Stroke color** swatch; a flyout is displayed. In this flyout, make sure **#000000** is entered in the Hex edit box and press the ENTER key.

**Note**
*You can hide the body and face of honey bee by hiding the **face and body** layer in the **Timeline** panel. To do so, turn off the **Show or Hide All Layers** option of the **face and body** layer, as shown in Figure 2-20.*

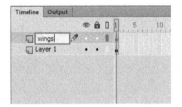

*Figure 2-19  Naming the layers in the **Timeline** panel*         *Figure 2-20  Hiding the **face and body** layer in the **Timeline** panel*

3.  Choose the **Fill color** swatch; a flyout is displayed. In this flyout, choose the No Color button. Next, make sure **3** is entered in the **Stroke** edit box and draw a horizontal oval in the **wings** layer, refer to Figure 2-21.

4.  Choose **Selection Tool** and select the oval. Next, create a copy of the oval by using the ALT key.

5.  Make sure the copied oval is selected and choose **Free Transform Tool** from the **Tools** panel; the oval is enclosed inside the transform bounding box. Next, place the cursor on the upper right transform point and drag it inward; the size of the oval is reduced, refer to Figure 2-21.

6.  Select the original oval and choose **Free Transform Tool** from the **Tools** panel. Place the cursor around any corner transform point available outside the transform bounding box; the cursor is changed to a rotating arrow icon. Now, rotate the oval anti clockwise approximately to 40 degrees, refer to Figure 2-22. Similarly, using **Free Transform Tool** rotate the copied oval clockwise approximately to 30 degrees to get the shape of a wing. Click in the Pasteboard to deselect **Free Transform Tool**.

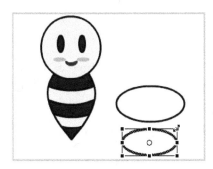

*Figure 2-21  Resizing the oval*

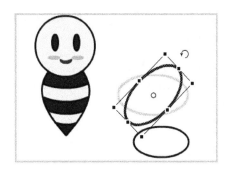

*Figure 2-22  Rotating the ovals*

7.  Choose the small oval using **Selection Tool** and place it on the large oval. Next, click anywhere in the Pasteboard such that none of the body parts is selected. Now, delete the stroke of the large oval that is overlapping the small oval, as shown in Figure 2-23. Figure 2-24 shows the final shape of the ovals after deleting the stroke.

*Figure 2-23  Selecting the stroke that is to be deleted*

*Figure 2-24  The ovals after deleting the stroke*

8.  Marquee select the entire wing and create a copy of the wing using the ALT key, refer to Figure 2-25. Next, select the copy of the wing using **Selection Tool**. Now, choose **Modify > Transform > Flip Horizontal** from the menubar; the wing is flipped horizontally, as shown in Figure 2-26.

9.  Drag the **face and body** layer above the **wings** layer in the **Timeline** panel. Next, place the wings behind the body, refer to Figure 2-27.

*Figure 2-25  The copy of the wing*

*Figure 2-26  The copy of the wing flipped horizontally*

*Figure 2-27  The wings placed behind the body*

## Creating the Antennae of Honey Bee

In this section, you will create the antennae of honey bee in the **face and body** layer.

1.  Select the **face and body** layer. Choose **Line Tool** from the **Tools** panel. In the **Fill and Stroke** area of the **Properties** panel, make sure **3** is entered in the **Stroke** edit box. In the **face and body** layer, draw a line segment on the head of the honey bee.

2.  Change the curvature of the line segment using **Selection Tool**, as shown in Figure 2-28.

3.  Choose **Oval Tool** from the **Tools** panel; the tool properties are displayed in the **Properties** panel.

4.  In the **Fill and Stroke** area of the **Properties** panel, choose the **Stroke color** swatch; a flyout is displayed. In this flyout, make sure **#000000** is entered in the Hex edit box and press the ENTER key. Next, choose the **Fill color** swatch; a flyout is displayed. In this flyout, enter **#FFFF00** in the Hex edit box and press the ENTER key.

5.  Press and hold the SHIFT key and drag the cursor to create a small circle anywhere in the Stage. Place the circle on the tip of the line segment using **Selection Tool**, as shown in Figure 2-29.

*Figure 2-28*  *Changing the curvature of the line segment*    *Figure 2-29*  *Placing the circle on the tip of the line segment*

6   Select the antenna using **Selection Tool**. Next, make a copy of the antenna using the ALT key and then flip it horizontally by choosing **Modify > Transform > Flip Horizontal** from the menubar. You can select multiple objects using the SHIFT key.

7.  Position the antennae at appropriate places using the **Selection Tool**. Figure 2-30 shows the complete honey bee.

*Figure 2-30  The honey bee*

8.  Save the flash file with the name *c02tut1* at the location *\Documents\Flash_Projects\c02_tut\c02_ tut_01*.

9.  Press CTRL+ENTER to view the final output of the vector graphic honey bee. You can also view the final rendered image of the honey bee by downloading the file *c02_flash_cc_rndr.zip* from *www.cadcim.com*. The path of the zip file is mentioned at the beginning of the TUTORIALS section.

## Tutorial 2

In this tutorial, you will create an advertisement banner with the name 'The Coffee Shop', as shown in Figure 2-31.                                   **(Expected time: 30 min)**

*Figure 2-31  The advertisement banner with the name 'The Coffee Shop'*

The following steps are required to complete this tutorial:

a.  Create a new Flash document.
b.  Set the width and height of the Stage.
c.  Create a coffee bean.
d.  Create a decorative pattern using **Line Tool** and **Oval Tool**.
e.  Download the images.
f.  Use bitmaps as fill.
g.  Insert text using **Text Tool**.

## Creating a New Flash Document
In this section, you will create a new Flash document.

1.  Choose **File > New** from the menubar; the **New Document** dialog box is displayed.

2.  In the **New Document** dialog box, choose **ActionScript 3.0** from the **General** tab and then choose the **OK** button; a new Flash document is displayed.

## Setting the Width and Height of the Stage
In this section, you will set the width and height of the Stage to define the exact area required for creating 'The Coffee Shop' ad banner.

1.  Click in the Stage; the **Document** properties are displayed in the **Properties** panel.

2.  In the **Properties** area of the **Properties** panel, choose the **Edit document properties** button, as shown in Figure 2-32; the **Document Settings** dialog box is displayed, refer to Figure 2-33.

*Figure 2-32  Choosing the **Edit document properties** button*

3.  Enter the values **600** (**width**) and **250** (**height**) in the **Dimensions** edit boxes of the **Documents Settings** dialog box and choose the **OK** button, refer to Figure 2-33.

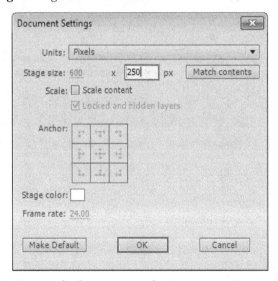

*Figure 2-33  Setting the dimensions in the **Documents Settings** dialog box*

### Creating a Coffee Bean

The shape of the coffee bean is roughly an oval shape. You will start creating the coffee bean by drawing an oval.

1.  Choose **Oval Tool** from the **Tools** panel. In the **Fill and Stroke** area of the **Properties** panel, choose the **Stroke color** swatch; a flyout is displayed. In this flyout, choose the No Color button.

2.  Choose the **Fill color** swatch; a flyout is displayed. In this flyout, enter **#663300** in the Hex edit box and press the ENTER key. Next, draw a vertical oval anywhere in the Pasteboard, as shown in Figure 2-34.

3.  Select half of the oval shape using **Selection Tool**, refer to Figure 2-35 and then press the DEL key; the selected fill is deleted.

**Figure 2-34** *Creating an oval shape*        **Figure 2-35** *Selecting half of the oval shape*

4.  Select the semi-oval shape.

5.  Choose the **Color** button to display the **Color** panel.

6.  Select the **Linear gradient** fill style from this **Color type** drop-down list; the gradient definition bar is displayed at the bottom of the **Color** panel, as shown in Figure 2-36. The pointers below the bar indicate the colors in the **Linear Gradient** fill. The **Linear gradient** fill style is used to blend colors on a linear path.

7.  Double-click on the left pointer below the gradient definition bar; a flyout is displayed, as shown in Figure 2-37. Next, make sure **#000000** is entered in the Hex edit box of the flyout and press the ENTER key. Similarly, double-click on the right pointer; a flyout is displayed. Next, enter **#663300** in the Hex edit box and press the ENTER key; a linear gradient fill is applied to the semi-oval shape.

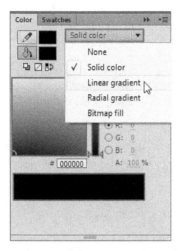

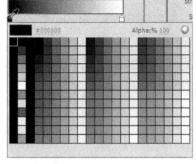

***Figure 2-36*** *Selecting* ***Linear gradient***
*from the* ***Color type*** *drop-down list*

***Figure 2-37*** *The flyout displayed on*
*double-clicking the left pointer*

8.  Select the semi-oval shape and make a copy to create the second half of the coffee bean.
    Next, flip it horizontally by choosing **Modify > Transform > Flip Horizontal** from the
    menubar. Position it next to the first semi-oval shape of the coffee bean, as shown in
    Figure 2-38.

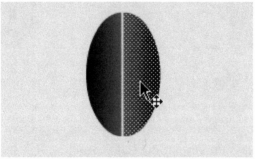

***Figure 2-38*** *Positioning semi-ovals to create*
*coffee bean*

9.  Choose **Lasso Tool** from the **Tools** panel; the properties of this tool are displayed in the
    **Properties** panel.

10. Select the outlines of the inner edges of the coffee bean using **Lasso Tool**, refer to
    Figure 2-39. Next, press the DEL key; the selected fill of the inner edges is deleted, refer
    to Figure 2-40.

***Figure 2-39*** *Selecting the outlines of the inner edges of the coffee bean*

***Figure 2-40*** *The coffee bean after deleting the outlines of the inner edges*

11. Now, you need to fill the color in the gap between the coffee beans. To do so, choose **Brush Tool** from the **Tools** panel; the properties of this tool are displayed in the **Properties** panel. In the **Fill and Stroke** area of the **Properties** panel, choose the **Fill color** swatch; a flyout is displayed. In this flyout, enter **#090400** in the Hex edit box and press the ENTER key. In the Options section of the **Tools** panel, choose the **Brush Mode** button; a flyout is displayed. In this flyout, choose the **Paint Behind** mode.

12. Choose the **Brush size** button in the Options section of the **Tools** panel; a flyout containing different sizes of the brush is displayed. In this flyout, choose the largest size of the brush, as shown in Figure 2-41.

13. Move the cursor over the gap between the coffee beans, press and hold the left mouse button, and then drag the cursor over the gap. Next, release the mouse button; the fill automatically shifts behind the coffee bean as the **Paint Behind** mode of **Brush Tool** was selected.

***Figure 2-41*** *Choosing the largest size of the brush*

The **Paint Behind** mode of **Brush Tool** is used to paint the blank area of the Stage while leaving the strokes and the fills unaffected in the same layer, refer to Figure 2-42.

***Figure 2-42*** *The **Paint Behind** mode of the **Brush Tool***

14. Select the coffee bean using **Selection Tool** and then create a copy of it. Next, rotate the coffee bean by using **Free Transform Tool** and position it, refer to Figure 2-43.

    Next, you will convert the coffee beans into a graphic symbol because it will be used later to create a decorative pattern using different tools.

15. Select coffee beans using **Selection Tool** and then choose **Modify > Convert to Symbol** from the menubar; the **Convert to Symbol** dialog box is displayed, as shown in Figure 2-44.

*Figure 2-43*  *Rotating and positioning the coffee bean*           *Figure 2-44*  *The **Convert to Symbol** dialog box*

16. In this dialog box, type **coffee beans** as the name of the symbol in the **Name** text box. Next, select **Graphic** as the symbol type from the **Type** drop-down list and then choose the **OK** button; a graphic symbol named *coffee bean* is saved in the **Library** panel. You can now delete the *coffee bean* instance from the Pasteboard as it is saved in the **Library** panel.

    The **Library** panel in Flash stores all the media files such as bitmaps, graphics, sound files, and video clips that you import and symbols that you create in a Flash document. By default, the **Library** panel is located next to the **Properties** panel in the **Essentials** workspace. Alternatively, choose **Window > Library** from the menubar to display the **Library** panel.

    Next, you will create a decorative pattern using **Line Tool** and **Oval Tool**. Before creating the decorative pattern, you will draw a layout of the advertisement banner and divide it into sections.

17. Choose **Rectangle Tool** from the **Tools** panel; the properties of this tool are displayed in the **Properties** panel.

18. In the **Fill and Stroke** area of the **Properties** panel, choose the **Stroke color** swatch; a flyout is displayed. In this flyout, enter **#000000** in the Hex edit box and press the ENTER key. Next, choose the **Fill color** swatch; a flyout is displayed. In this flyout, choose the No Color button and make sure **1** is entered in the **Stroke** edit box.

19. Draw a rectangle with the dimensions equal to the dimensions of the Stage. Now, choose **Line Tool** and draw line segments to divide the rectangle into sections. Figure 2-45 shows the advertisement banner layout, with the sections named to provide you an idea of positioning the images and text.

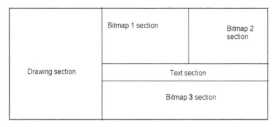

*Figure 2-45  The layout for 'The Coffee Shop' advertisement banner*

## Creating Decorative Pattern Using Line Tool and Oval Tool

In this section, you will create complex patterns and decorations easily and quickly by using the **Line Tool** and **Oval Tool**.

1. Choose **Paint Bucket Tool** from the **Tools** panel; the properties of this tool are displayed in the **Properties** panel. In the **Fill and Stroke** area of the **Properties** panel, choose the **Fill color** swatch; a flyout is displayed. In this flyout, enter **#E07E33** in the Hex edit box and press the ENTER key. Next, click in the Drawing section of the advertisement banner layout in the Stage; the color is applied in this section, refer to Figure 2-46.

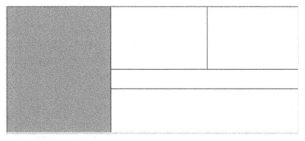

*Figure 2-46  The color applied in the Drawing section*

2. Choose the **Line Tool** from the **Tools** panel; the properties of this tool are displayed in the **Properties** panel. In the **Fill and Stroke** area of the **Properties** panel, choose the **Stroke color** swatch; a flyout is displayed. In this flyout, enter **#FFFFFF** in the Hex edit box and press the ENTER key. Make sure **1** is entered in the **Stroke** edit box.

3. Next, press and hold the SHIFT key and draw a vertical line segment (stroke) on the pasteboard, as shown in Figure 2-47.

4. Choose **Selection Tool**. Next, place the cursor over the stroke and drag it to the right; the curvature bends outward, as shown in Figure 2-48.

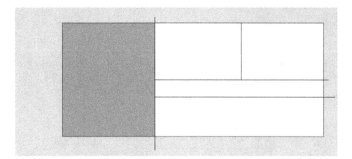 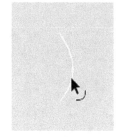

***Figure 2-47***  *Creating a line segment*          ***Figure 2-48***  *Changing the curvature of the stroke*

5.  Choose **Oval Tool** from the **Tools** panel. In the **Fill and Stroke** area of the **Properties** panel, choose the **Fill color** swatch; a flyout is displayed. In this flyout, choose the No Color button located on the upper right side of this flyout.

6.  Choose the **Stroke color** swatch; a flyout is displayed. In this flyout, make sure **#FFFFFF** is entered in the Hex edit box and press the ENTER key. Next, create two small ovals on the pasteboard, as shown in Figure 2-49.

7.  Choose **Selection Tool**. Marquee select the newly created shapes. Next, choose **Modify > Convert to Symbol** from the menubar; the **Convert to Symbol** dialog box is displayed, as shown in Figure 2-50.

 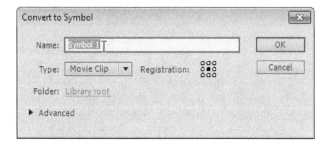

***Figure 2-49***  *Creating two ovals on the pasteboard*          ***Figure 2-50***  *The **Convert to Symbol** dialog box*

8.  In this dialog box, type **pattern** as the name of the symbol in the **Name** text box. Next, select **Graphic** as the symbol type from the **Type** drop-down list and then choose the **OK** button; a graphic symbol named *pattern* is saved in the **Library** panel. You can now delete the *pattern* instance from the Pasteboard as it is saved in the **Library** panel.

9.  Select and drag the *pattern* symbol from the **Library** panel and place it in the Drawing section of the layout, as shown in Figure 2-51. Next, reduce the size of the pattern as required using the **Transform Tool**.

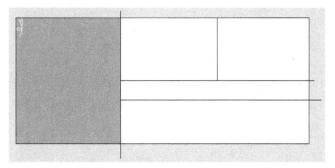

**Figure 2-51** *Pattern symbol placed in the Drawing section*

10. Create copies of the *pattern* using the ALT key and place them randomly in the Drawing section, as shown in Figure 2-52.

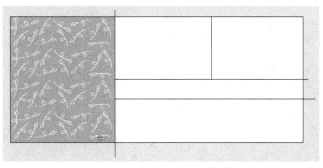

**Figure 2-52** *Copies of the pattern symbol placed randomly in the Drawing section*

11. Now, you need to select and drag the *coffee beans* symbol from the **Library** panel and place it in the Drawing section of the layout, as shown in Figure 2-53. Next, reduce the size of the pattern using the **Transform Tool** as required.

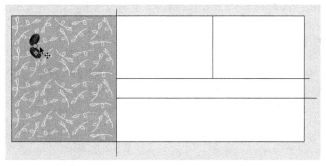

**Figure 2-53** *Coffee beans symbol placed in the Drawing section*

12. Create copies of the *coffee beans* using the ALT key and place them randomly in the Drawing section, as shown in Figure 2-54.

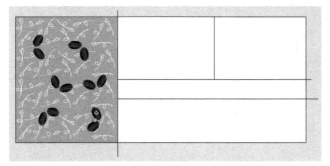

**Figure 2-54**  *Copies of the coffee beans symbol are placed in the Drawing section*

## Downloading the Images

In this section, you will download the bitmap images for using them as **Bitmap Fill**.

1.  Download the images used in this tutorial from the following links:

    *http://www.sxc.hu/photo/1287441, http://www.sxc.hu/photo/1289296, and http://www.sxc.hu/photo/1097233*

    Save them with the names: *cafe latte.jpg, cup.jpg, and beans.jpg,* respectively at the location */Documents/Flash_Projects/c02_tut/Resources.*

**Note**
*Footage Courtesy:* **Gareth Weeks** *(http://www.sxc.hu/profile/garwee),* **ilker** *(http://www.sxc.hu/profile/ilco),* **Rob Owen-Wahl** *(http://www.sxc.hu/profile/lockstockb)*

## Using Bitmaps as Fill

In this section, you will use bitmaps as fill.

1.  Choose **Paint Bucket Tool** from the **Tools** panel. Next, choose the **Color** button; the **Color** panel is displayed. In the **Color** panel, select **Bitmap fill** from the **Color type** drop-down list; the **Import to Library** dialog box is displayed.

2.  In the **Import to Library** dialog box, choose **Documents > Flash_Projects > c02_tut > Resources > cup.jpg**. Next, choose the **Open** button; the selected image is displayed in the **Color** panel as bitmap swatch, refer to Figure 2-55.

3.  In the **Color** panel, choose the **Import** button; the **Import to Library** dialog box is displayed. In this dialog box, browse to the location *Documents/Flash_Projects/c02_tut/Resources* folder and import *cafe latte.jpg,* and *beans.jpg.* These images are displayed in the **Color** panel as bitmap swatches, as shown in Figure 2-55, and are saved in the **Library** panel, as shown in Figure 2-56.

*Figure 2-55* *The bitmap swatches*

*Figure 2-56* *The **Library** panel*

4.  In the **Color** panel, make sure the **Fill color** button is chosen. Next, click on the **cup.jpg** swatch using the color picker, as shown in Figure 2-57. Next, move the cursor in the Bitmap 1 section in the Stage and click; the *cup.jpg* image is applied as fill in this section.

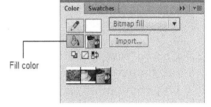

*Figure 2-57* *Choosing cup.jpg as fill*

5.  For the Bitmap 2 section, choose the **cafe latte.jpg** swatch in the **Color** panel.

6.  For the Bitmap 3 section, choose the **beans.jpg** swatch in the **Color** panel.

If the images that are used as fill for Bitmap sections do not fit properly, then you need to resize the bitmap fill. To resize a bitmap fill, for example the **cup** fill, choose **Gradient Transform Tool** from the **Tools** panel and click on the **cup** fill in the Stage; the gradient bounding box with transform handles is displayed around the **cup** fill. Move the cursor over the arrow located at the bottom left handle of the gradient bounding box; the cursor changes to a double-headed arrow. Drag the double-headed arrow outward to fit the **cup** fill, refer to Figure 2-58. Figure 2-59 shows the complete view of Bitmap sections.

*Figure 2-58* *Scaling the cup.jpg using **Gradient Transform Tool***

*Figure 2-59  The Bitmap sections*

## Inserting Text Using Text Tool

Now, you need to add text to complete this advertisement banner.

1.  Choose **Insert > Timeline > Layer** from the menubar; a new layer is created. Next, rename the new layer as **Text**. Alternatively, you can choose the **New Layer** button in the **Timeline** panel to create a new layer.

2.  Choose **Text Tool** from the **Tools** panel; the properties of **Text Tool** are displayed in the **Properties** panel. In this panel, make sure **Static Text** is selected in the **Text type** drop-down list, refer to Figure 2-60.

3.  Make sure the orientation of the text is horizontal. If it is not horizontal, change it to horizontal by using the **Change orientation of text** drop-down list in the **Properties** panel, refer to Figure 2-60.

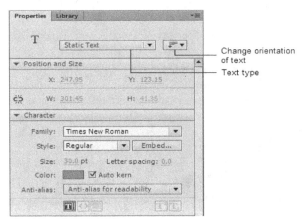

*Figure 2-60  Text Tool options in the Properties panel*

4.  In the **Character** area of the **Properties** panel, choose the **Gill Sans Ultra Bold** font from the **Family** drop-down list. Next, set the font size to **30** in the **Size** edit box. Next, choose the swatch located on the right to **Color**; a flyout is displayed. In this flyout, enter **#000000** in the Hex edit box.

5.  Click in the Stage; the text box is displayed. In this text box, type **The Coffee Shop**. Next, choose **Selection Tool** and position the text at the center of the Text section, as shown in Figure 2-61.

***Figure 2-61*** *The Coffee Shop advertisement banner*

6.  Save the flash file with the name *c02tut2* at the location *\Documents\Flash_Projects\c02_tut\ c02_tut_02*.

7.  Press CTRL+ENTER to view the final output of the advertisement banner. You can also view the final rendered image of the advertisement banner by downloading the file *c02_flash_cc_rndr.zip* from *www.cadcim.com*. The path of the zip file is mentioned in the beginning of the TUTORIALS section.

# HOT KEYS

In Flash, you can use the keyboard shortcuts to invoke the commonly used commands. The shortcut keys are referred to as hot keys. With the help of these keys, you can work faster and more efficiently. Some of the most important keys and their functions are listed below.

**Hot keys and their function**

| Key | Function |
|---|---|
| CTRL+N | Creates a new document |
| CTRL+O | Opens the existing Flash file |
| CTRL+W | Closes the active Flash file |
| CTRL+S | Saves the active Flash file |
| CTRL+Z | To undo the last step |
| CTRL+Y | To redo the last step |

**Hot keys for invoking tools**

| Key | Tool |
|---|---|
| V | Selection Tool |
| A | Subselection Tool |
| Q | Free Transform Tool |
| F | Gradient Transform Tool |
| W | 3D Rotation Tool |
| G | 3D Translation Tool |
| L | Lasso Tool |

| P | Pen Tool |
|---|---|
| = | Add Anchor Point Tool |
| - | Delete Anchor Point Tool |
| C | Convert Anchor Point Tool |
| T | Text Tool |
| N | Line Tool |
| R | Rectangle Tool and Rectangle Primitive Tool |
| O | Oval Tool and Oval Primitive Tool |
| Y | Pencil Tool |
| B | Brush Tool |
| K | Paint Bucket Tool |
| S | Ink Bottle Tool |
| I | Eyedropper Tool |
| E | Eraser Tool |
| H | Hand Tool |
| Z | Zoom Tool |

**Some Important Hot keys**

| Keys | Function |
|---|---|
| CTRL+R | Imports elements to the Stage |
| CTRL+F8 | Creates new symbols |
| F8 | Converts objects to symbols |
| CTRL+B | Breaks apart elements |
| CTRL+G | Groups elements |
| CTRL+SHIFT+G | Ungroups elements |
| CTRL+ENTER | Tests the movie |
| CTRL+U | Opens preferences settings |

## Self-Evaluation Test

**Answer the following questions and then compare them to those given at the end of this chapter:**

1. Which of the following options of the **Brush Tool** is used to paint behind the strokes and fills in the same layer?

   (a) **Paint Fills**              (b) **Paint Behind**
   (c) **Paint Selection**          (d) **Paint Inside**

2.   The _____ key helps you to draw a perfect circle while using **Oval Tool**.

3.   The _____ graphics are produced by using geometrical primitives such as points, lines, curves, and shapes.

4.   The _____ option provides a platform for colors to blend on the linear path.

5.   The _____ option is used to apply bitmap images as a fill.

6.   The **Linear gradient** option is used to create linear gradient strokes. (T/F)

7.   You can create a new symbol by pressing CTRL+R. (T/F)

8.   You can close the active Flash file by pressing CTRL+W. (T/F)

9.   L is the shortcut key for invoking **Lasso Tool**. (T/F)

10.  CTRL+ENTER is used to test a movie. (T/F)

## Review Questions

**Answer the following questions:**

1.   Which of the following combinations of shortcut keys is used for creating a new document?

     (a) CTRL+N                                                (b) CTRL+B
     (c) CTRL+G                                                (d) CTRL+U

2.   _____ is the shortcut key for invoking **Add Anchor Point Tool.**

3.   _____ is the shortcut key for invoking **Free Transform Tool**.

4.   The _____ option is used to snap objects along the edges of other objects.

5.   _____ is the shortcut key for invoking **3D Rotation Tool**.

6.   _____ is the shortcut key for invoking **Rectangle Tool** and **Rectangle Primitive Tool**.

7.   You can ungroup the elements by pressing CTRL+G. (T/F)

8.   You can invoke Text Tool by using the shortcut key 'T'. (T/F)

# EXERCISE

## Exercise 1

Using various tools, create the advertisement banner for 'The Flower Shop', as shown in Figure 2-62. You can view the final rendered image of the banner by downloading the file *c02_flash_cc_exr.zip* from *www.cadcim.com*. The path of the file is as follows: *Textbooks > Animation and Visual Effects > Flash > The Adobe Flash Professional CC: A Tutorial Approach.*

**(Expected time: 30 min)**

Download the bitmaps used in this exercise from the following links:

*http://www.sxc.hu/photo/1340073 (Courtesy: http://www.sxc.hu/profile/alex27)*
*http://www.sxc.hu/photo/1338574 (Courtesy: http://www.sxc.hu/profile/Roxanne727)*
*http://www.sxc.hu/photo/1284438 (Courtesy: http://www.sxc.hu/profile/robby_m)*
*http://www.sxc.hu/photo/1077716 (Courtesy: http://www.sxc.hu/profile/bjearwicke)*
*http://www.sxc.hu/photo/1323129 (Courtesy: http://www.sxc.hu/profile/misscheeky)*

**Figure 2-62** *The advertisement banner with the name 'The Flower Shop'*

# Chapter 3

# Working with Symbols and Instances

## Learning Objectives

*After completing this chapter, you will be able to:*
- *Create new symbols*
- *Edit the symbols and instances*
- *Create and edit button symbols*
- *Import Adobe Photoshop files in Flash*

# INTRODUCTION

In Flash, you can create movies of small file size. One way to keep the file size small is to create symbols. There are three categories of symbols in Flash namely graphics, buttons, and movie clips. Once a symbol is created in a Flash document, it is automatically saved in its library and can be used later in any of the Flash documents.

The Graphic symbols are the basic category of symbols. These symbols are generally used for static images. They do not support ActionScript, filters, or blending modes.

The Button symbols are used to create buttons for interactivity. A button symbol contains four keyframes. Each keyframe is used to define the behavior when the mouse pointer interacts with the button symbol. You can apply filters, blending modes, and color effects to the button symbols. These symbols require ActionScript to perform an action.

The Movie Clip symbols are the most powerful symbols in Flash and are generally used for animation. A movie clip symbol contains its own independent Timeline. You can add an animation to the movie clip Timeline as you do in the main Timeline and play both the animations simultaneously, making complex animations simpler. You can also apply filters, color effects, and blending modes to a movie clip and its instances. An instance is the copy of a symbol located in the Stage or inside a symbol. In addition, you can use ActionScripts to control movie clips and make them respond to the user.

## Creating Symbols

In Flash, you can create symbols in two ways which are discussed next.

1.  Create a new Flash document. Next, choose **Insert > New Symbol** from the menubar; the **Create New Symbol** dialog box will be displayed. In this dialog box, specify a name for the symbol in the **Name** text box and select the required symbol type from the **Type** drop-down list. Next, choose the **OK** button; the symbol-editing mode will be displayed. In this mode, you can draw or import the graphics in the symbol.

2.  Select an object or existing graphic in the stage that you need to convert into a symbol. Next, choose **Modify > Convert to Symbol** from the menubar; the **Convert to Symbol** dialog box will be displayed. Next, specify a name for the symbol in the **Name** text box and select the required symbol type from the **Type** drop-down list. Then, choose the **OK** button; the selected object or graphic will be converted into a symbol and will be saved in the document library.

# TUTORIALS

Before you start the tutorials, you need to download the *c03_flash_cc_tut.zip* file from *www.cadcim.com*. The path of the file is as follows: *Textbooks > Animation and Visual Effects > Flash > The Adobe Flash Professional CC: A Tutorial Approach.*

Next, extract the contents of the zip file to *\Documents\Flash_Projects.*

## Tutorial 1

In this tutorial, you will create and edit a graphic symbol and its instances.

**(Expected time: 15 min)**

The following steps are required to complete this tutorial:

a. Open the Flash document.
b. Convert the shape into a graphic symbol.
c. Create and edit the instance of the symbol.
d. Edit the symbol.
e. Break the link of the instance from its symbol.

### Opening the Flash Document

In this section, you will open the Flash document.

1. Choose **File > Open** from the menubar; the **Open** dialog box is displayed.

2. Choose **Documents > Flash_Projects > c03_tut > c03_tut_01 > c03_tut_01_start.fla**. Next, choose the **Open** button from the dialog box; the Flash document is displayed, as shown in Figure 3-1.

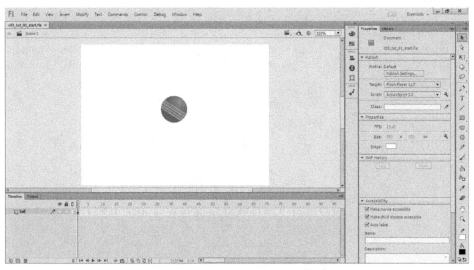

*Figure 3-1* *The c03_tut_01_start.fla document displayed*

### Converting the Shape into a Graphic Symbol

In this section, you will convert the object into a graphic symbol.

1. Make sure the **Selection Tool** is chosen in the **Tools** panel. Next, marquee select the circular shape in the Stage and choose **Modify > Convert to Symbol** from the menubar; the **Convert to Symbol** dialog box is displayed, as shown in Figure 3-2.

*Figure 3-2* The *Convert to Symbol* dialog box

2.  In the **Convert to Symbol** dialog box, type **cricket ball** as the name of the symbol in the **Name** text box and then select **Graphic** from the **Type** drop-down list. Next, choose the **OK** button; the graphic symbol with the name *cricket ball* is created and saved in the Library and an instance of it is created in the Stage, refer to Figure 3-3.

When you convert a shape or graphic into a symbol, its instance is created in the stage and the symbol itself is placed inside the **Library** panel. The graphic symbols are the basic category of symbols. These symbols are generally used to convert still images or objects into symbol.

**Note**
*Select the* **cricket ball** *symbol in the* **Library** *panel to view it in the Item preview window if it is not selected, as shown in Figure 3-3. The Item preview window displays the selected symbol in the* **Library** *panel. The Library in Flash stores all the files such as bitmaps, graphics, sound files, and the video clips that you import. It also stores the symbols that are created in a Flash document.*

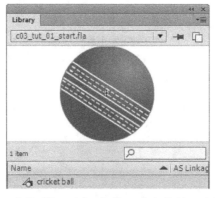

*Figure 3-3* The *cricket ball symbol displayed in the*
*Item preview window of the* **Library** *panel*

## Creating and Editing the Instance of the Symbol
In this section, you will create and edit the instances of the **cricket ball** symbol.

1.  Click on the *cricket ball* symbol icon (🔺) in the **Library** panel and drag it to the Stage; the second instance of the *cricket ball* symbol is created in the Stage. Alternatively, drag the *cricket ball* symbol from the Item preview window of the **Library** panel to the Stage to create its instance.

2. Place the second instance below the first instance in the Stage.

3. Make sure the **Selection Tool** from the **Tools** panel is selected and select the first instance of the *cricket ball*; the properties of the first instance are displayed in the **Properties** panel.

4. In the **Color Effect** area of the **Properties** panel, select **Alpha** from the **Style** drop-down list; the **Alpha** slider is displayed in the **Color Effect** area, as shown in Figure 3-4.

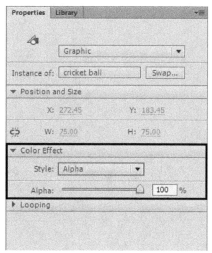

5. Set the value of the **Alpha** slider to **55**. Alternatively, enter **55** in the **Alpha** edit box and notice the change in the transparency of the first instance, as shown in Figure 3-5.

6. Make sure the **Selection Tool** from the **Tools** panel is selected and select the second instance in the Stage; the properties of the second instance are displayed in the **Properties** panel.

7. In the **Color Effect** area of the **Properties** panel, select **Brightness** from the **Style** drop-down list; the **Bright** slider is displayed in the **Color Effect**

*Figure 3-4  The **Alpha** slider in the Color Effect area*

area. Next, set the value of **Bright** slider to **-60**; the second instance of the symbol turns dark, as shown in Figure 3-6.

*Figure 3-5  The first instance*

*Figure 3-6  The second instance*

**Note**
*You can create any number of instances of a symbol and change their respective properties from the **Properties** panel without affecting the other instances. To edit a symbol's property and enter the symbol-editing mode, double-click on the icon of the symbol in the **Library** panel.*

## Editing the Symbol
In this section, you will edit the *cricket ball* symbol in the symbol-editing mode.

1. Double-click on the icon of the *cricket ball* graphic symbol (🄰) in the **Library** panel to enter into the symbol-editing mode. Alternatively, double-click on the *cricket ball* graphic symbol image in the Item Preview window of the **Library** panel; the *cricket ball* graphic symbol is displayed in the Stage with its Timeline in the symbol-editing mode, refer to Figure 3-7.

**Tip:** *You can also edit a symbol by choosing **Edit > Edit Symbols** from the menubar or by pressing CTRL+E.*

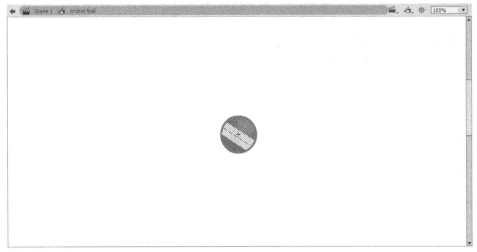

*Figure 3-7*  *The cricket ball graphic symbol in the symbol-editing mode*

2.  Select the upper fill of the *cricket ball* graphic symbol and choose the **Color** button  located at the upper left corner of the **Properties** panel; the **Color** panel is displayed.

3.  In this panel, double-click on the left pointer of the gradient definition bar; a flyout is displayed. In this flyout, enter **#FFFFFF** in the Hex edit box and press the ENTER key. Next, double-click on the right pointer; a flyout is displayed. In this flyout, enter **#000000** in the Hex edit box and press the ENTER key. Figure 3-8 displays the selected fill and its gradient definition bar.

4.  Repeat Step 2 for the middle and lower fills of the *cricket ball*. Next, double-click on the stroke of the border of the *cricket ball* to select the stroke entirely; the **Shape** properties are displayed in the **Properties** panel.

5.  In the **Fill and Stroke** area of the **Properties** panel, choose the **Stroke color** swatch; a flyout is displayed. In this flyout, enter **#000000** in the Hex edit box and press the ENTER key. Notice that the changes that you make to the symbol also affect the instances of the symbol in the Stage. The ball will turn black in the **Library** panel and in the Stage, refer to Figure 3-9.

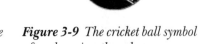

*Figure 3-8*  *The gradient definition bar of the upper fill inside the cricket ball symbol*

*Figure 3-9*  *The cricket ball symbol after changing the color*

6.  Click on **Scene 1** to return to the main Timeline.

## Breaking the Link of the Instance from its Symbol

In this section, you will break the link of the *cricket ball* instance from its symbol.

1.  Choose **Selection Tool** from the **Tools** panel, if it is not selected and select the first instance of *cricket ball* symbol in the Stage.

2.  Choose **Modify > Break Apart** from the menubar or press CTRL+B; the first instance of *cricket ball* is delinked from its symbol. The instance is now an independent object and is no longer linked to the symbol. Now, you can modify the symbol without affecting the instance or vice-versa.

3.  Double-click on the icon of the *cricket ball* graphic symbol (🎨) in the **Library** panel to enter into the symbol-editing mode.

4.  Make sure the **Selection Tool** from the **Tools** panel is selected and select the upper fill of the ball. Next, choose the **Color** button located at the upper left corner of the **Properties** panel; the **Color** panel is displayed.

5.  In this panel, double-click on the right pointer of the gradient definition bar; a flyout is displayed. In this flyout, enter **#0000CC** in the Hex edit box and press the ENTER key; the color of the *cricket ball* graphic symbol in the **Library** panel is changed, as shown in Figure 3-10.

6.  Click on **Scene 1** to return to the main Timeline; the color of the second instance is changed as it is still linked to the symbol. The first instance remains unchanged as it is no more linked to the symbol, refer to Figure 3-11.

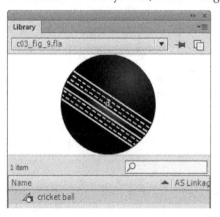

***Figure 3-10*** *Displaying the change in color of the cricket ball graphic symbol*

***Figure 3-11*** *The first instance without any change*

7.  Save the flash file with the name *c03tut1* at the location *\Documents\Flash_Projects\ c03_tut\c03_tut_01*.

8.  Press CTRL+ENTER to view the final output of the instance and the symbol. You can also view the final rendered image of the instance by downloading the file *c03_flash_cc_rndr.zip* from *http://www.cadcim.com*. The path of the zip file is mentioned at the beginning of the TUTORIALS section.

## Tutorial 2

In this tutorial, you will create a button symbol, as shown in Figure 3-12 and then define its states.                                                          **(Expected time: 20 min)**

*Figure 3-12* *The button symbol*

The following steps are required to complete this tutorial:

a.   Create a new Flash document.
b.   Create a shape.
c.   Convert the shape into a button symbol.

### Creating a New Flash Document

In this section, you will create a new Flash document.

1.   Choose **File > New** from the menubar; the **New Document** dialog box is displayed.

2.   In the **New Document** dialog box, choose **ActionScript 3.0** from the **General** tab and then choose the **OK** button; a new Flash document is displayed.

### Creating a Shape

In this section, you will create the shape of the button symbol.

1.   Choose **Rectangle Primitive Tool** from the **Tools** panel.

2.   Choose the **Color** button located at the upper left of the **Properties** panel; the **Color** panel is displayed. In this panel, select the fill style as **Linear gradient** from the **Color type** drop-down list.

3.   Draw a rectangle in the Stage; the tool properties are displayed in the **Properties** panel.

4.   In the **Rectangle Options** area of the **Properties** panel, enter **7** in the **Rectangle corner radius** edit box and press the ENTER key; the shape of the corners is changed, as shown in Figure 3-13.

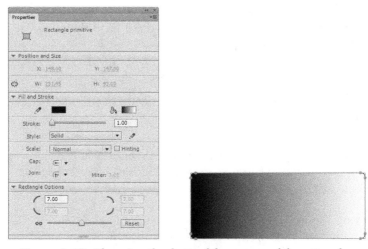

*Figure 3-13*  *Changing the shape of the corners of the rectangle*

5.  Choose **Gradient Transform Tool** from the **Tools** panel and click on the fill of the rectangle in the Stage; the gradient transform bars are displayed around the fill.

6.  Move the cursor over the rotation handle of the gradient transform bar located at the upper right corner of the bars and drag the cursor to the left to rotate the gradient transform bars to approximately 90 degrees, as shown in Figure 3-14.

7.  Move the cursor over the arrow located on the gradient transform bar; the shape of the cursor changes to a double-headed arrow indicating that now you can scale the fill. Next, drag the cursor inward and scale the gradient fill approximately to 50%, as shown in Figure 3-15. The rectangular shape of the button symbol is created in the Stage.

*Figure 3-14*  *Rotating the gradient fill*          *Figure 3-15*  *Scaling the gradient fill*

## Converting the Shape into a Button Symbol

In this section, you will convert the rectangle into a button symbol and edit it.

1.  Double-click on **Layer 1** (default layer name) in the **Timeline** panel and rename it as **Buttons**.

2. Choose **Selection Tool** from the **Tools** panel and make sure the rectangle in the Stage is selected. Next, choose **Modify > Convert to Symbol** from the menubar or press the F8 key; the **Convert to Symbol** dialog box is displayed.

3. In the **Convert to Symbol** dialog box, type **Home** in the **Name** text box and select **Button** from the **Type** drop-down list. Next, choose the **OK** button; a button symbol with the name *Home* is created and saved in the Library.

**Note**

*In Flash, when you create a new button or convert a shape into a button symbol, a new Timeline is created for the corresponding button symbol, which is visible only in the button symbol's editing mode. To make the Timeline visible, double-click on that button symbol.*

4. Double-click on the icon of the *Home* button symbol icon () in the **Library** panel to enter the editing mode. Alternatively, choose **Edit > Edit Symbols** from the menubar. Figure 3-16 shows the editing mode of the *Home* button symbol.

**Note**

*Figure 3-17 shows the Timeline of the Home button symbol. This Timeline contains four frames that define different states of the button symbol. The **Up** frame is used to define the appearance of the button when the cursor is not placed over it. Flash automatically places the original button symbol in the **Up** frame.*

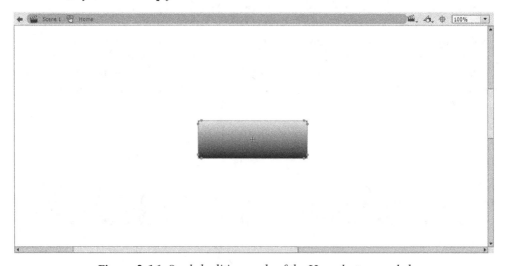

*Figure 3-16   Symbol-editing mode of the Home button symbol*

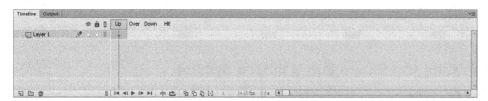

*Figure 3-17   The Timeline of the Home button symbol*

5. In the **Timeline** panel, select the **Over** frame. Next, press the F6 key or choose **Insert >Timeline > Keyframe** from the menubar; a keyframe is inserted in the blank frame.

    The **Over** frame of the button symbol is used to define the appearance of the symbol when the mouse pointer is over it.

**Note**

*The keyframe is a frame that represents a new symbol instance in the Timeline. You can also add the ActionScript code to the keyframe to control certain actions in a document.*

6. Make sure the **Selection Tool** is chosen from the **Tools** panel and the rectangle in the Stage is selected.

7. Choose the **Color** button located at the upper left corner of the **Properties** panel; the **Color** panel is displayed. In the **Color** panel, double-click on the right pointer of the gradient definition bar; a flyout is displayed. In this flyout, enter **#999999** in the Hex edit box and press the ENTER key.

8. Select the **Down** frame and press the F6 key to insert a keyframe. Next, select the fill of the rectangle in the Stage.

9. Choose the **Color** button; the **Color** panel is displayed. In the **Color** panel, double-click on the right pointer of the gradient definition bar; a flyout is displayed. In this flyout, enter **#333333** in the Hex edit box and press the ENTER key.

    The **Down** frame of the button symbol is used to define the appearance of the button, when the user clicks on it.

10. Select the **Hit** frame and press the F7 key to insert a blank keyframe. Create a new layer above **Layer 1** using the **New Layer** button.

11. Choose **Rectangle Tool** from the **Tools** panel; the properties of this tool are displayed in the **Properties** panel. In the **Fill and Stroke** area of the **Properties** panel, choose the **Stroke color** swatch; a flyout is displayed. In this flyout, make sure **#000000** is selected in the Hex edit box and press the ENTER key. Choose the **Fill color** swatch; a flyout is displayed. In this flyout, enter **#0000CC** in the Hex edit box.

12. In **Layer 2**, select **Hit** frame and press the F7 key to insert a blank keyframe. Next, choose the **Onion Skin** button; the frame range before and after the current frame range becomes visible. Now, create a rectangle covering the rectangle of the button symbol, as shown in Figure 3-18.

    The **Hit** frame of the button symbol represents the area of the screen that will respond on clicking. The rectangle created in this frame defines the hit area of the button.

**Note**

*The hit area is not visible in the Stage and in the preview window.*

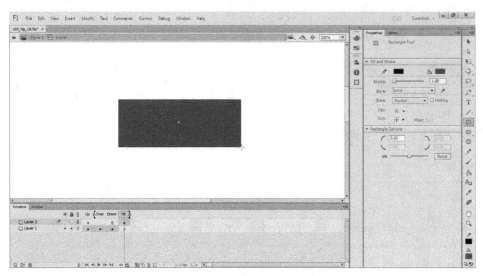

*Figure 3-18  Rectangle in the **Hit** frame*

13. Press CTRL+ENTER; the preview window is displayed showing the *Home* button instance. Move the mouse pointer over the *Home* button instance to see its **Over** state and click on it to see its **Down** state. Figures 3-19 and 3-20 shows the **Over** and **Down** states of the *Home* button instance, respectively.

*Figure 3-19  The **Over** state of the button symbol*

*Figure 3-20  The **Down** state of the button symbol*

Notice that the rectangle you created in the **Hit** frame is not visible in the preview window. Click anywhere in the preview window, except on the hit area (rectangle) you created in the **Hit** frame; the button symbol shows no change.

14. Close the preview window to return to the Flash document.

15. In the **Layer 2** of the **Timeline** panel, select the **Hit** frame; the rectangle in the Stage is selected.

16. Choose **Selection Tool** from the **Tools** panel and click on the rectangle; the **Shape** properties are displayed in the **Properties** panel.

17. In the **Position and Size** area of the **Properties** panel, set the value of **W** to **270** and the value of **H** to **170**. Next, set the value of **X** to **-140** and the value of **Y** to **-86**; the rectangle is positioned and resized, as shown in Figure 3-21.

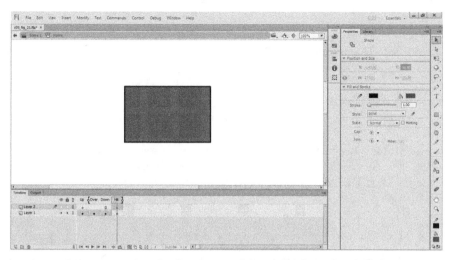

*Figure 3-21  Increasing the dimensions of the rectangle in the Flash document*

18. Press CTRL+ENTER; the preview window is displayed showing the *Home* button. In the preview window, move the cursor over the hit area of the button and notice the changes in it.

    By increasing the dimensions of the rectangle in the **Hit** frame, you can define the hit area of the button symbol (instance). Now, the appearance of the button changes not merely by clicking on the symbol itself, but also on placing the cursor over the hit area and clicking in the hit area.

19. Save the flash file with the name *c03tut2* at the location *\Documents\Flash_Projects\c03_tut\ c03_tut_02*.

20. Press CTRL+ENTER to view the final output of the button symbol. You can also view the final rendered file of the button symbol by downloading the file *c03_flash_cc_rndr.zip* from *http://www.cadcim.com*. The path of the zip file is mentioned at the beginning of the TUTORIALS section.

## Tutorial 3

In this tutorial, you will convert the objects into movie clip symbols and apply **Glow** filter to them, as shown in Figure 3-22.                                                    **(Expected time: 10 min)**

*Figure 3-22  The **Glow** filter applied to movie clips symbols*

The following steps are required to complete this tutorial:

a.   Open the Flash document.
b.   Convert the shapes into the movie clip symbols.

## Opening the Flash Document

In this section, you will open the Flash document required for this tutorial.

1.   Choose **File > Open** from the menubar; the **Open** dialog box is displayed. In this dialog box, choose **Documents > Flash_Projects > c03_tut > c03_tut_03 > c03_tut_03_start.fla**. Next, choose the **Open** button; the Flash document is displayed, as shown in Figure 3-23.

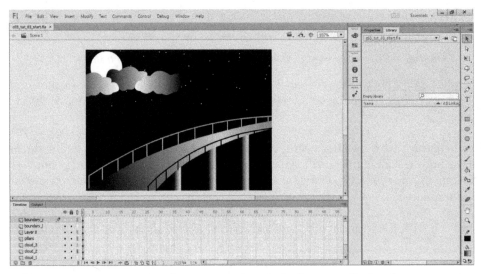

*Figure 3-23*  *The c03_tut_03_start.fla document displayed*

## Converting the Shapes into Movie Clip Symbols

In this section, you will convert the shapes into movie clips symbols.

1.   Select the **Moon** layer in the **Timeline** panel; the circle (moon) behind the clouds is selected in the Stage.

2.   Press the F8 key; the **Convert to Symbol** dialog box is displayed. In this dialog box, type **moon_mc** as the symbol name in the **Name** text box and select **Movie Clip** as the symbol type from the **Type** drop-down list. Next, choose the **OK** button; the moon shape is converted into a movie clip symbol with the name *moon_mc*.

3.   In the **Filters** area of the **Properties** panel, choose the Add filter button located at  the bottom of the **Filters** area; a flyout is displayed showing various filters, as shown in Figure 3-24.

*Figure 3-24  The flyout displayed on choosing the **Add filter** button*

4.  Choose **Glow** from this flyout; the **Glow** area with various properties is displayed in the **Filters** area, as shown in Figure 3-25.

5.  In the **Glow** area, set the value of **Blur X** and **Blur Y** to **50** each and **Strength** value to **150**.

6.  Click on the swatch on the right to **Color**; a flyout is displayed. In this flyout, enter **#FFFFFF** in the Hex edit box and press the ENTER key.

7.  Select **High** from the **Quality** drop-down list. After setting these values, you will notice the glow effect displayed around the circle (moon) in the Stage, as shown in Figure 3-26.

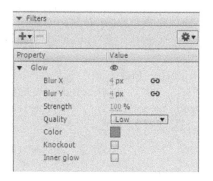

*Figure 3-25  The **Glow** area*  *Figure 3-26  The effect of the **Glow** filter on the moon*

8.  In the **Timeline** panel, select the **Stars** layer; the dots (stars) are selected in the Stage.

9.  Press the F8 key; the **Convert to Symbol** dialog box is displayed. In this dialog box, type the symbol name as **stars** in the **Name** text box and make sure the symbol type **Movie Clip** is selected in the **Type** drop-down list. Next, choose the **OK** button; the dots are converted into a movie clip symbol with the name *stars*.

10. At the bottom of the **Filters** area, choose the **Add filter** button; a flyout is displayed showing various filters. Choose **Glow** from this flyout; the **Glow** area with various properties is displayed in the **Filters** area.

11. In the **Glow** area, set the **Strength** value to **150**. Click on the swatch on the right of **Color**; a flyout is displayed. In this flyout, enter **#FFFFFF** in the Hex edit box and press the ENTER key.

12. Select **High** from the **Quality** drop-down list; the glow effect is displayed around the dots in the Stage, as shown in Figure 3-27.

*Figure 3-27  The glow effect on dots*

13. Save the flash file with the name *c03tut3* at the location *\Documents\Flash_Projects\c03_tut\ c03_tut_03*.

14. Press CTRL+ENTER to view the final output of the tutorial. You can also view the final rendered file of the tutorial by downloading the file *c03_flash_cc_rndr.zip* from *http://www.cadcim.com*. The path of the zip file is mentioned at the beginning of the TUTORIALS section.

## Tutorial 4

In this tutorial, you will import Adobe Photoshop artwork into Flash.

**(Expected time: 10 min)**

The following steps are required to complete this tutorial:

a.   Create a new Flash document.
b.   Import Photoshop file.

### Creating a New Flash Document

In this section, you will create a new Flash document.

1.   Choose **File > New** from the menubar; the **New Document** dialog box is displayed.

2.   In the **New Document** dialog box, choose **ActionScript 3.0** from the **General** tab and then choose the **OK** button; a new Flash document is displayed.

## Importing the Photoshop File

To create a complex artwork, you may prefer other applications such as Adobe Illustrator or Adobe Photoshop. In this section, you will learn to import artwork created in Adobe Photoshop to Flash.

1. Choose **File > Import > Import to Stage** from the menubar; the **Import** dialog box is displayed. In this dialog box, choose **Documents > Flash_Projects > c03_tut > Resources > shapes.psd**; the **Import "Shapes.psd" to Stage** dialog box is displayed, as shown in Figure 3-28.

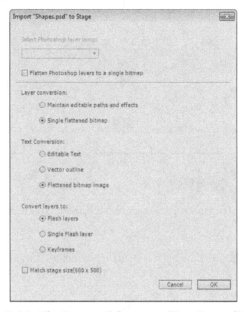

*Figure 3-28  The **Import "shapes.psd" to Stage** dialog box*

2. Choose the **OK** button; every object created in separate layers in Photoshop is placed in the same manner in Flash with name of the layers as **Shape 1**, **Shape 2**, **Shape 3,** and so on, as shown in Figure 3-29.

3. Save the flash file with the name *c03tut3* at the location *\Documents\Flash_Projects\c03_tut\ c03_tut_04*.

4. Press CTRL+ENTER to view the final output. You can also view the final rendered file of the tutorial by downloading the file *c03_flash_cc_rndr.zip* from *http://www.cadcim.com*. The path of the zip file is mentioned at the beginning of the TUTORIALS section.

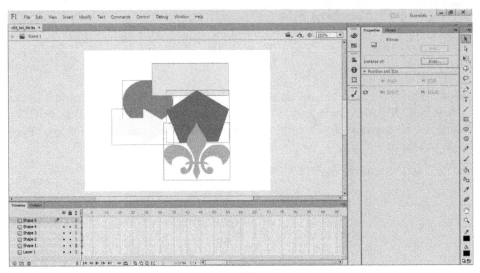

*Figure 3-29  The separate layers imported in the Flash document*

## Self-Evaluation Test

**Answer the following questions and then compare them to those given at the end of this chapter:**

1.  Which of the following shortcut keys is used to insert a keyframe?

    (a) F2                                    (b) F4
    (c) F8                                    (d) F6

2.  The _____ window displays the selected symbol in the **Library** panel.

3.  An _____ is a copy of a symbol.

4.  The _____ symbols are generally used for animating static images.

5.  The _____ symbols are used to create buttons for interactivity.

6.  A button symbol contains its own independent Timeline. (T/F)

7.  The **Over** state of a button symbol is used to define the appearance of the button when the cursor is placed over it. (T/F)

8.  You can apply blending modes and filters to a graphic symbol. (T/F)

## *Review Questions*

**Answer the following questions:**

1. Which of the following combinations of the shortcut keys is used for applying the **Break Apart** command?

    (a) CTRL+C                          (b) CTRL+B
    (c) CTRL+G                          (d) CTRL+U

2. The _____, _____, and _____ are the three categories of symbols in Flash.

3. The _____ area of a button symbol is not visible in the Stage and in the preview window.

4. _____, _____, _____, and _____ are the four states of a button symbol.

5. The _____ represents a new symbol instance in the Timeline.

6. The _____ state of a button symbol represents how the button will appear when the user clicks on it.

7. The _____ command is used to delink the instance from its symbol.

# EXERCISES

## Exercise 1

Create the buttons for a website, as shown in Figure 3-30, using various drawings and editing tools, functions, and button symbol frames. You can view the final rendered file of the buttons by downloading the file *c03_flash_cc_exr.zip* from *http://www.cadcim.com*. The path of the file is as follows: *Textbooks > Animation and Visual Effects > Flash > The Adobe Flash Professional CC: A Tutorial Approach.*            **(Expected time: 20 min)**

*Figure 3-30  The buttons for website*

## Exercise 2

Create a night scene, as shown in Figure 3-31, using various tools, functions, and filters. You can view the final rendered file of the tutorial by downloading the file *c03_flash_cc_exr.zip* from *http://www.cadcim.com*. The path of the file is mentioned in Exercise 1.

           **(Expected time: 40 min)**

*Figure 3-31* The night scene

# Chapter 4

## Creating Animation

### Learning Objectives

*After completing this chapter, you will be able to:*
- *Create motion tween animations*
- *Create animation inside symbols*
- *Use mask layers*
- *Create shape tween animations*
- *Create 3D animations*

# INTRODUCTION

Animation is an illusion of motion created by displaying a series of 2D or 3D images or artwork. Basically, when image passes before our eyes, our eyes retain an image for a fragment of second. But when a series of images are viewed in a continuous flow, our eyes get tricked and perceive it as a real moving object. This happens due to an optical phenomenon called persistence of vision.

Animation is one of the important features of Flash. In Flash, you can animate the position, color, transparency, size, filters, and so on of an object. You can also animate path of motion of an object.

There are twelve basic Principles of Animation. The principles were introduced by the Disney animators Ollie Johnston and Frank Thomas in their book *The Illusion of Life: Disney Animation*. The main purpose of these principles is to create animation abiding basic laws of physics.

## Squash and Stretch

The squash and stretch principle is considered to be the most important and commonly used principle of animation. It helps determine the rigidity and mass of an object by deforming its shape during an action. For example, a bouncing ball squashes when it hits the ground and stretches before and after it hits the ground.

## Anticipation

The preparation for an action is called anticipation. Anticipations are also called the backward actions. A backward action prepares the audience for the real action that is about to be performed by a character; for example, the action that takes place before a person is about to jump, run, or get up from a chair.

## Staging

Staging refers to presenting an idea such that it is clearly and effectively communicated to the audience. It involves posing the characters, setting a scene, fixing camera, lighting, and almost everything that is required for the scene.

## Straight Ahead Action and Pose to Pose

Straight ahead is one of the oldest methods of animation. In this method, you start working on the first drawing and simultaneously work on all other drawings till the end of animation. In pose to pose, you do the basic blocking in the scene. Blocking implies setting the key poses and roughly estimating the frames in which each of the key poses should be keyframed. After blocking the scene, you need to add anticipation, and finally tweak and shuffle poses wherever required.

## Follow Through and Overlapping Action

Actions generally continue after their termination point. The principle of Follow through involves the animation that occurs after the action ends. Overlapping of action means starting a new action before the first action completes. Overlapping is the technique with which you can start different actions at different speed and timing, so that the animation does not appear mechanical.

## Slow In and Slow Out

Slow in and slow out deals with the spacing of the in-between drawings between the extreme poses to apply an effect of ease in and ease out in a scene. It helps soften the action and makes it more realistic.

## Arcs

Most actions performed by living beings occur along an arched trajectory. Arcs create motion that is less stiff than action that occurs along a straight path. The arcs are used to make the look of the animation more natural and as well as to ensure it flows better. Using arcs, you can make the movement of the characters more life-like without any visual obstruction.

## Secondary Action

Secondary actions are added to the main action to create interest and realism in animation such as a person walking and simultaneously swinging his arms. For example, a character throws a basketball into the rim. The primary or main action is to throw basketball into the rim and adjust the shape of the ball and the secondary action is the effect of the ball on the rim after the ball hits it.

## Timing

Timing refers to the number of drawings or frames for an action and its movement in a scene. Timing is important for establishing a character's mood, emotion, and reaction.

## Exaggeration

Exaggeration means presenting an action in an extreme form. Exaggeration can be done by modifying the physical features of a character.

## Solid Drawing

The principle of solid drawing is based on weight, depth, balance, and illusion of three dimensions which are together applied to an animation. It means taking into account the three-dimensional space in animation. The animator needs to understand the basics of three-dimensional shapes, anatomy, weight, balance, light, and shadow.

## Appeal

Appeal means something that a person likes to see, a quality of charm and magnetism in an actor. A character is considered to be appealing only when it looks real and connects to the audience.

# TUTORIALS

Before you start the tutorials, you need to download the *c04_flash_cc_tut.zip* file from *www.cadcim.com*. The path of the file is as follows: *Textbooks > Animation and Visual Effects > Flash > Adobe Flash Professional CC: A Tutorial Approach.*

Next, extract the contents of the zip file to *\Documents\Flash_Projects*.

**Note**
*The tutorial zip file that you have downloaded from the CADCIM website contains a folder **Resources**. This folder contains all resources related to this chapter.*

## Tutorial 1

In this tutorial, you will create a walk cycle using the frame by frame animation method.
**(Expected time: 30 min)**

The following steps are required to complete this tutorial:

a.  Open the Flash document.
b.  Position the first instance in the Timeline.
c.  Position other instances in the Timeline.

### Opening the Flash Document
In this section, you will open the Flash document.

1.  Choose **File > Open** from the menubar; the **Open** dialog box is displayed.

2.  In this dialog box, choose **Documents > Flash_Projects > c04_tut > c04_tut_01 > c04_tut_01_start.fla**. Next, choose the **Open** button; the Flash document is displayed.

3.  Choose the Workspace switcher button; a flyout is displayed. In this flyout, choose **Animator**; the **Essentials** workspace is changed to the **Animator** workspace, as shown in Figure 4-1.

**Note**
*The **Animator** workspace is a preset workspace of Flash. This workspace is arranged in such a manner that makes it easy for animators to animate objects in Flash. By default, the **Motion Presets** panel is active in this workspace.*

The **Library** panel of this document contains various movie clip symbols, as shown in Figure 4-2. Each movie clip symbol in the **Library** panel is a pose of the walk cycle.

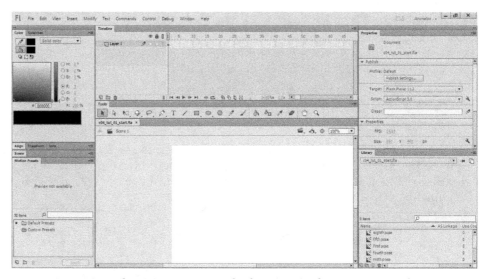

***Figure 4-1*** *The c04_tut_01_start.fla document in the **Animator** workspace*

***Figure 4-2*** *The movie clip symbols in the **Library** panel*

## Positioning the First Instance in the Timeline

In this section, you will place the first instance in the Timeline.

1. In the **Timeline** panel, select frame **1** of **Layer 1**.

2. Drag the *first pose* movie clip from the **Library** panel to the Stage; an instance of this movie clip is created in the Stage.

3. In the **Align** area of the **Align** panel, select the **Align to stage** check box. Next, choose the **Align horizontal center** button and then the **Align vertical center** button; the first pose of the walk cycle is displayed in the Stage, as shown in Figure 4-3.

***Figure 4-3*** *The first instance of the walk cycle*

4. Choose **View > Rulers** from the menubar; the ruler bars are displayed on the top and left sides of the Stage, as shown in Figure 4-4.

   **Rulers** are used to measure the width and height of Flash elements. When the ruler bars are displayed, you can also use guides to position the objects in the Stage.

5. Press and hold the cursor on the horizontal ruler bar and drag the cursor to the Stage; a guide is created in the Stage. Drag the guide and place it below the *first pose* instance in the Stage, as shown in Figure 4-5.

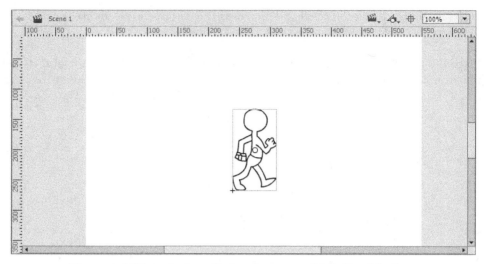

*Figure 4-4* *The ruler bars displayed on top and left side of the Stage*

*Figure 4-5* *The guide placed below the first pose instance*

## Positioning the Other Instances in the Timeline

In this section, you will position the remaining instances in the Timeline.

1.  In **Layer 1**, select frame **4**.

2.  Choose **Insert > Timeline > Blank Keyframe** from the menubar or press the F7 key; a blank keyframe is inserted on frame **4**.

    Blank Keyframe is a keyframe with no content.

3.  Choose the **Onion Skin** button located at the bottom of the **Timeline** panel; the Start Onion Skin and End Onion Skin markers are displayed in the Timeline Header.

    The **Onion Skin** button is used to view the number of frames simultaneously in the Stage. By default, you can see the contents of only the current frame in the Stage. This button is also used to view the progress of an animation. All the frames between the Start Onion Skin and End Onion Skin markers are superimposed as one frame.

4.   Select frame **4**, if it is not selected and then drag the *second pose* movie clip from the **Library** panel to the Stage; its instance is created in the Stage.

5.   Place the *second pose* instance next to the *first pose* instance, as shown in Figure 4-6. Note that you can view the instances of frame **1** and frame **4** simultaneously in the Stage as frame **1** and frame **4** lie between the Onion Skin markers, as shown in Figure 4-7.

*Figure 4-6* *The second pose instance placed next to the first pose instance*

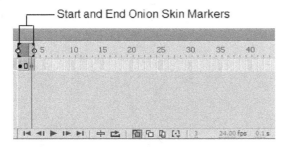

*Figure 4-7* *The Onion Skin markers in the Timeline Header*

6.   Create blank keyframes after an interval of every three frames and place the respective movie clips on each frame. Refer to Table 4-1 for frame number and the movie clip to be placed. Figure 4-8 displays the walk cycle after placing the *sixth pose* instance and Figure 4-9 displays the walk cycle after placing the *ninth pose* instance.

**Note**
*The Onion Skin option makes the pose in the previous frames appear in the shaded form. Drag the Onion Skin markers in the Timeline Header to increase the Onion Skin range.*

***Table 4-1*** *Frames and their respective movie clips*

| Frame | Movie clip |
|---|---|
| Frame 7 | third pose |
| Frame 10 | fourth pose |
| Frame 13 | fifth pose |
| Frame 16 | sixth pose |
| Frame 19 | seventh pose |
| Frame 22 | eighth pose |
| Frame 25 | ninth pose |

***Figure 4-8*** *Placing the sixth pose instance*   ***Figure 4-9*** *Placing the ninth pose instance*

7.  Press CTRL+ENTER to preview the animation.

8.  Save the flash file with the name *c04tut1* at the location *\Documents\Flash_Projects\c04_tut\ c04_tut_01*.

9.  Press CTRL+ENTER to view the final output of the walk cycle. You can also view the final rendered file of the walk cycle by downloading the file *c04_flash_cc_rndr.zip* from *www.cadcim.com*. The path of the zip file is mentioned at the beginning of the TUTORIALS section.

## Tutorial 2

In this tutorial, you will create the bouncing ball animation.   **(Expected time: 30 min)**

The following steps are required to complete this tutorial:

a.  Create a new Flash document.
b.  Create a symbol.
c.  Create a motion tween animation.

## Creating a New Flash Document

In this section, you will create a new Flash document.

1.  Choose **File > New** from the menubar; the **New Document** dialog box is displayed. In this dialog box, choose **ActionScript 3.0** from the **Type** area in the **General** tab.

2.  Set the value of **Frame rate** to **30**, as shown in Figure 4-10 and then choose the **OK** button; a new Flash document is displayed.

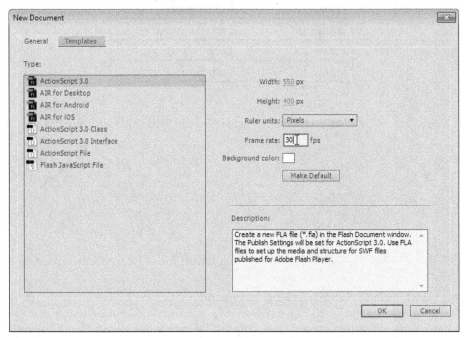

*Figure 4-10  Changing the value of the **Frame rate** in the **New Document** dialog box*

 **Note**
*Frame rate determines the speed at which a movie is played. By default, the frame rate is set to 24 frames per second. You can change the frame rate using the **Timeline** and the **Properties** panels, refer to Figures 4-11 and 4-12.*

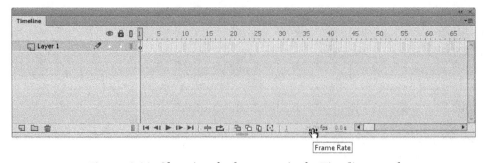

*Figure 4-11  Changing the frame rate in the **Timeline** panel*

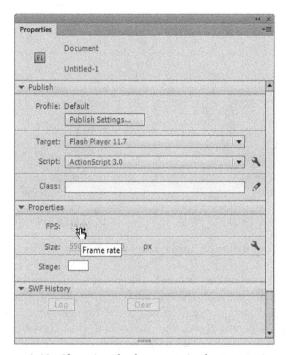

***Figure 4-12***  *Changing the frame rate in the* ***Properties*** *panel*

## Creating a Movie Clip Symbol

In this section, you will create a movie clip symbol.

1.  Choose **Oval Tool** from the **Tools** panel; the properties of this tool are displayed in the **Properties** panel. In the **Fill and Stroke** area of the **Properties** panel, choose the **Stroke color** swatch; a flyout is displayed. In this flyout, make sure **#000000** is entered in the Hex edit box.

2.  In the **Color** panel, select **Radial gradient** fill style from the **Color type** drop-down list. Now, hold the SHIFT key and draw a circle in the Stage.

    The **Radial gradient** option is used to blend colors radially in the outward direction starting from the center point.

3.  Choose **Selection Tool** from the **Tools** panel and select the fill of the circle in the Stage.

4.  In the **Color** panel, double-click on the left pointer of the gradient definition bar; a flyout is displayed. In this flyout, enter **#F5EEEE** in the Hex edit box. Similarly, double-click on the right pointer to display a flyout. In this flyout, enter **#660000** in the Hex edit box.

5.  Choose **Gradient Transform Tool** from the **Tools** panel; the gradient transform circle is displayed around the fill in the Stage. Next, place the cursor at the center of the circle ( on ▒ icon) and drag it upward; the fill is moved upward, as shown in Figure 4-13. Now, place the cursor on the radial scaling arrow and drag the cursor outward, as shown in Figure 4-14.

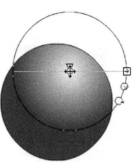
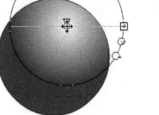
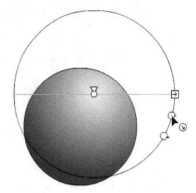

*Figure 4-13* Moving the fill upward                    *Figure 4-14* Scaling the fill

6.   Choose **Selection Tool** from the **Tools** panel and marquee select the circle in the Stage.

7.   Press the F8 key; the **Convert to Symbol** dialog box is displayed. In this dialog box, type the symbol name as **ball_mc** in the **Name** text box and select **Movie Clip** as the symbol type from the **Type** drop-down list. Next, select the bottom center square of the **Registration** grid for specifying the registration point of the symbol, as shown in Figure 4-15, and then choose the **OK** button; a movie clip with the name *ball_mc* is created and saved in the **Library** panel.

*Figure 4-15* The **Convert to Symbol** dialog box

**Note**
*The registration point is a point inside the symbol that is registered as (0,0) on the X and Y axes.*

8.   Make sure the *ball_mc* instance is selected in the Stage. In the **Position and Size** area of the **Properties** panel, set the value of **X** to **263.50** and **Y** to **137**; the *ball_mc* instance is placed at the specified position in the Stage.

## Creating a Motion Tween Animation
In this section, you will create a motion tween animation.

1.   In the **Timeline** panel, rename **Layer 1** as **Ball**.

2. In the **Ball** layer, right-click on frame **1**; a flyout is displayed. In this flyout, choose **Create Motion Tween**. Alternatively, choose **Insert > Motion Tween** from the menubar; the layer is converted into a tween layer and 30 frames are added to the layer, refer to Figure 4-16.

 **Note**
*When a layer is converted into a tween layer, the standard number of frames that are added to the tween layer is equal to the frame rate. Motion tween layers display a tween icon on the left of the layer name, as shown in Figure 4-16.*

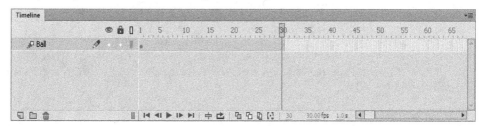

*Figure 4-16  The **Ball** tween layer displaying the tween icon*

3. Drag the Playhead and place it on frame **30**, if it is not already placed there. Next, press and hold the SHIFT key and drag the *ball_mc* instance to the bottom of the Stage, as shown in Figure 4-17; a keyframe is created on frame **30** and the motion path is displayed in the Stage.

 **Tip:** *Holding the SHIFT key while dragging the object helps you to move the object in a straight line.*

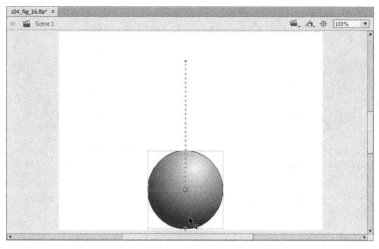

*Figure 4-17  Dragging the ball_mc instance*

4. Click in the blank area of the Stage to deselect the *ball_mc* instance.

5. In the **Timeline** panel, select the **Ball** layer; the tween span also gets selected. Move the cursor on the tween span in this layer, as shown in Figure 4-18.

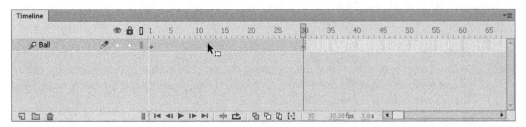

**Figure 4-18** *Moving the cursor on the tween span*

6. Press and hold the ALT key and drag the cursor; a copy of the tween span is created. Now, place the copy of the tween span next to the original tween span in the **Ball** layer, as shown in Figure 4-19.

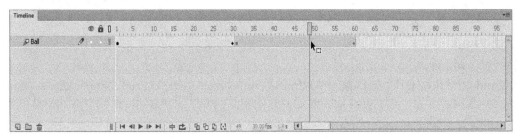

**Figure 4-19** *Placing the copied tween span*

7. Preview the animation (test the movie) by pressing CTRL+ENTER. You will notice that the ball falls twice instead of bouncing. This is because the position of the *ball_mc* instance is same in initial keyframes in both the tween spans, as shown in Figures 4-20 and 4-21.

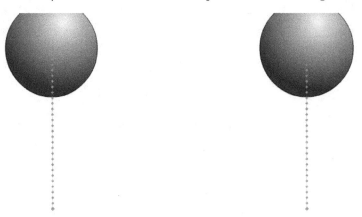

**Figure 4-20** *The ball_mc instance on frame 1*

**Figure 4-21** *The ball_mc instance on frame 31*

8. Close the preview window to return to the document.

9. In the **Ball** layer, right-click on the copied frame span; a flyout is displayed. In this flyout, choose **Reverse Keyframes**; the initial and final keyframes of this span are reversed, as shown in Figures 4-22 and 4-23.

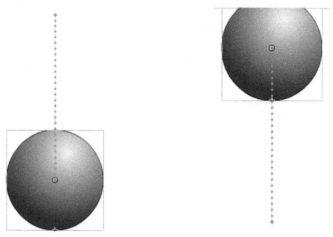

*Figure 4-22*  *The ball_mc instance at frame 31*   *Figure 4-23*  *The ball_mc instance at frame 60*

**Note**
*The Reverse Keyframes option is used to reverse an animation.*

10. Press CTRL+ENTER to preview the animation, the ball starts bouncing, but its animation is not smooth. Close the preview window to return to the document.

**Note**
*Figures 4-22 and 4-23 display the equally spaced dots in the motion path which implies that the object is moving with the same speed throughout the animation.*

Now, you will give a realistic look to the motion of the bouncing ball.

11. Select a frame between frame **1** and **30**; the **Motion Tween** properties are displayed in the **Properties** panel.

12. In the **Ease** area of the **Properties** panel, set the value of **Ease** to **-100**; the space between the dots in the motion path changes. Now, the dots are spaced at shorter distances in the beginning and longer distances at the end of the motion path, as shown in Figure 4-24. This means that the animation is easing-in as the ball moves slowly at the beginning and fast at the end of animation. Figure 4-24 shows the spacing of the dots after easing-in.

**Note**
*Easing is used to change the speed of an object in animation. It allows you to speed up or slow down the start or end of an animation to give motion a realistic effect.*

13. Select a frame between frame **31** and **60**; the **Motion Tween** properties are displayed in the **Properties** panel.

14. In the **Ease** area of the **Properties** panel, set the value of **Ease** to **100**; the space between the dots in the motion path changes. The dots in the motion path are spaced at longer distances in the end and shorter distances in the beginning, as shown in Figure 4-25. This means that the animation is easing-out as the ball moves fast in the beginning and slow at the end of the animation.

 **Tip:** *The speed of the animation depends upon the distance between the dots in the motion path. The more is the distance between the dots, faster will be the animation. Similarly, lesser the distance between the dots, slower will be the animation.*

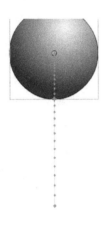    

*Figure 4-24  Easing-in*              *Figure 4-25  Easing-out*

15. Save the flash file with the name *c04tut2* at the location *\Documents\Flash_Projects\c04_tut\ c04_tut_02*.

16. Press CTRL+ENTER to view the final output of the bouncing ball animation. You can also view the final rendered file of the bouncing ball animation by downloading the file *c04_flash_cc_rndr.zip* from *www.cadcim.com*. The path of the zip file is mentioned at the beginning of the TUTORIALS **section**.

## Tutorial 3

In this tutorial, you will create an animated movie clip symbol. Next, you will animate the symbol in the main Timeline, refer to Figure 4-26.                        **(Expected time: 45 min)**

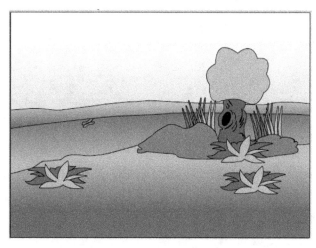

*Figure 4-26* *The animation on frame 31*

The following steps are required to complete this tutorial:

a.   Open the Flash document.
b.   Animate the wings of the butterfly in the symbol.
c.   Animate the butterfly in the main Timeline.

## Opening the Flash Document

In this section, you will open the Flash document.

1.   Choose **File > Open** from the menubar; the **Open** dialog box is displayed.

2.   In this dialog box, choose **Documents > Flash_Projects > c04_tut > c04_tut_03 > c04_tut_03_start.fla**. Next, choose the **Open** button from the dialog box; the Flash document is displayed, as shown in Figure 4-27.

     In *c04_tut_03_start.fla*, all the layers are hidden except **butterfly** layer, refer to Figure 4-27.

3.   Choose **Animator** from the Workspace flyout. Next, choose **Zoom Tool** from the **Tools** panel and click thrice in the center of the Stage to zoom in to **800%**. Alternatively, enter **800** in the Zoom edit box located at the extreme right of the Scene area and press the ENTER key, refer to Figure 4-28.

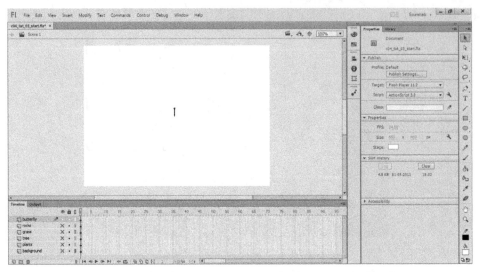

**Figure 4-27**  *The c04_tut_03_start.fla document displayed*

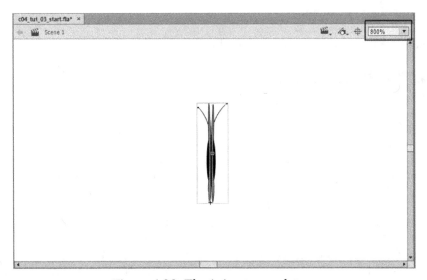

**Figure 4-28**  *The **Animator** workspace*

## Animating the Wings of the Butterfly in the Symbol

In this section, you will animate the wings of the butterfly.

1.  Choose **Selection Tool** and double-click on the *butterfly* instance in the Stage; the symbol-editing mode of the *butterfly* instance is displayed. Notice that in the **Timeline** panel, the parts of the *butterfly* instance are distributed in layers, as shown in Figure 4-29.

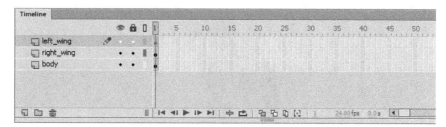

*Figure 4-29  The Timeline of the butterfly instance*

2.   In the **right_wing** layer, right-click on frame **1**; a flyout is displayed. In this flyout, choose **Create Motion Tween**; the layer is converted into a tween layer and 24 frames are added to the layer.

The **Create Motion Tween** option allows you to animate the motion of an object. When a layer is converted into a tween layer, you can select any frame to move and rotate the object.

3.   In the **Timeline** panel, move the cursor close to the end of the tween layer span; the cursor changes to a double-headed arrow. Drag the end of tween span back to frame **8**, refer to Figure 4-30.

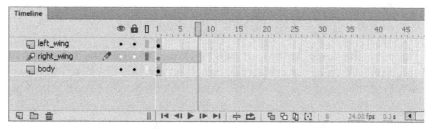

*Figure 4-30  Shortening the tween span*

4.   In the **body** layer, select frame **8** and choose **Insert > Timeline > Frame** from the menubar; the static frames are added and the elements in the **body** layer remain visible till frame **8**.

 **Tip:** *Press F5 to add static frames. Static frames are not a part of tween frames.*

5.   In the **right_wing** layer, place the Playhead on frame **8**, if it is not placed and press the F6 key; a keyframe is inserted and the properties of the *rightwing* instance on frame **1** are copied to frame **8**.

6.   In the **right_wing** layer, place the Playhead on frame **5** and then click on the *rightwing* instance in the Stage; the properties of this instance are displayed in the **Properties** panel.

7.   Make sure that the **Lock width and height values together** button is off ( ). In the **Position and Size** area of the **Properties** panel, set the value of **W** to **92**; the width of the wing is increased, as shown in Figure 4-31.

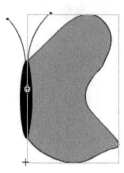

*Figure 4-31 Increasing the width of the wing on frame* **5**

8. In the **left_wing** layer in the **Timeline** panel, right-click on frame **1**; a flyout is displayed. In this flyout, choose **Create Motion Tween**; the layer is converted into a tween layer and 24 frames are added to the layer.

9. Decrease the tween span till frame **8**. Next, place the Playhead on frame **8** and press the F6 key; the properties of the *leftwing* instance in frame **1** are copied to frame **8**.

10. Place the Playhead on frame **5** and then click on the *leftwing* instance in the Stage; the properties of this instance are displayed in the **Properties** panel.

11. Make sure that the **Lock width and height values together** button is off (⟲). In the **Position and Size** area of the **Properties** panel, set the value of **W** to **92**; the width of the wing increases, as shown in Figure 4-32. Next, click on **Scene 1** to return to the Stage.

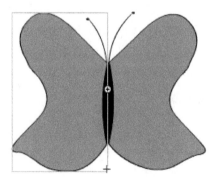

*Figure 4-32 The wings on frame* **5**

12. Enter **100** in the Zoom edit box.

13. In the **Timeline** panel, choose the **Lock or Unlock All Layers** button located in the Timeline Header; all the layers are locked, as shown in Figure 4-33.

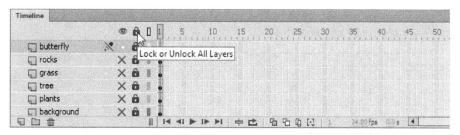

*Figure 4-33  The **Lock or Unlock All Layers** button in the Timeline Header*

14. Choose the **Lock or Unlock All Layers** button of the **butterfly** layer; the **butterfly** layer is unlocked, as shown in Figure 4-34.

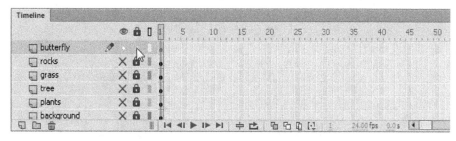

*Figure 4-34  The **butterfly** layer unlocked*

**Note**

*When a layer is locked in the **Timeline** panel, the layer will freeze and no changes can be made in that layer.*

## Animating the Butterfly Instance in the Main Timeline

In this section, you will animate the butterfly instance in the main Timeline.

1. Right-click on the **butterfly** layer; a flyout is displayed. In this flyout, choose **Add Classic Motion Guide**; a new layer is added above the **butterfly** layer with the name **Guide: butterfly**. This layer is the guide layer of the **butterfly** layer, refer to Figure 4-35.

   The guide layer consists of guide icon on the left of the layer name, as shown in Figure 4-35. In guide layers, you can create strokes that act as path for instances, groups, or texts to be followed.

*Figure 4-35  The guide layer of the **butterfly** layer*

2.  In the **Timeline** panel, double-click on the **Show or Hide All Layers** button to make all the layers visible, refer to Figure 4-36.

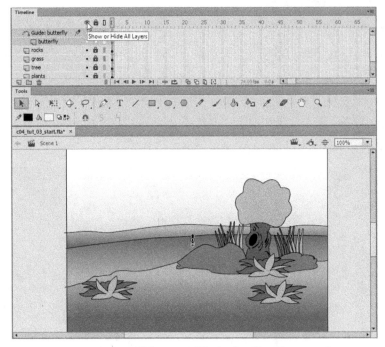

*Figure 4-36  All layers visible in the **Timeline** panel*

3.  Choose **Pencil Tool** from the **Tools** panel. In the **Guide: butterfly** layer, select frame **1** and draw the path, as shown in Figure 4-37.

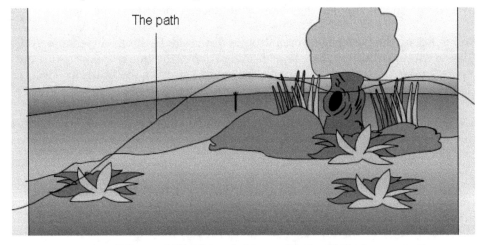

*Figure 4-37  The path drawn with **Pencil Tool***

4.  In the **Guide: butterfly** layer, select frame **96**. Next, hold the SHIFT key and select frame **96** of the **background** layer and then press the F5 key; the static frames are added till frame **96** of each layer, refer to Figure 4-38.

*Figure 4-38* *The Timeline of layers after adding the static frames*

5.  Select the **butterfly** layer. Next, choose **Selection Tool** from the **Tools** panel. In the Options section of the **Tools** panel, choose the **Snap to Objects** option.

6.  Select frame **1** of the **butterfly** layer. Drag the **+** icon of the *butterfly* instance in the Stage to the left end of the path in the Pasteboard; a black circle is displayed on the *butterfly* instance when it is snapped to the path.

7.  Choose **Modify > Transform > Rotate 90° CW** from the menubar; the *butterfly* instance is placed horizontally to the left end of the motion guide path, as shown in Figure 4-39.

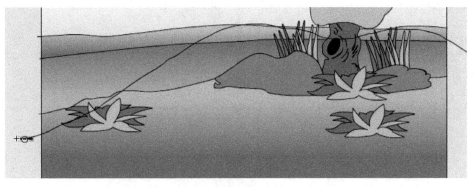

*Figure 4-39* *Snapping the butterfly instance to the left end of the path*

8.  In the **butterfly** layer, select frame **96** and press the F6 key; a keyframe is inserted. Next, drag the *butterfly* instance and place it on the right end of the path.

9.  Make sure that the *butterfly* instance is selected in the Stage. Choose **Free Transform Tool** from the **Tools** panel. Next, rotate the *butterfly* instance in the clockwise direction approximately to 20 degrees, refer to Figure 4-40.

10. In the **butterfly** layer, right-click on a frame between frame **1** and frame **96**; a flyout is displayed. In this flyout, choose **Create Classic Tween**; an arrow is created between frame **1** and frame **96**, representing the classic tween animation, refer to Figure 4-41.

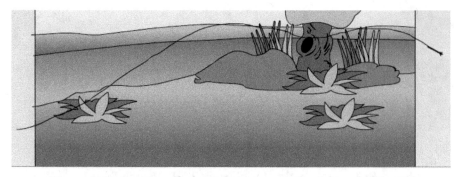

*Figure 4-40  Snapping the butterfly instance to the right end of the path*

*Figure 4-41  The **butterfly** layer after adding classic tween*

The **Create Classic Tween** option is used to create specific animated effects that cannot be created using span-based tweens, for example, applying eases to a group of frames instead of the entire tween. You can also apply two or more color effects to a classic tween. To a motion tween, you can apply only one color effect.

11. In the **butterfly** layer, select a frame between frame **1** and frame **96**; the **Frame** properties are displayed in the **Properties** panel. In the **Tweening** area of the **Properties** panel, select the **Orient to path** check box, as shown in Figure 4-42.

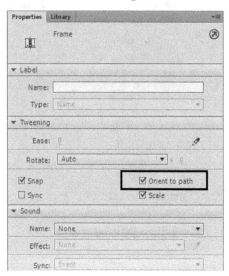

*Figure 4-42  The **Tweening** area with the **Orient to Path** check box selected*

The **Orient to path** option is used to maintain a constant orientation of the object relative to its path.

12. Select the **butterfly** and **Guide: butterfly** layers in the **Timeline** panel using SHIFT key. Next, drag the layers and place them below the **tree** layer, as shown in Figure 4-43.

*Figure 4-43* *Changing the position of the layers in the* **Timeline** *panel*

13. Click in the pasteboard; the document properties are displayed in the **Properties** panel. In the **Properties** area of the **Properties** panel, set the value of **FPS** to **30**.

14. Save the flash file with the name *c04tut3* at the location *\Documents\Flash_Projects\c04_tut\ c04_tut_03*.

15. Press CTRL+ENTER to view the final output of the butterfly animation. You can also view the final rendered file of the butterfly animation by downloading the file *c04_flash_cc_rndr.zip* from *www.cadcim.com*. The path of the zip file is mentioned at the beginning of the TUTORIALS **section**.

## Tutorial 4

In this tutorial, you will animate a chopper following a car running on the highway in a cityscape scene, refer to Figure 4-44.

**(Expected time: 45 min)**

*Figure 4-44* *The chopper and the car at frame 36*

The following steps are required to complete this tutorial:

a.  Open the Flash document.
b.  Create the stars.
c.  Animate the car.
d.  Animate the chopper.

## Opening the Flash Document
In this section, you will open the Flash document.

1.  Choose **File > Open** from the menubar; the **Open** dialog box is displayed.

2.  In this dialog box, choose **Documents > Flash_Projects > c04_tut > c04_tut_04 >
    c04_tut_04_start.fla**. Next, choose the **Open** button; the Flash document is displayed, as
    shown in Figure 4-45.

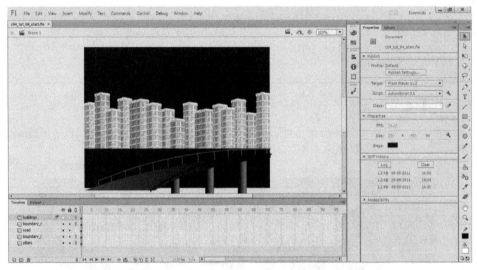

*Figure 4-45  The c04_tut_04_start.fla document displayed*

## Creating the River
In this section, you will create the river.

1.  Choose the **New Layer** button in the **Timeline** panel to create a new layer and rename it
    to **river**. Next, drag and place the **river** layer below the **pillars** layer.

2.  Choose **Rectangle Tool** from the **Tools** panel; the properties of this tool are displayed in
    the **Properties** panel.

3.  In the **Fill and Stroke** area of the **Properties** panel, choose the **Stroke color** swatch; a
    flyout is displayed. In this flyout, choose the **No Color** button.

4.  Make sure the **river** layer is selected and create a rectangle in the Stage.

5.  Choose **Selection Tool** and then select the rectangle in the Stage; the **Shape** properties are displayed in the **Properties** panel.

6.  In the **Position and Size** area of the **Properties** panel, set the value of **X** and **Y** to **-55** and **250**, respectively. Next, set the values of **W** and **H** to **720** and **195**, respectively.

7.  In the **Color** panel, select **Bitmap fill** from the **Color type** drop-down list. Next, choose the **Import bitmap** button; the **Import to Library** dialog box is displayed. In this dialog box, choose **Documents > Flash_Projects > c04_tut > Resources > water.jpg**. Now, choose the **Open** button; the selected image is displayed in the **Color** panel as bitmap swatch and is applied to the selected fill of the rectangle in the Stage, as shown in Figure 4-46.

*Figure 4-46 The bitmap applied to the rectangle as fill*

8.  Choose **Gradient Transform Tool** from the **Tools** panel; the gradient transform bars are displayed around the rectangle (fill). Place the cursor on the arrow located at the lower left corner gradient transform bar; the cursor is changed into a double-headed arrow. Next, drag the cursor to left to scale the fill, as shown in Figure 4-47.

*Figure 4-47 Scaling the fill*

## Creating the Stars

In this section, you will create the stars.

1.  Choose the **New Layer** button in the **Timeline** panel; a new layer is created. Rename this layer to **stars** and place it below the **river** layer.

2.  Choose **Brush Tool** from the **Tools** panel; the properties of this tool are displayed in the **Properties** panel.

3.  In the **Fill and Stroke** area of the **Properties** panel, choose the **Fill color** swatch; a flyout is displayed. In this flyout, enter **#FFFFFF** in the Hex edit box and press the ENTER key.

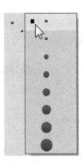

4.  Choose the **Brush size** button in the Options section of the **Tools** panel; a flyout containing different sizes for the brush is displayed. In this flyout, choose the smallest brush size, as shown in Figure 4-48.

5.  Select the **stars** layer. Next, click at different places in the upper area of the Stage; a pattern of dots is displayed in the Stage that appears like stars, as shown in Figure 4-49.

*Figure 4-48* *Choosing the smallest brush size*

*Figure 4-49* *Creating the stars*

## Animating the Car
In this section, you will animate the car.

1.  Choose the **New Layer** button in the **Timeline** panel; a new layer is created. Rename this layer to **car**.

2.  Drag and place the **car** layer above the **buildings** layer.

3.  Select the **car** layer in the **Timeline** panel. Next, drag the *car_mc* movie clip from the **Library** panel to the Stage; an instance of the movie clip is created in the Stage.

4.  Choose **Selection Tool** from the **Tools** panel and position the *car_mc* instance in the beginning of the road (on the left), as shown in Figure 4-50.

5.  Choose **Free Transform Tool** from the **Tools** panel; the transform box is displayed around the car. Next, rotate the *car_mc* instance to match with the arc of the road, as shown in Figure 4-51.

6.  In the **car** layer, right-click on the frame **1**; a flyout is displayed. In this flyout, choose **Create Motion Tween**; the **car** layer is converted into a tween layer and 24 frames are added to the layer.

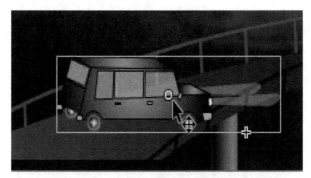

**Figure 4-50** *Positioning the car_mc instance*

**Figure 4-51** *Rotating the car_mc instance*

7. Select 120th frame of all layers using the SHIFT key. Next, press the F5 key; static frames are inserted till frame **120** of all layers.

8. Place the Playhead on frame **60**.

9. Choose **Selection Tool** and select the *car_mc* instance in the Stage. Next, drag the instance to the end of the road (on the right); a motion path is created, as shown in Figure 4-52.

**Figure 4-52** *Positioning the car_mc instance on frame* **60**

10. Choose **Free Transform Tool** from the **Tools** panel and rotate the *car_mc* instance to match with the arc of the road, as shown in Figure 4-53.

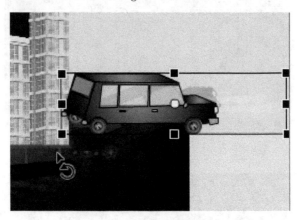

*Figure 4-53*  *Rotating the car*

11. Choose **Selection Tool** from the **Tools** panel and select the *car_mc* instance. Next, position it on the level of the road, as shown in Figure 4-54.

*Figure 4-54*  *Positioning the car*

12. Lock all the layers and then unlock the **car** layer.

13. Make sure the **Selection Tool** is chosen in the **Tools** panel and place the cursor beneath the dotted motion path; an arc appears below the cursor indicating that you can change the shape of the motion path. Now, drag the cursor upward to match the shape of the motion path with the arc of the road, as shown in Figure 4-55.

*Figure 4-55* *Changing the curvature of the motion path*

## Animating the Chopper

In this section, you will animate the chopper.

1.  Choose the **New Layer** button in the **Timeline** panel; a new layer is created. Rename this layer to **chopper**.

2.  Drag the *chopper_mc* movie clip from the **Library** panel in the Pasteboard; an instance of the movie clip is created. Next, position it on the left of the Stage (in the Pasteboard), as shown in Figure 4-56.

*Figure 4-56* *Positioning the chopper_mc instance on frame 1*

3.  Right-click on frame **1** of the **chopper** layer; a flyout is displayed. In this flyout, choose **Create Motion Tween**; the layer is converted into a tween layer.

4.  Place the Playhead on frame **120**. Next, drag the *chopper_mc* instance diagonally downward on the other side of the Stage to create a diagonal motion path, as shown in Figure 4-57.

5.  Place the Playhead on frame **60**. Next, choose **Free Transform Tool** from the **Tools** panel; the transform box is displayed around the *chopper_mc* instance. Next, rotate this instance approximately to 45 degrees clockwise, as shown in Figure 4-58.

6.  Place the Playhead on frame **90** and rotate the *chopper_mc* instance approximately 20 degree anti-clockwise, as shown in Figure 4-59.

*Figure 4-57* *The chopper_mc instance on frame **60***

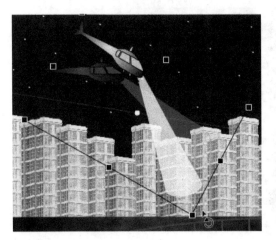

*Figure 4-58* *Rotating chopper_mc instance by 45 degrees clockwise on frame **60***

*Figure 4-59* *Rotating chopper_mc instance by 20 degrees anti-clockwise on frame **90***

7.  Click on the tween span of the **chopper** layer; the **Motion Tween** properties are displayed in the **Properties** panel. In the **Ease** area of the **Properties** panel, set the value of **Ease** to **100**.

8.  Drag and place the **boundary_r** layer above the **chopper** layer, as shown in Figure 4-60.

*Figure 4-60  Boundary_r layer is placed above the chopper layer*

9.  Save the flash file with the name *c04tut4* at the location *\Documents\Flash_Projects\c04_tut\ c04_tut_04*.

10. Press CTRL+ENTER to view the final output of the tutorial. You can also view the final rendered file of the tutorial by downloading the file *c04_flash_cc_rndr.zip* from *www.cadcim.com*. The path of the zip file is mentioned at the beginning of the TUTORIALS **section**.

## Tutorial 5

In this tutorial, you will use the mask layer to create ripple animation, refer to Figure 4-61.

**(Expected time: 20 min)**

*Figure 4-61  The ripple animation on frame 6*

The following steps are required to complete this tutorial:

a.   Create a new Flash document.
b.   Download the image.
c.   Import the image.
d.   Create a movie clip.
e.   Return to the main Timeline.

## Creating a New Flash Document

In this section, you will create a new Flash document.

1.   Choose **File > New** from the menubar; the **New Document** dialog box is displayed.

2.   In this dialog box, choose **ActionScript 3.0** from the **General** tab and then choose the **OK** button; a new Flash document is displayed.

## Downloading an Image

In this section, you will download the image.

1.   Open the link *www.sxc.hu/photo/797111*; a page is displayed.

2.   Download the image used in this tutorial and then save it with the name *scene.jpg* at the location */Documents/Flash_Projects/c04_tut/Resources*.

**Note**
*Footage Courtesy:* **Kyle Sorensen** *(http://www.sxc.hu/profile/sparta41)*

## Importing the Image

In this section, you will import the image and edit its properties.

1.   Rename **Layer 1** to **Image**.

2.   Select frame **1** and press CTRL+R; the **Import** dialog box is displayed. In this dialog box, choose **Documents > Flash_Projects > c04_tut > Resources > scene.jpg**. Next, choose the **Open** button; the selected image is displayed in the Stage, as shown in Figure 4-61.

3.   In the **Match size** area of the **Align** panel, choose the **Match width and height**  button; the width and height of the *scene.jpg* is equal to that of the Stage.

4.   In the **Align** area of the **Align** panel, choose the **Align horizontal center** and **Align vertical center** buttons; the image is aligned exactly to the Stage.

5.   Press the F8 key; the **Convert to Symbol** dialog box is displayed. In this dialog box, type the name of the symbol as **scene_mc** in the **Name** text box and make sure the **Movie Clip** is selected as the symbol type in the **Type** drop-down list. Next, choose the **OK** button; the *scene.jpg* is converted into a movie clip symbol.

6. Select the *scene_mc* instance in the Stage, if it is not selected; the properties of this instance are displayed in the **Properties** panel. In the **Color Effect** area of the **Properties** panel, select **Alpha** from the **Style** drop-down list; the **Alpha** slider is displayed in the **Properties** panel. Next, set the value of **Alpha** to **99**.

## Creating a Movie Clip

In this section, you will create a new movie clip.

1. Press CTRL+F8; the **Create New Symbol** dialog box is displayed. In this dialog box, enter the name of the symbol as **ripple_mc** in the **Name** text box and make sure **Movie Clip** is selected as the symbol type in the **Type** drop-down list. Next, choose the **OK** button; the **ripple_mc** symbol-editing mode is displayed in the Scene area.

2. From the **Library** panel, drag the *scene_mc* movie clip to the **ripple_mc** symbol-editing mode in the Scene area; an instance of *scene_mc* is created in the *ripple_mc* movie clip.

3. In the **Color Effect** area of the **Properties** panel, select **Alpha** from the **Style** drop-down list; the **Alpha** slider is displayed in the **Properties** panel. Next, set the value of **Alpha** to **0**; the instance of the *scene_mc* movie clip turns transparent, refer to Figure 4-62.

4. Right-click on frame **1**; a flyout is displayed. In this flyout, choose **Create Motion Tween**. Next, decrease the frame span to frame **20**.

5. Place the Playhead on frame **5**, select *scene_mc* in the Stage, and then set the value of **Alpha** to **99**.

6. Place the Playhead on frame **15** and press the F6 key to insert a keyframe. Next, move the Playhead on frame **20** and insert another keyframe.

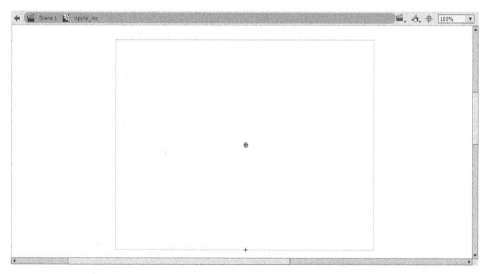

*Figure 4-62  The scene_mc instance on frame 1*

7.  Select the *scene_mc* instance in the Stage; the properties of this instance are displayed in the **Properties** panel. In the **Color Effect** area of the **Properties** panel, set the value of **Alpha** to **0%**.

8.  Move the Playhead on frame **5**, and then select the *scene_mc* instance in the Stage; the properties of the instance are displayed in the **Properties** panel.

9.  In the **Position and Size** area of the **Properties** panel, set the value of **W** to **545** and the value of **H** to **395**.

10. Place the Playhead on frame **20** and then select the *scene_mc* instance in the Stage. In the **Position and Size** area of the **Properties** panel, set the value of **W** to **555** and the value of **H** to **405**.

11. Choose the **New Layer** button in the **Timeline** panel; **Layer 2** is created. Lock the **Layer 1**.

12. In the **Timeline** panel, double-click on the layer icon of the **Layer 1**, as shown in Figure 4-63; the **Layer Properties** dialog box is displayed. In this dialog box, click on the **Outline color** swatch; a flyout is displayed. In this flyout, enter **#000000** in the Hex edit box and press the ENTER key. Select the **View layer as outlines** check box, refer to Figure 4-64. Next, choose the **OK** button. Now, click on **Scene 1** to return to main Timeline and double click on the *ripple_mc* symbol icon in the

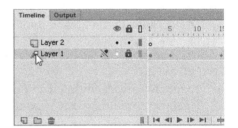

*Figure 4-63  The layer icon of the Layer 1*

**Library** panel, refer to Figure 4-65; the objects in the layer are represented only by their outlines, as shown in Figure 4-66.

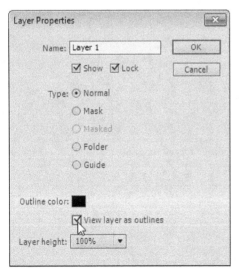

*Figure 4-64  The Layer Properties dialog box displayed on double-clicking on the layer icon*

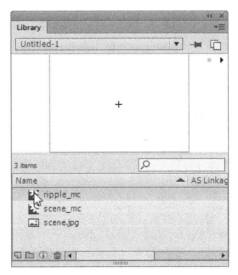

*Figure 4-65  Ripple_mc symbol icon shown in the Library panel*

*Figure 4-66  The objects in the layer displayed as outline*

13. Choose **Oval Tool** from the **Tools** panel; the properties of this tool are displayed in the **Properties** panel.

14. In the **Fill and Stroke** area of the **Properties** panel, choose the **Fill color** swatch; a flyout is displayed. In this flyout, enter **#FF0000** in the Hex edit box and press the ENTER key. Next, choose the **Stroke color** swatch; a flyout is displayed. In this flyout, choose the **No color** button.

15. Enter **800** in the Zoom edit box to zoom in to the Stage. In **Layer 2**, move the Playhead on frame **1** and create an oval horizontally.

16. Choose **Selection Tool** and select the oval in the Stage; the **Shape** properties are displayed in the **Properties** panel. In the **Position and Size** area of the **Properties** panel, set the value of **W** to **47** and **H** to **19**.

17. Press CTRL+C; a copy of oval is copied to clipboard. Next, choose **Edit > Paste in Place** from the menubar. Alternatively, press CTRL+SHIFT+V; the copy of the oval is placed on the original oval.

18. Choose **Free Transform Tool** from the **Tools** panel; the transform box is displayed around the oval. Next, move the cursor on the upper right corner transform point. Press and hold SHIFT and drag the cursor inward, as shown in Figure 4-67.

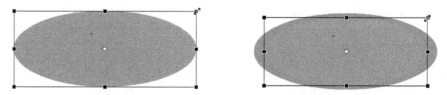

*Figure 4-67  Dragging the cursor inward*

19. Choose **Selection Tool** from the **Tools** panel and select the original oval behind the copied oval, as shown in Figure 4-68. Next, select the copy of the oval (small oval) and press the DEL key; a hollow oval is created, as shown in Figure 4-69.

**Figure 4-68** *Selecting the original oval*          **Figure 4-69** *A hollow oval*

 **Tip:** *For viewing the outline of a layer when the content in that layer is transparent, choose the Show All layers As Outlines button corresponding to that layer.*

20. Enter **100** in the Zoom edit box to zoom out of the Stage. Next, select frame **1**. Choose the **Selection Tool** from the **Tools** panel, if it is not selected and select the oval; the **Shape** properties are displayed in the **Properties** panel.

21. In the **Position and Size** area of the **Properties** panel, set the value of **X** to **83** and **Y** to **171**; the oval is placed at the bottom of the *scene_mc* instance, as shown in Figure 4-70.

22. Select frame **20** and press F6 to insert a keyframe.

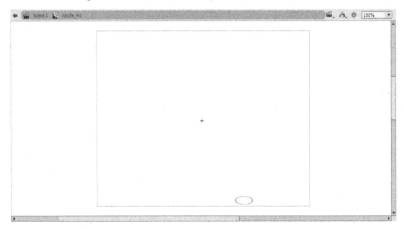

**Figure 4-70** *Oval placed at the bottom of the instance*

23. Choose **Free Transform Tool** from the **Tools** panel; the transform box is displayed around the oval. Next, move the cursor on the middle right transform point. Press and hold the SHIFT key and drag the cursor outward. In the **Position and Size** area of the **Properties** panel, set the value of **W** to **173** and **H** to **19**.

24. In **Layer 2**, right-click on a frame between frame **1** and **20**; a flyout is displayed. In this flyout, choose **Create Shape Tween**; the layer is converted into a shape tween layer and all frames are tinted green, as shown in Figure 4-71.

The **Create Shape Tween** option is used to create the animation of a shape changing into another shape. For example, draw a shape on a frame and change that shape or draw another shape on another frame. Flash then interpolates the intermediate shapes for the in-between frames.

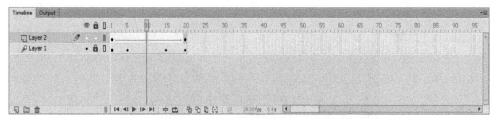

***Figure 4-71*** *The shape tween frames*

25. Right-click on **Layer 2**; a flyout is displayed. In this flyout, choose **Mask**; the layer is converted into the mask layer and the mask icon is displayed on the left of the layer name, as shown in Figure 4-72.

The mask layer is used to display portions of layer below it. The shape that is placed on the mask layer acts as a window that shows the area of the layer beneath it.

 **Note**
*Strokes cannot be masked.*

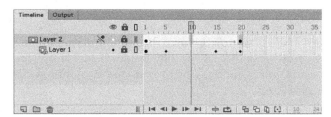

***Figure 4-72*** *The mask layer*

## Returning to the Main Timeline
In this section, you will return to main Timeline.

1.  Click on **Scene 1** to return to main Timeline.

2.  Select frame **30** of the **Image** layer and press the F5 key.

3.  Choose the **New layer** button; a new layer is created. Drag the *ripple_mc* movie clip in the Stage from the **Library** panel; an instance of the movie clip is created.

4.  Choose **Selection Tool** from the **Tools** panel and select the *ripple_mc* instance in the Stage, if it is not selected; the properties of this instance are displayed in the **Properties** panel. In the **Position and Size** area of the **Properties** panel, set the value of **X** to **230** and **Y** to **203**; the instance is positioned at specified place in the Stage, as shown in Figure 4-73.

*Figure 4-73* *Placing the ripple_mc instance in the Stage*

5.  Select frame **20** of **Layer 2** (new layer) and press the F5 key to insert static frames.

6.  Press CTRL+ENTER to preview the final ripple animation.

7.  Save the flash file with the name *c04tut5* at the location *\Documents\Flash_Projects\c04_tut\ c04_tut_05*.

8.  Press CTRL+ENTER to view the final output of the ripple animation. You can also view the final rendered file of the ripple animation by downloading the file *c04_flash_cc_rndr.zip* from *www.cadcim.com*. The path of the zip file is mentioned at the beginning of the TUTORIALS **section**.

## Tutorial 6

In this tutorial, you will convert an image into a movie clip symbol and then create a 3D animation using 3D tools, as shown in Figure 4-74.                      **(Expected time: 20 min)**

*Figure 4-74* *The 3D animation on frame 33*

The following steps are required to complete this tutorial:

a.   Create a new Flash document.
b.   Download an image.
c.   Import the image.
d.   Convert the image into a movie clip symbol.
e.   Animate the instance.
f.   Create a rectangle.

## Creating a New Flash Document
In this section, you will create a new Flash document.

1.   Choose **File > New** from the menubar; the **New Document** dialog box is displayed.

2.   In this dialog box, choose **ActionScript 3.0** from the **General** tab and then choose the **OK** button; a new Flash document is displayed.

## Downloading the Image
In this section, you will download the image.

1.   Open the link *www.sxc.hu/photo/287602*; a page is displayed.

2.   Download the image from this page and then save it with the name *dance.jpg* at the location */Documents/Flash_Projects/c04_tut/Resources*.

**Note**
*Footage Courtesy:* **Fabrizio turco** *(http://www.sxc.hu/profile/zirak)*

## Importing the Image
In this section, you will import the image in Flash.

1.   Select frame **1** in **Layer 1** and press CTRL+R; the **Import** dialog box is displayed. In this dialog box, choose **Documents > Flash_Projects > c04_tut > Resources > dance.jpg**. Next, choose the **Open** button; the selected image is displayed in the Stage, as shown in Figure 4-75.

2.   Select the *dance.jpg* in the Stage; the **Bitmap** properties are displayed in the **Properties** panel.

3.   In the **Position and Size** area of the **Properties** panel, set the value of **W** to **285** and the value of **H** to **169**; the size of the image is reduced.

*Figure 4-75  The dance.jpg in the Stage*

## Converting the Image into a Movie Clip Symbol

In this section, you will convert the image into a movie clip symbol and then modify the properties of its instance.

1. Select *dance.jpg* in the Stage and press the F8 key; the **Convert to Symbol** dialog box is displayed.

2. In this dialog box, type the name of the symbol as **dance_mc** in the **Name** text box and make sure **Movie Clip** is selected in the **Type** drop-down list. Next, choose the **OK** button; the *dance_mc* movie clip is saved in the **Library** panel and its instance is created in the Stage.

3. Place the *dance_mc* instance in the Pasteboard, as shown in Figure 4-76.

*Figure 4-76  Placing the dance_mc instance in the Pasteboard*

4. In the **Filters** area of the **Properties** panel, choose the **Add filter** button located at the bottom; a flyout is displayed. In this flyout, choose **Bevel**; the **Bevel** filter is applied on the instance and the properties of this filter are displayed in the **Filters** area.

5.  In the **Bevel** area, select **High** from the **Quality** drop-down list. Next, click on the **Highlight** swatch; a flyout is displayed. In this flyout, enter **#CCCCCC** in the Hex edit box and make sure the value of **Angle** is set to **45**, as shown in Figure 4-77.

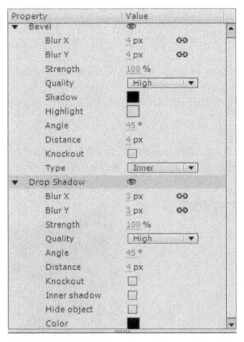

*Figure 4-77  The Bevel and Drop Shadow areas in the Properties panel*

6.  Choose the **Add filter** button; a flyout is displayed. In this flyout, choose **Drop Shadow**; a shadow of the instance is created behind it.

7.  In the **Drop Shadow** area of the **Properties** panel, set the value of both **Blur X** and **Blur Y** to **3**. Next, select **High** from the **Quality** drop-down list, refer to Figure 4-77. Figure 4-78 shows the *dance_mc* instance after applying the **Bevel** and **Drop Shadow** filters.

*Figure 4-78  The instance after applying the Bevel and Drop Shadow filters*

## Animating the Instance

In this section, you will animate the instance.

1. Right-click on frame **1**; a flyout is displayed. In this flyout, choose **Create Motion Tween**; the layer is converted into a tween layer and standard frames are added to the layer. Next, increase the tween span till frame **96**.

2. Place the Playhead on frame **1** and choose **Window > Transform** from the menubar; the **Transform** panel is displayed, as shown in Figure 4-79. In the **3D Rotation** area of the **Transform** panel, set the value of **Y** to **-84**; the instance rotates about the Y-axis, as shown in Figure 4-80.

3. Place the Playhead on frame **96** and drag the *dance_mc* instance on the other side of the Stage, as shown in Figure 4-81. In the **3D Rotation** area of the **Transform** panel, set the value of **Y** to **84**.

*Figure 4-79*   *The **Transform** panel*

*Figure 4-80*   *The dance_mc instance on frame 1*

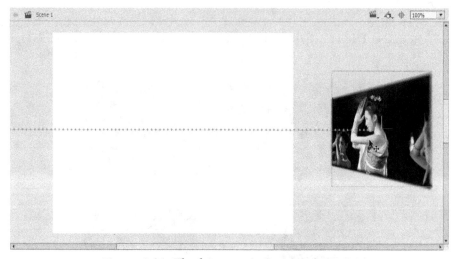

*Figure 4-81*   *The dance_mc instance on frame 96*

4. Select the tween span; the **Motion Tween** properties are displayed in the **Properties** panel. In the **Ease** area of the **Properties** panel, set the value of **Ease** to **100**.

## Creating a Rectangle

In this section, you will create a rectangle using **Rectangle Tool**.

1. Choose the **New Layer** button in the **Timeline** panel to create a new layer.

2. Choose **Rectangle Tool** from the **Tools** panel; the properties of this tool are displayed in the **Properties** panel.

3. In the **Fill and Stroke** area of the **Properties** panel, choose the **Stroke color**; a flyout is displayed. In this flyout, choose the **No color** button.

4. In the **Color** panel, select the **Linear gradient** fill style from the **Color type** drop-down list. In the new layer, create a rectangle approximately to the size of the Stage.

5. Choose **Selection Tool** from the **Tools** panel and select the fill in the stage. Next, choose **Gradient Transform Tool** from the **Tools** panel. Now, rotate the gradient fill 90 degrees anti-clock wise. Now, scale the fill to the size of the Stage, refer to Figure 4-82.

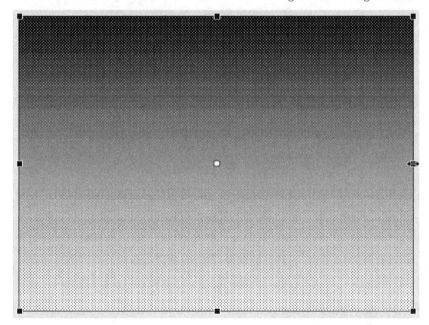

*Figure 4-82  The rectangle after transforming the gradient fill*

6. Place **Layer 2** below **Layer 1**, as shown in Figure 4-83; the rectangle is placed behind the *dance_mc* instance, as shown in Figure 4-84.

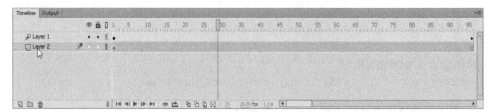

*Figure 4-83  Placing **Layer 2** below **Layer 1***

***Figure 4-84**  The rectangle placed behind dance_mc instance*

7.  Save the flash file with the name *c04tut6* at the location *\Documents\Flash_Projects\c04_tut\ c04_tut_06*.

8.  Press CTRL+ENTER to view the final output of the tutorial. You can also view the final rendered file of the tutorial by downloading the file *c04_flash_cc_rndr.zip* from *www.cadcim.com*. The path of the zip file is mentioned at the beginning of the **TUTORIALS** section.

## Self-Evaluation Test

**Answer the following questions and then compare them to those given at the end of this chapter:**

1.  What is the default frame rate in Flash?

(a) 24 fps                          (b) 25 fps
(c) 26 fps                          (d) 27 fps

2. The _____ key helps to drag the objects in a straight line.

3. The _____ command is used to reverse the keyframes.

4. _____ is used to slow-in and slow-out the speed of an object in animation.

5. The _____ check box is used to maintain a constant orientation of the object relative to its path.

6. FPS stands for _____.

7. In _____ layers, you can create stroke that act as path for instances, groups, or text to be followed.

8. The _____ button is used to lock and unlock the layers.

9. The more the distance between the dots in the motion path, the faster will be the speed of animation. The less the distance between the dots, the slower will be the speed of animation. (T/F)

10. Press F5 to add keyframes. (T/F)

## Review Questions

**Answer the following questions:**

1. Which of the following shortcut keys is used for invoking the **Paste in Place** command?

   (a) CTRL+SHIFT+U          (b) CTRL+SHIFT+V
   (c) CTRL+SHIFT+P          (d) CTRL+SHIFT+X

2. Which of the following shortcut keys is used for inserting a static frame?

   (a) F3          (b) F5
   (c) F7          (d) F9

3. The _____ layer is used to display the portions of a graphic of the layer below it.

4. The _____ are used to measure the width and height of Flash elements.

5. The _____ option is used to create the animation of one shape morphing into another.

6. The _____ is the point inside the symbol that is registered ( 0,0 ) on the X and Y axes.

7. The _____ are used to position the objects in the Stage.

8.   The **Bevel** and **Drop Shadow** are types of blending modes. (T/F)

# EXERCISES

## Exercise 1

Using the shape tween and mask layer, animate a pencil, as shown in Figure 4-85. You can view the final output of this exercise by downloading *c04_flash_cc_exr.zip* file from *www.cadcim.com*. The path of the file is as follows: *Textbooks > Animation and Visual Effects > Flash > The Adobe Flash Professional CC: A Tutorial Approach.*                    **(Expected time: 20 min)**

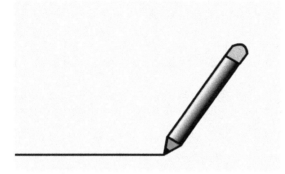

*Figure 4-85  The pencil animation on frame 38*

## Exercise 2

Using motion tween, mask layer, and movie clip filters, create a golf ball animation, as shown in Figure 4-86.  You can view the final output of this exercise by downloading *c04_flash_cc_exr.zip* file from *www.cadcim.com*. The path of the file is mentioned in Exercise 1.

**(Expected time: 40 min)**

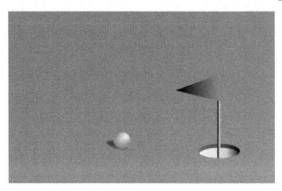

*Figure 4-86  The final output at frame 26*

**Answers to Self-Evaluation Test**
**1.** a, **2.** SHIFT, **3. Reverse Keyframes, 4.** Easing, **5. Orient to path, 6.** Frames Per Second, **7.** guide, **8. Lock or Unlock All Layers, 9.** F, **10.** F

# Chapter 5

# Understanding ActionScript 3.0

## Learning Objectives

**After completing this chapter, you will be able to:**

* *Understand the basics of ActionScript 3.0*
* *Add interactivity to button symbols*
* *Create a photo gallery*
* *Create an analog clock*
* *Control the Timeline using labels*
* *Load XML using ActionScript 3.0*
* *Create class in Flash*

# INTRODUCTION

Flash CC uses ActionScript 3.0, an object-oriented programming language, to create interactive applications. The object-oriented programming language is the fundamental style of computer programming. It uses an object as an entity of any type that can be manipulated by the commands of a programming language, such as a value, variable, function, and data structure that consists of data fields and methods.

**Note**

*ActionScript 3.0 is based on ECMAScript, the international standardized programming language for scripting. It has been standardized by Ecma International in the ECMA-262 specification and ISO/IEC 16262. This scripting style is widely used in the form of the programming languages such as JavaScript, JScript, and ActionScript.*

ActionScript is executed by the ActionScript Virtual Machine (AVM) built in the Flash Player. ActionScript 3.0 introduces new ActionScript Virtual Machine, AVM2. The new AVM2 virtual machine has been introduced in Flash Player 9. ActionScript code is transformed into bytecode format by a compiler. The bytecode is a type of language that is understood by computers. ActionScript 3.0 consists of many classes and features. ActionScript 3.0 includes new features of the core language, such as statements, expressions, conditions, loops, and types that speed up the development process.

# THE Actions PANEL

The **Actions** panel is a platform to create the ActionScript code for an object or frame. To display the **Actions** panel, choose **Window > Actions** from the menubar; the **Actions** panel is displayed for the selected frame or object, as shown in Figure 5-1.

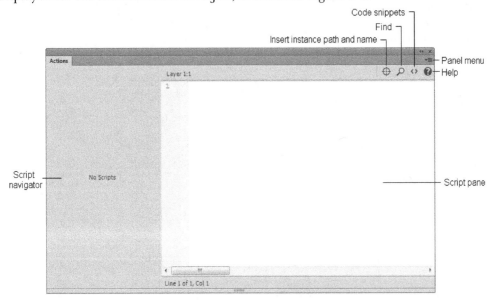

*Figure 5-1  The Actions panel*

**Note**

*Script navigator is visible only when you type the ActionScript code on the script pane.*

## Script pane

The Script pane is the area where you type the ActionScript code.

## Script navigator

When an item is selected in the Script navigator, the script associated with that item is displayed in the script pane and the Playhead is placed on the frame which contains the script in the Timeline.

### Insert a target path

 The **Insert a target path** tool is used to set an absolute or relative target path for an action in the script.

### Find

 The **Find** tool is used to find and replace the element or text in the script.

### Help

 The **Help** tool is used to display the information for the selected ActionScript element in the Script pane.

# TUTORIALS

Before you start the tutorials, you need to download the *c05_flash_cc_tut.zip* file from *www.cadcim.com*. The path of the file is as follows: *Textbooks > Animation and Visual Effects > Flash > The Adobe Flash Professional CC: A Tutorial Approach.*

Next, extract the contents of the *c05_flash_cc_tut.zip* file to *\Documents\Flash_Projects*.

## Tutorial 1

In this tutorial, you will create a photo gallery using the drawing and editing tools. Next, you will add ActionScript to the button instances of the gallery to navigate it. Figure 5-2 shows the first frame of the photo gallery. **(Expected time: 30 min)**

The following steps are required to complete this tutorial:

a. Create a new Flash document.
b. Create a rectangle.
c. Create the text.
d. Download and import the images.
e. Edit the images.
f. Create the buttons.
g. Add interactivity to the buttons.

*Figure 5-2*  *The photo gallery*

## Creating a New Flash Document

In this section, you will create a new Flash document.

1.  Choose **File > New** from the menubar; the **New Document** dialog box is displayed.

2.  In the **New Document** dialog box, choose **ActionScript 3.0** from the **Type** area in the **General** tab.

3.  Choose the **Background color** swatch; a flyout is displayed. In this flyout, enter **#000000** in the Hex edit box and press the ENTER key. Next, choose the **OK** button; a new Flash document is displayed and the color of the Stage is changed according to the specified value for the **Background color** swatch.

## Creating a Rectangle

In this section, you will create a rectangle in the Stage.

1.  Choose the Workspace switcher button in the application bar; a flyout is displayed. In this flyout, make sure the **Essentials** workspace is chosen. Next, choose **Reset 'Essentials'** from the flyout; a warning message box is displayed with the message **"Are you sure you want to reset 'Essentials' to its original layout?"**. Choose the **Yes** button to reset the arrangement of panels.

2.  Choose **Rectangle Tool** from the **Tools** panel; the properties of **Rectangle Tool** are displayed in the **Properties** panel.

3. In the **Fill and stroke** area of the **Properties** panel, choose the **Stroke color** swatch; a flyout is displayed. In this flyout, choose the No Color button.

4. Choose the **Fill color** swatch; a flyout is displayed. In this flyout, enter **#FFFFFF** in the Hex edit box and press the ENTER key.

5. Create a rectangle in the Stage.

6. Choose **Selection Tool** from the **Tools** panel and select the rectangle; the **Shape** properties are displayed in the **Properties** panel.

7. In the **Position and size** area of the **Properties** panel, set the value of **W** to **521** and **H** to **335**; the rectangle is resized.

8. In the **Position and size** area of the **Properties** panel, set the value of **X** to **15** and **Y** to **0**; the rectangle is positioned in the Stage, as shown in Figure 5-3.

9. Rename **Layer 1** as **background**. Next, select frame **6** of this layer and press the F5 key to insert static frames.

*Figure 5-3  The rectangle positioned in the Stage*

## Creating the Text
In this section, you will create the text.

1. Choose the **New Layer** button in the **Timeline** panel; a new layer is created. Rename this layer as **Gallery**. In this layer, select frame **1**.

2. Choose **Text Tool** from the **Tools** panel; the properties of this tool are displayed in the **Properties** panel.

3.  In the **Character** area of the **Properties** panel, select **Impact** from the **Family** drop-down list. Set the value of the **Size** to **135**. Next, click on the swatch right to **Color**; a flyout is displayed. In this flyout, enter **#000000** in the Hex edit box and press the ENTER key, refer to Figure 5-4.

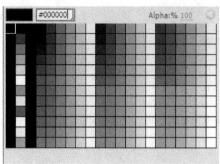

*Figure 5-4* *Entering the color value for the text*

4.  Click and drag the cursor in the Stage; a text box is displayed. In this text box, type **Wildlife**.

5.  Choose **Selection Tool** from the **Tools** panel.

6.  In the **Filters** area of the **Properties** panel, choose the **Add filter** button located at the bottom; a flyout is displayed. In this flyout, choose the **Glow** filter; the **Glow** area is displayed in the **Filters** area.

7.  In the **Glow** area, set the value of **Strength** to **150**. Select **High** from the **Quality** drop-down list. Next, click on the swatch located on right to **Color**; a flyout is displayed. In this flyout, enter **#FFFF00** in the Hex edit box and press the ENTER key.

8.  To position the text in the Stage, make sure the **Selection Tool** is chosen in the **Tools** panel.

9.  In the **Position and Size** area of the **Properties** panel, set the value of **X** to **50** and **Y** to **180**; the text is positioned in the Stage, as shown in Figure 5-5.

*Figure 5-5  The text positioned in the Stage*

## Downloading and Importing the Images

In this section, you will download and import the images.

1.  Download the images used in this tutorial from the links listed below.

    *http://www.sxc.hu/photo/1347762, http://www.sxc.hu/photo/670506, http://www.rgbstock.com/ largephoto/Ayla87/mQhtW86.jpg, http://www.rgbstock.com/largephoto/Ayla87/mfjExU4.jpg, and http://www.rgbstock.com/largephoto/Ayla87/mfjE8Xi.jpg*

    **Note**
    *Footage Courtesy: (http://www.sxc.hu/profile/jivemm),* **Marcelo Gerpe** *(http://www.sxc.hu/ profile/gmarcelo),* **Ayla87** *(http://www.rgbstock.com/gallery/Ayla87)*

2.  Save the images with the names: *lion.jpg, aligator.jpg, swans.jpg, lemur.jpg, and mongoose.jpg,* respectively at the location */Documents/Flash_Projects/c05_tut/Resources.*

3.  Choose **File > Import > Import to Library** from the menubar; the **Import to Library** dialog box is displayed.

4.  In the **Import to Library** dialog box, choose **Documents > Flash_Projects > c05_tut > Resources > lion.jpg**. Next, choose the **Open** button from the dialog box; the **lion.jpg** is displayed in the **Library** panel.

5.  Repeat steps 3 and 4 and import *aligator.jpg, swans.jpg, lemur.jpg,* and *mongoose.jpg.*

## Editing the Images

In this section, you will edit the images.

1.  In the **Gallery** layer, select frame **2** and press the F7 key to insert a blank keyframe. Alternatively, choose **Insert > Timeline > Blank Keyframe** from the menubar. Insert a blank keyframe on each frame till frame **6**, as shown in Figure 5-6.

*Figure 5-6  Inserting blank keyframes till frame 6*

 **Note**
*There is no content in the blank keyframe. It is used to add content or make the content disappear.*

2.  Select frame **2**. Next, drag *lion.jpg* from the **Library** panel to the Stage. In the **Position and Size** area of the **Properties** panel, set the value of **W** to **515** and **H** to **330**; the image is resized.

3.  In the **Position and Size** area of the **Properties** panel, set the value of **X** to **18** and **Y** to **2**; the image is positioned, as shown in Figure 5-7.

*Figure 5-7  Positioning lion.jpg in the Stage*

4.  Repeat Steps 2 and 3 and place an image on each frame till frame **6**.

## Creating the Buttons
In this section, you will create buttons for navigation in the photo gallery.

1.  Create a new layer above the **Gallery** layer using the **New Layer** button and rename it as **Buttons**.

2.  Choose **Rectangle Primitive Tool** from the **Tools** panel; the tool properties are displayed in the **Properties** panel.

3. In the **Fill and stroke** area of the **Properties** panel, choose the **Stroke color** swatch; a flyout is displayed. In this flyout, enter **#FFFF00** in the Hex edit box and press the ENTER key. Next, choose the **Fill color** swatch; a flyout is displayed. In this flyout, enter **#33CC66** in the Hex edit box and press the ENTER key.

4. In the **Fill and stroke** area of the **Properties** panel, set the value of **Stroke** to **2**. Next, in the **Rectangle Options** area, enter **5** in the **Rectangle corner radius** edit box, as shown in Figure 5-8.

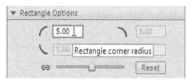

5. In the **Buttons** layer, create a rectangle.

*Figure 5-8 The Rectangle Options area*

6. In the **Position and size** area of the **Properties** panel, set the value of **W** to **110** and **H** to **35**. Next, set the value of **X** to **90** and **Y** to **345**; the rectangle is resized and positioned, as shown in Figure 5-9.

*Figure 5-9 Positioning the rectangle*

7. Choose **Selection Tool** from the **Tools** panel and select the rectangle in the Stage and press the F8 key; the **Convert to Symbol** dialog box is displayed. In this dialog box, type **prev** in the **Name** text box and select **Button** from the **Type** drop-down list. For specifying registration point of the symbol, select the center square of the **Registration** grid, if it is not selected and then choose the **OK** button; the rectangle is converted into a button symbol with the name *prev* and its instance is created in the Stage.

8. In the **Position and size** area of the **Properties** panel, set the value of **X** to **110** and **Y** to **360**; the rectangle is slightly positioned to its left. Double-click on the *prev* button symbol in the Stage.

9. In the **Layer 1** of the **Timeline** panel, select the **Over** frame and press the F6 key to insert a keyframe. Next, select the rectangle in the Stage.

10. In the **Fill and stroke** area of the **Properties** panel, choose the **Fill color** swatch; a flyout is displayed. In this flyout, enter **#33CC00** in the Hex edit box and press the ENTER key; the over state of the button is defined, as shown in Figure 5-10.

11. Select the **Down** frame and press the F6 key to insert a keyframe. Next, select the rectangle in the Stage.

12. In the **Fill and stroke** area of the **Properties** panel, choose the **Fill color** swatch; a flyout is displayed. In this flyout, enter **#339966** and press the ENTER key; the down state of the button is defined, as shown in Figure 5-11.

*Figure 5-10  The over state*           *Figure 5-11  The down state*

13. In the **Timeline** panel, create a new layer using the **New Layer** button and rename it as **Text**.

14. Choose **Text Tool** from the **Tools** panel; the properties of this tool are displayed in the **Properties** panel.

15. In the **Character** area of the **Properties** panel, make sure the **Impact** option from the **Family** drop-down list is selected. Next, set the value of **Size** to **26**. Click on the swatch located on the right of **Color**; a flyout is displayed. In this flyout, enter **#FFFFFF** in the Hex edit box and press the ENTER key, refer to Figure 5-12.

16. Click and drag the cursor in the Stage; the text box is displayed. In this text box, type **Previous**.

17. Choose **Selection Tool** from the **Tools** panel and position the text at the center of the symbol, as shown in Figure 5-13.

*Figure 5-12  The **Character** area*          *Figure 5-13  Positioning the text*

18. Click on **Scene 1** to return to the main Timeline.

19. Select the *prev* button instance in the Stage, if it is not selected; the properties of this instance are displayed in the **Properties** panel.

20. In the **Filters** area of the **Properties** panel, choose the **Add filter** button; a flyout is displayed. In this flyout, choose the **Bevel** filter; the **Bevel** area is displayed in the **Filters** area, refer to Figure 5-14.

21. In the **Bevel** area, set the value of **Strength** to **60** and select **High** from the **Quality** drop-down list. The **Bevel** filter is applied on the *prev* button instance, as shown in Figure 5-15.

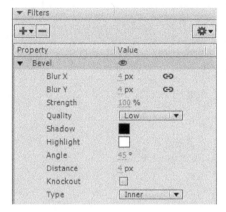

*Figure 5-14  The **Bevel** filter area*

*Figure 5-15  The prev button symbol after applying the **Bevel** filter*

22. In the **Library** panel, make sure the *prev* button symbol is selected.

23. Choose the triangle located at the extreme right of the **Library** panel; the menu of the **Library** panel is displayed, as shown in Figure 5-16. In this menu, choose **Duplicate**; the **Duplicate Symbol** dialog box is displayed with the name of symbol as *prev copy*, as shown in Figure 5-17.

24. In the **Duplicate Symbol** dialog box, type **nxt** in the **Name** text box and choose the **OK** button; a duplicate of the *prev* button symbol is created in the **Library** panel with the symbol name as *nxt*.

25. Drag the *nxt* button symbol from the **Library** panel to the Stage; its instance is created in the Stage.

26. Double-click on the *nxt* button instance in the Stage. In the **Text** layer of the **Timeline** panel, erase the **Previous** and type **Next** in the text box in the Stage.

27. Click on **Scene 1** to return to the main Timeline.

28. Choose the **Selection Tool** and select the *prev* button symbol in the Stage .

29. In the **Filters** area of the **Properties** panel, select the **Bevel** filter and choose the **Options** button located at the right of the **Filters** area; a flyout is displayed, refer to Figure 5-18. In this flyout, choose **Copy Selected filter**; the **Bevel** filter with its properties are copied.

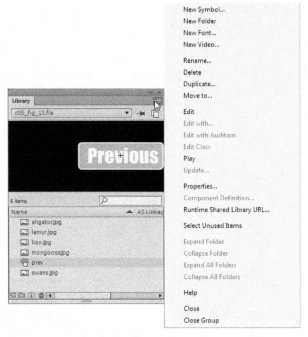

*Figure 5-16* *The menu of* ***Library*** *panel displayed*

*Figure 5-17* *The* ***Duplicate Symbol*** *dialog box*

*Figure 5-18* *The flyout displayed on*            *Figure 5-19* *The nxt button symbol*
*choosing the* ***Options*** *button*

30. Select the *nxt* button symbol in the Stage. In the **Filters** area of the **Properties** panel, choose the **Options** button; a flyout is displayed. In this flyout, choose **Paste filters**; the **Bevel** filter and its properties are applied on this button symbol, refer to Figure 5-19.

31. In the **Position and size** area of the **Properties** panel, set the value of **X** to **440** and the value of **Y** to **360**; the *nxt* button instance is positioned, as shown in Figure 5-20.

*Figure 5-20  The prev and nxt button symbols in the Stage*

## Adding Interactivity to the Buttons

In this section, you will add interactivity to the button symbols.

1. Select the *prev* button symbol in the Stage; the properties of this symbol are displayed in the **Properties** panel. In this panel, type **prev** in the **Instance name** text box, as shown in Figure 5-21.

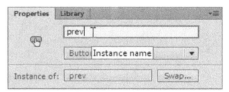

*Figure 5-21  The **Instance name** text box*

  **Note**
*The instance name is the name that you assign to symbols to address them with ActionScript.*

2. Select the *nxt* instance in the Stage; the instance properties are displayed in the **Properties** panel. Now in this panel, type *nxt* in the **Instance name** text box.

3. In the **Timeline** panel, create a new layer above the **Buttons** layer using the **New Layer** button and rename it as **Actions**.

4. In the **Actions** layer, select frame **1** and choose **Windows > Actions** from the menubar; the **Actions** panel is displayed. Alternatively, press the F9 key. Now, place the **Actions** panel next to the **Motion Editor** panel, as shown in Figure 5-22.

  **Note**
*In Flash CC, the ActionScript code is assigned to the frame and not to the object.*

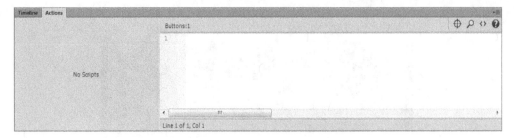

*Figure 5-22*   *The **Actions** panel displayed*

5. In the Script pane of the **Actions** panel, type the following script:

```
1  stop()
2
3  /* Clicking on the specified symbol instance moves the Playhead to
   the previous frame and stops the movie.
4  */
5
6  prev.addEventListener(MouseEvent.CLICK,gotopreviousframe);
7
8  function gotopreviousframe(event:MouseEvent):void
9  {
10    prevFrame();
11 }
12
13 /* Clicking on the specified symbol instance moves the Playhead to
   the next frame and stops the movie.
14 */
15
16 nxt.addEventListener(MouseEvent.CLICK,gotonextframe);
17
18 function gotonextframe(event:MouseEvent):void
19 {
20    nextFrame();
21 }
```

**Explanation**

Line 1
**stop()**
In this line, the **stop** () command is used to stop the Playhead in the Timeline.

Lines 3 and 4
**/* Clicking on the specified symbol instance moves the playhead to the previous frame and stops the movie.**
**\*/**
These lines are comments. Comments are added to explain the script and they are not executed during the run time.

Line 6
**prev.addEventListener(MouseEvent.CLICK,gotopreviousframe);**
In this line, *prev* is the instance name of the **prev** button instance. The **gotopreviousframe** is a function created to go to the previous frame. **MouseEvent.CLICK** executes the function when the **prev** button instance is clicked. The **addEventListener** essentially subscribes the function to the specified event. When the event occurs, the function's actions are carried out. The events are the codes that determine which instructions are to be carried out and when they are to be carried out.

Lines 8-11
**function gotopreviousframe(event:MouseEvent):void**
**{**
    **prevFrame();**
**}**
This code defines the function **gotopreviousframe** which is used to go to previous frame when the event occurs. The function is used to specify the actions that are to be performed in response to the event.

Lines 18-21
**function gotonextframe(event:MouseEvent):void**
**{**
    **nextFrame();**
**}**
This code defines the function **gotonextframe** which is used to go to the next frame when the event occurs.

6.  Save the flash file with the name *c05tut1* at the location *\Documents\Flash_Projects\c05_tut\ c05_tut_01*.

7.  Press CTRL+ENTER to view the final output of the tutorial. You can also view the final rendered file of the tutorial by downloading the file *c05_flash_cc_rndr.zip* from *www.cadcim.com*. The path of the file is mentioned at the beginning of the TUTORIALS section.

## Tutorial 2

In this tutorial, you will create and animate an analog clock, as shown in Figure 5-23.
**(Expected time: 30 min)**

The following steps are required to complete this tutorial:

a.  Create a new Flash document.
b.  Create the dial of the clock.
c.  Create the hands of the clock.
d.  Animate the hands of the clock using ActionScript.

**Figure 5-23** *The analog clock*

## Creating a New Flash Document

In this section, you will create a new Flash document.

1.  Choose **File > New** from the menubar; the **New Document** dialog box is displayed.

2.  In this dialog box, choose **ActionScript 3.0** from the **General** tab and then choose the **OK** button; a new Flash document is displayed.

## Creating the Dial of the Clock

In this section, you will create the dial of the analog clock.

1.  Choose the Workspace switcher button in the application bar; a flyout is displayed. In this flyout, make sure the **Essentials** workspace is chosen.

2.  In the **Timeline** panel, rename **Layer 1** as **background**.

3.  Choose **Oval Tool** from the **Tools** panel; the properties of this tool are displayed in the **Properties** panel.

4.  In the **Fill and Stroke** area of the **Properties** panel, choose the **Stroke color** swatch; a flyout is displayed. In the flyout, enter **#000000** in the Hex edit box and press the ENTER key. Next, choose the **Fill color** swatch; a flyout is displayed. In this flyout, enter **#000000** in the Hex edit box and press the ENTER key.

5.  Select the **background** layer and create a circle in the Stage. Next, marquee select the circle with **Selection Tool**; the **Shape** properties are displayed in the **Properties** panel.

6.  In the **Position and Size** area of the **Properties** panel, set the value of **W** and **H** to **248**.

7.  Choose the **Align** button located on the left of the **Properties** panel, as shown in Figure 5-24; the **Align** panel is displayed. In this panel, make sure the **Align to stage** check box is selected, refer to Figure 5-25.

8.  In the **Align** area of the **Align** panel, choose the **Align horizontal center** button and then the **Align vertical center** button, refer to Figure 5-25. The circle is positioned at the center of the Stage, as shown in Figure 5-26.

*Figure 5-24  The **Align** button located on the left of the **Properties** panel*

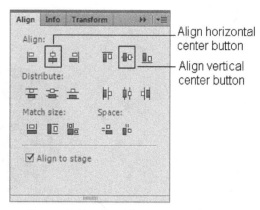

*Figure 5-25  The **Align** area in the **Align** panel*

*Figure 5-26  The circle positioned at the center of the Stage*

9.  Using the guides, divide the circle into four equal quarters, as shown in Figure 5-27.

10. In the **Timeline** panel, create a new layer using the **New Layer** button and rename it as **numbers**.

11. Choose **Text Tool** from the **Tools** panel; the properties of this tool are displayed in the **Properties** panel.

12. In the **Character** area of the **Properties** panel, select **Harrington** from the **Family** drop-down list and set the value of **Size** to **30**. Next, click on the swatch right to **Color**; a flyout is displayed. In this flyout, enter **#FFFFFF** in the Hex edit box and press the ENTER key.

13. Select the **numbers** layer in the **Timeline** panel. Next, click and drag the cursor in the Stage; a text box is displayed. In this text box, type **12**.

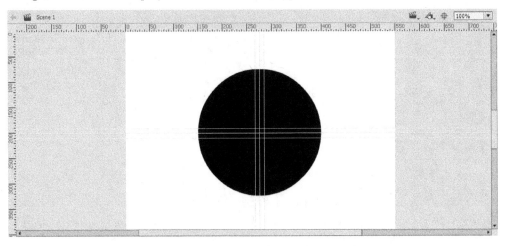

*Figure 5-27* *Dividing the circle into four equal quarters*

14. In the **Filters** area of the **Properties** panel, choose the **Add filter** button; a flyout is displayed. In this flyout, choose the **Glow** filter; the **Glow** area is displayed in the **Filters** area. In this area, set the **Blur X** and **Blur Y** value to **10** and **Strength** value to **150**. Select **High** from the **Quality** drop-down list. Next, click on the swatch located on the right of **Color**; a flyout is displayed. In this flyout, enter **#FFFFFF** in the Hex edit box and press the ENTER key; the **Glow** filter is applied on the text.

15. Choose **Selection Tool** from the **Tools** panel. In **Position and Size** area of the **Properties** panel, set the value of **X** to **260** and **Y** to **72**; a text box with **12** (numeral) is positioned at the top of the circle, as shown in Figure 5-28.

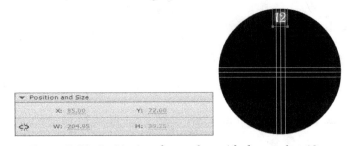

*Figure 5-28* *Positioning the text box with the number 12*

16. Create a copy of the text box with the number **12** using the ALT key, refer to Figure 5-29. Next, double-click on the copy of the text box and erase **12** using the BACKSPACE key. Now, type **3**, refer to Figure 5-30.

**Figure 5-29**  *Creating a copy of the text box*

**Figure 5-30**  *The letter 3 typed in the text box*

17. Choose **Selection Tool** from the **Tools** panel. In the **Position and Size** area of the **Properties** panel, set the value of **X** to **367** and **Y** to **181**; the text box with numeral **3** is positioned on the right of the circle, as shown in Figure 5-31.

18. Refer to Step 16 to create text boxes with numeral **6** and **9**. For text box with the **6** numeral set the value of **X** to **255** and **Y** to **287**; the text box with numeral **6** is positioned at the bottom of the circle, as shown in Figure 5-32.

19. For text box with numeral **9**, set the value of **X** to **145** and **Y** to **180**; the text box with numeral **9** is positioned on the left of the circle, as shown in Figure 5-32.

**Figure 5-31**  *Positioning the 3 text box*      **Figure 5-32**  *Positioning the 6 and 9 text boxes*

Next, you will create the hands of the clock.

## Creating the Hands of the Clock
In this section, you will create hands of the clock.

1. Create a new layer using the **New Layer** button in the **Timeline** panel and rename it as **hourhand**.

2. Choose **Rectangle Tool** from the **Tools** panel; the properties of this tool are displayed in the **Properties** panel. In the **Fill and Stroke** area of the **Properties** panel, choose the **Stroke color** swatch; a flyout is displayed. In this flyout, choose the No Color button.

3. Choose the **Fill color** swatch; a flyout is displayed. In this flyout, make sure **#FFFFFF** is entered in the Hex edit box and press the ENTER key.

4. Select the **hourhand** layer and create a rectangle in the Pasteboard. Next, choose **Selection Tool** from the **Tools** panel and then select the rectangle in the Pasteboard.

5. In the **Position and Size** area of the **Properties** panel, set the value of **W** to **3** and **H** to **65**.

6. Press the F8 key; the **Convert to Symbol** dialog box is displayed. In this dialog box, type **hour** in the **Name** text box. Select **Movie Clip** from the **Type** drop-down list and select bottom center square of the **Registration** grid for specifying the registration point of the symbol. Next, choose the **OK** button; the *hour* movie clip symbol is saved in the **Library** panel and its instance is created in the Stage.

7. Choose **Free Transform Tool** from the **Tools** panel; the *hour* instance is bounded with the transform box. Hover the cursor over the center point; a small circle appears beneath the cursor, as shown in Figure 5-33.

8. Drag the anchor point and place it on the bottom center transform point, as shown in Figure 5-34.

*Figure 5-33* The anchor point      *Figure 5-34* Changing the
                                                     position of anchor point

9. Choose **Selection Tool** from the **Tools** panel and select the **hour** instance in the Pasteboard, if it is not selected. In the **Filters** area of the **Properties** panel, choose the **Add filter** button; a flyout is displayed. In this flyout, choose the **Glow** filter; the **Glow** area is displayed in the **Filters** area.

10. In the **Glow** filter area, set the value of **Strength** to **150** and select **High** from the **Quality** drop-down list; the **Glow** filter is applied on the *hour* instance, as shown in Figure 5-35.

11. In the **Properties** panel, type **hr_mc** in the **Instance name** text box, as shown in Figure 5-36.

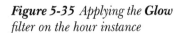
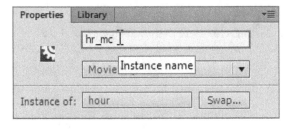

*Figure 5-35* Applying the **Glow**      *Figure 5-36* Assigning the instance
filter on the hour instance                name to the hour instance

12. In the **Timeline** panel, create a new layer above the **hourhand** layer using the **New Layer** button and rename it as **minutehand**. In this layer, create a rectangle in the Pasteboard. Next, choose **Selection Tool** from the **Tools** panel and then select the rectangle.

13. In the **Position and Size** area of the **Properties** panel, set the value of **W** to **3** and the value of **H** to **83**.

14. Press the F8 key; the **Convert to Symbol** dialog box is displayed. In this dialog box, type **minute** in the **Name** text box. Make sure the **Movie Clip** is selected from the **Type** drop-down list and select the bottom center square of the **Registration** grid for specifying registration point of the symbol. Next, choose the **OK** button; the *minute* movie clip symbol is saved in the **Library** panel and its instance is created in the Stage.

15. Choose **Free Transform Tool** from the **Tools** panel; the *minute* instance is bound with transform box.

16. Drag the anchor and place it on the bottom center transform point.

17. Choose **Selection Tool** from the **Tools** panel and select the *minute* instance, if it is not selected. In the **Filters** area of the **Properties** panel, choose the **Add filter** button; a flyout is displayed. In this flyout, choose the **Glow** filter; the **Glow** area is displayed in the **Filters** area.

18. In the **Glow** area, set the value of **Strength** to **150** and then select **High** from the **Quality** drop-down list. Click on the swatch located on the right of **Color**; a flyout is displayed, as shown in Figure 5-37. In this flyout, enter **#0000FF** in the Hex edit box and press the ENTER key; the **Glow** filter is applied on the *minute* instance, refer to Figure 5-38.

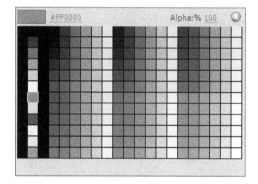

*Figure 5-37  Entering glow color in the Hex edit box*

*Figure 5-38  The minute instance after applying the Glow filter*

19. In the **Properties** panel, type **min_mc** in the **Instance name** text box.

20. In the **Timeline** panel, create a new layer above the **minutehand** layer using the **New Layer** button and rename it as **secondhand**. In this layer, create a rectangle in the Pasteboard using **Rectangle Tool**.

21. Choose **Selection Tool** from the **Tools** panel and select the rectangle in the Pasteboard, if it is not selected. In the **Position and Size** area of the **Properties** panel, set the value of **W** to **3** and **H** to **100**.

22. Press the F8 key; the **Convert to Symbol** dialog box is displayed. In this dialog box, type **second** in the **Name** text box. Make sure **Movie Clip** is selected from the **Type**

drop-down list and select the bottom center square of the **Registration** grid for specifying the registration point of the symbol. Next, choose the **OK** button; the *second* movie clip symbol is saved in the **Library** panel and its instance is created in the Stage.

23. Choose **Free Transform Tool** from the **Tools** panel; the *minute* instance is bound with transform box.

24. Drag the center point and place it on the bottom center transform point using **Free Transform Tool**.

25. Choose **Selection Tool** from the **Tools** panel and then select the **second** instance. In the **Filters** area of the **Properties** panel, choose the **Add filter** button; a flyout is displayed. In this flyout, choose the **Glow** filter; the **Glow** filter area is displayed in the **Filters** panel.

26. In the **Glow** filter area, set the value of **Strength** to **150** and then select **High** from the **Quality** drop-down list. Click on the swatch right to **Color**; a flyout is displayed. In this flyout, enter **#00FF00** in the Hex edit box and press the ENTER key. Next, select the **Knockout** check box, refer to Figure 5-39. Figure 5-40 shows the *second* instance after applying the **Glow** filter.

 **Note**
*The **Knockout** option is used to hide the object and display only the glow.*

27. In the **Properties** panel, type **sec_mc** in the **Instance name** text box.

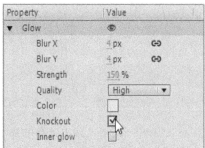
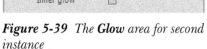

**Figure 5-39** *The **Glow** area for second instance*          **Figure 5-40** *The second instance after applying the **Glow** filter*

28. Make sure the **Selection Tool** from the **Tools** panel is selected and marquee select *hour*, *minute* and *second* instances in the Pasteboard.

29. Choose the **Align** button; the **Align** panel is displayed. In this panel, make sure the **Align to stage** check box is clear.

30. In the **Align** area of the **Align** panel, choose the **Align bottom edge** button and then choose the **Align horizontal center** button; the instances are placed on top of each other, having the same alignment.

31. In the **Position and Size** area of the **Properties** panel, set the value of **X** to **274** and **Y** to **100**; the instances are positioned at the center of the circle, as shown in Figure 5-41.

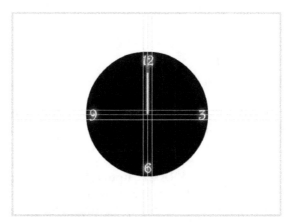

**Figure 5-41** *Positioning the instances at the center of the circle*

32. Create a new layer above the **secondhand** and rename it as **cover**.

33. Choose **Oval Tool** from the **Tools** panel; the properties of this tool are displayed in the **Properties** panel. In the **Fill and Stroke** area of the **Properties** panel, choose the **Stroke color** swatch; a flyout is displayed. In this flyout, make sure the No color button is chosen.

34. Choose the **Fill color** swatch; a flyout is displayed. In this flyout, make sure **#FFFFFF** is entered in the Hex edit box. Select the **cover** layer and create a circle in the Pasteboard.

35. Choose **Selection Tool** and select the circle. In the **Position and Size** area of the **Properties** panel, set the value of **W** and **H** to **10**.

36. In the **Position and Size** area of the **Properties** panel, set the value of **X** to **269** and **Y** to **194**; the circle is positioned in the center of the clock.

## Animating the Hands of the Clock using ActionScript

In this section, you will animate the hands of the clock.

1. Create a new layer above the **cover** layer and rename it as **AS3**. In this layer, make sure frame **1** is selected and press the F9 key; the **Actions** panel is displayed. In this panel, type the following code:

```
1  var date:Date;
2
3  addEventListener(Event.ENTER_FRAME, updateHour);
4
5  function updateHour(event:Event):void{
6  date = new Date();
7  hr_mc.rotation = date.getHours()*30 + (date.getMinutes()/2);
8  min_mc.rotation = date.getMinutes()*6 + (date.getSeconds()/10);
9  sec_mc.rotation = date.getSeconds()*6 + (date.getMilliseconds()/
   (1000/6));
10 }
```

### Explanation

Line 1
**var date:Date;**
Here, **var** is a keyword for variable and is used to declare a variable in ActionScript. The keywords are reserved words that are used to perform a specific task. The **date** is a variable and the **Date** is the object that is used to get time from the computer system. The variables are words in codes that store different values or data.

Line 3
**addEventListener(Event.ENTER_FRAME, updateHour)**
The **addEventListener** subscribes the function to the specified event. Here **updateHour** is the function. In this line, the code loops the actions contained within it every time the movie is tested.

Lines 7-9
In these lines, the code gets all the information from your system clock, and incorporates it into Flash.

Line 7
**hr_mc.rotation = date.getHours()*30 + (date.getMinutes()/2);**
Here **hr_mc** is the instance name of the *hour* instance. The **.rotation** function is used to define the rotation of an object. So, here rotation of hour hand is defined. The hour hand of the clock rotates 30 degrees in 60 minutes, which means 0.5 degrees per minute. There are 12 hours in a full rotation of a clock, so you need to multiply hours by 30 (12 x 30 = 360), **date.getHours()*30**. To get a motion, add one degree for every two minutes, that is, **getMinutes()/2**.

Line 8
**min_mc.rotation = date.getMinutes()*6 + (date.getSeconds()/10);**
Here **min_mc** is the instance name of the *minute* instance. The **.rotation** function is used to define the rotation of an object. So, here rotation of minute hand is defined. Again, since there are 60 minutes in an hour and you want the minute hand to rotate a full 360°. So, you need to multiply the 60 minutes by 6. (60 x 6 = 360). The seconds are there to help create a continuous sweep. Every minute is 6° of rotation and every second is 6° of rotation, so with every second that goes by, this code adds one degree to the minute hand.

Line 9
**sec_mc.rotation = date.getSeconds()*6 + (date.getMilliseconds()/(1000/6));**
Here **sec_mc** is the instance name of the *second* instance. The **.rotation** function is used to define the rotation of an object. So, here rotation of second hand is defined. There are 60 seconds in a minute and the second hand rotates 360°. So you need to multiply the 60 seconds by 6 (60 x 6 = 360). The milliseconds take 6 degrees of rotation (one second), therefore, current milliseconds divide by possible milliseconds (1000), then divide that fraction by the 6 degrees to get the milliseconds rotation.

2.  Save the flash file with the name *c05tut2* at the location *\Documents\Flash_Projects\c05_tut\ c05_tut_02*.

3. Press CTRL+ENTER to view the final output of the tutorial. You can also view the final rendered file of the tutorial by downloading the file *c05_flash_cc_rndr.zip* from *www.cadcim.com*. The path of the file is mentioned at the beginning of the TUTORIALS section.

## Tutorial 3

In this tutorial, you will add interactivity to the button symbols using the **Code Snippets** panel.                                                                    **(Expected time: 15 min)**

The following steps are required to complete this tutorial:

a. Open the Flash document.
b. Import button from the external library.
c. Create ActionScript for interactivity of button.

### Opening the New Flash Document

In this section, you will open the Flash document.

1. Choose **File > Open** from the menubar; the **Open** dialog box is displayed.

2. Choose **Documents > Flash_Projects > c05_tut > c05_tut_03 > c05_tut_03_start.fla**. Next, choose the **Open** button from the dialog box; the Flash document is displayed.

3. In the **Properties** area of the **Properties** panel, click on the **Background color** swatch right of the **Stage** option; a flyout is displayed. In this flyout, enter **#000000** in the Hex edit box and press the ENTER key, refer to Figure 5-42.

### Importing Button from the External Library

In this section, you will import buttons from the buttons library.

1. In the **Timeline** panel, rename **Layer 1** as **buttons**.

2. Choose **Window > Components** from the menubar; the **Components** panel is displayed, as shown in Figure 5-43.

3. Drag the *Button* symbol from the **Components** panel to the Stage; the *Button* instance is displayed in the Stage and is saved in the **Library** panel. In the **Component Parameters** of the **Properties** panel, erase the text **Label** in the **label** text box and type **Enter**, as shown in Figure 5-44.

4. In the **Position and Size** area of the **Properties** panel, set the value of **W** to **144** and **H** to **42**. Next, set the value of **X** to **210** and **Y** to **170**; the **Enter** button instance is positioned at the center of the Stage, as shown in Figure 5-45. Next, type **enter_btn** as the instance name of the button in the **Instance name** edit box.

Figure 5-42  The **Background color** swatch

Figure 5-43  The **Components** panel

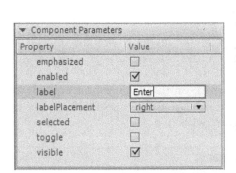

Figure 5-44  The **button** symbol

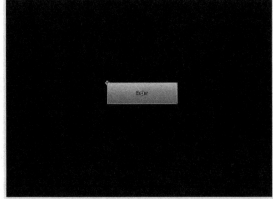

Figure 5-45  The **Enter** instance positioned in the
Stage

5.  In the **Timeline** panel, create a new layer using the **New Layer** button and rename it as
    **movieclip**.

6.  Select frame **15** and press the F7 key to insert a blank keyframe.

7.  Drag *pondscene* movie clip from the **Library** panel to the Stage; an instance of this movie
    clip is created in the Stage.

8.  In the **Properties** panel, set the value of **X** to **275** and **Y** to **200**; the instance is positioned
    at the center of the Stage on frame **15**, as shown in Figure 5-46.

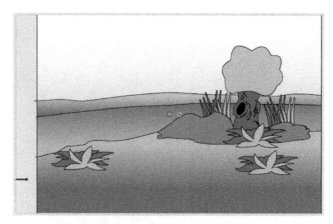

*Figure 5-46  Placing the pondscene instance on frame 15*

## Creating ActionScript for Interactivity of Button

In this section, you will create ActionScript for interactivity of buttons.

1.  Create a new layer above the **movieclip** layer and rename it as **Actions**.

2.  Select frame **1** and press the F9 key; the **Actions** panel is displayed. In the Script pane of the **Actions** panel, type the following script:

```
1   stop()
```

3.  In the **Actions** panel, choose the **Code Snippets** button located in the upper right of the **Actions** panel; the **Code Snippets** panel is displayed, as shown in Figure 5-47.

4.  In the **Code Snippets** panel, expand the **Timeline Navigation** folder and double-click on **Click to Go to Frame and Stop**; the **Adobe Flash Professional** message box is displayed, as shown in Figure 5-48. This message box displays the message that this action requires an object to be selected in the Stage. Next, choose the **OK** button to close this message box.

    The **Code Snippets** panel consists of set of ActionScript codes that are used for adding simple interactivity. This panel is useful for non-programmers who are new to **ActionScript 3.0**. It is used to add **ActionScript 3.0** code to the object and frame. You can add code that affects the behavior of an object in the Stage. You can also add code that controls the Timeline. You can save, import, and share your code. Choose **Windows > Code Snippets** from the menubar to display the **Code Snippets** panel. Alternatively, choose the **Code Snippets** button located in the upper right corner of the **Actions** panel. The codes are organized in folders that represent their function.

5.  Select the *Enter* button instance in the Stage and then double-click on the **Click to Go to Frame and Stop** in the **Code Snippets** panel; the ActionScript is displayed in the **Actions** panel. Next, change the value in the parenthesis after **gotoAndStop** to **15**, as shown in Figure 5-49.

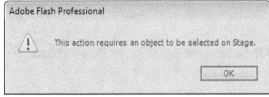

*Figure 5-47* The **Code Snippets** *panel*          *Figure 5-48* The **Adobe Flash CC** *message box*

```
10      enter_btn.addEventListener(MouseEvent.CLICK, fl_ClickToGoToAndStopAtFrame_2);
11
12      function fl_ClickToGoToAndStopAtFrame_2(event:MouseEvent):void
13    {
14          gotoAndStop(15);
15    }
16
```

*Figure 5-49* The **Click to Go to Frame and Stop** *code*

### Explanation

On clicking the *Enter* button instance, the Playhead moves to frame 15 in the Timeline and stops the movie.

**gotoAndStop(15);**
The value between parenthesis in a line of code is referred as arguments. In the code **gotoAndStop(15);** the argument instructs the script to go to frame **15**.

6.  Save the flash file with the name *c05tut3* at the location *\Documents\Flash_Projects\c05_tut\ c05_tut_03*.

7.  Press CTRL+ENTER to view the final output of the tutorial in the preview window. In this window, click on the *Enter* button instance; the *pondscene* instance is displayed. You can also view the final rendered file of the tutorial by downloading the file *c05_flash_cc_rndr.zip* from *www.cadcim.com*. The path of the file is mentioned at the beginning of the TUTORIALS section.

## Tutorial 4

In this tutorial, you will create the frame labels to control the Timeline, as shown in Figure 5-50. **(Expected time: 40 min)**

*Figure 5-50* *The frame labels*

The following steps are required to complete this tutorial:

a. Open the Flash Document.
b. Import buttons from library.
c. Create labels for frames.
d. Create ActionScript code frame labels.

### Opening the Flash Document

In this section, you will open the Flash document.

1. Choose **File > Open** from the menubar; the **Open** dialog box is displayed.

2. Choose **Documents > Flash_Projects > c05_tut > c05_tut_04 > c05_tut_04_start.fla**. Next, choose the **Open** button from the dialog box; the Flash document is displayed, as shown in Figure 5-51.

   This document consists of the **background**, **buttons**, **pages**, **labels**, and **actions** layers. The **background** layer consists of *undrcons.jpg*. The **pages** layer consists of the content on frame **1**, frame **5**, and frame **10**. The **buttons**, **labels**, and the **actions** layers are empty.

*Figure 5-51* *The c05_tut_04_start.fla document displayed*

## Importing Buttons from the Library

In this section, you will import buttons from the library.

1.  Select frame **1** on the **buttons** layer.

2.  In the **Buttons** folder of the **Library** panel, three button symbols are displayed, refer to Figure 5-52.

3.  Drag the *home* and *projects* button symbols to the Stage; their instances are created in the Stage.

4.  Select the *home* button instance in the Stage; the properties of the symbol are displayed in the **Properties** panel. Next, type **home_btn** in the **Instance name** text box.

5.  In the **Position and Size** area of the **Properties** panel, set the value of **X** to **74** and **Y** to **34,** as shown in Figure 5-53.

6.  Select the **projects** button symbol in the Stage; the properties of the symbol are displayed in the **Properties** panel. Next, type **projects_btn** in the **Instance name** text box.

7.  In the **Position and Size** area of the **Properties** panel, set the value of **X** to **162** and **Y** to **34**; the button symbols are positioned, as shown in Figure 5-53.

8.  In the **buttons** layer, select frame **5** and press the F7 key to insert a blank keyframe.

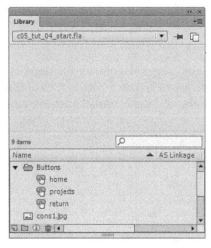
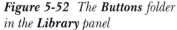

*Figure 5-52  The **Buttons** folder in the **Library** panel*          *Figure 5-53  The home and projects button instances*

9.  Similarly, select frame **2** and press the F7 key to insert a blank keyframe; the *home* and *projects* button instances disappear after frame **1**, as shown in Figure 5-54.

10. In the **buttons** layer, select frame **5**. Next, drag the *return* button symbol from the **Library** panel to the Stage.

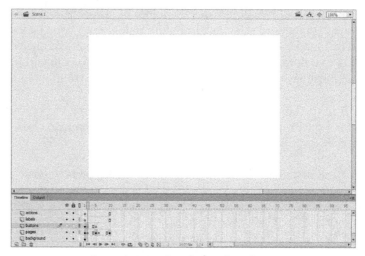

**Figure 5-54** *The Playhead on frame 2*

11. In the **Properties** panel, type **return_btn** as the instance name in the **Instance name** text box. In the **Position and Size** area of the **Properties** panel, set the value of **X** to **485** and **Y** to **370**.

12. In the **buttons** layer, insert a blank keyframe on frame **7** and then on frame **10**.

13. Next, drag the *return* button instance from the **Library** panel to the Stage.

14. In the **Properties** panel, type **back_btn** in the **Instance name** text box. In the **Position and Size** area of the **Properties** panel, set the value of **X** to **485** and **Y** to **370**.

## Creating Labels for Frames
In this section, you will create labels for frames.

1. Select frame **1** in the **labels** layer; the **Frame** properties are displayed in the **Properties** panel.

2. In the **Label** area of the **Properties** panel, type **Under Construction** in the **Name** text box, refer to Figure 5-55. In the **Timeline** panel, frame **1** is assigned a label name, *Under Construction* and a red flag is displayed in this frame, as shown in Figure 5-56.

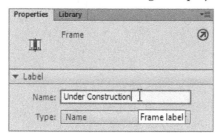

**Figure 5-55** *The **Label** area*

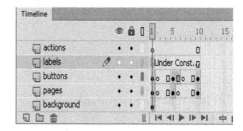

**Figure 5-56** *The labeled frame 1*

Frame labels enable you to assign a specific name to an individual frame. Frame labels are helpful when you have to refer to a frame in ActionScript code by its label, instead of frame numbers. It makes your code more readable. When you rearrange the Timeline and move the label to a different frame number, the ActionScript will still refer to the frame label. A frame must have a keyframe in it to assign a frame label.

3. Select frame **5** in the **labels** layer and insert a blank keyframe by pressing the F7 key. In the **Label** area of the **Properties** panel, type **Home** in the **Name** text box. In the **Timeline** panel, frame **5** is assigned a label name, *Home*, refer to Figure 5-57.

4. Repeat Step 3 and assign a label name to frame **10** as **Projects**, refer to Figure 5-57.

*Figure 5-57  The labeled frames*

## Creating ActionSript Code for Frame Labels

In this section, you will create ActionScript code for frame labels.

1. In the **actions** layer, select frame **1** and press the F9 key; the **Actions** panel is displayed. In this panel, type the following code:

```
1  stop()
2  home_btn.addEventListener(MouseEvent.CLICK, gotohome);
3
4  function gotohome(event:MouseEvent):void
5  {
6     gotoAndStop("Home");
7  }
8  projects_btn.addEventListener(MouseEvent.CLICK, gotoprojects);
9
10 function gotoprojects(event:MouseEvent):void
11 {
12    gotoAndStop("Projects");
13 }
```

**Explanation**

Line 1
**stop()**
In this line, the **stop** command is used to stop the Playhead in Timeline.

Line 2

**home_btn.addEventListener(MouseEvent.CLICK, gotohome);**

In this line, **home_btn** is the instance name of the **home** instance. The **gotohome** is a function created to command flash to go to the frame that is labeled as **Home**. **MouseEvent.CLICK** executes the function when the **home** button instance is clicked. The **addEventListener** essentially subscribes the function to the specified event. When the mouse click event occurs, the function is executed.

Lines 4 and 6

**function gotohome(event:MouseEvent):void**
**gotoAndStop("Home")**

In these lines, **gotohome** is a function that will be executed when the event will occur. When the user will click *home* instance, the Playhead will go to frame that has a label name **"Home"** .

In lines 8, 10, and 12 the same process is repeated to go to frame that has a label name **Projects**.

2. In the **actions** layer, select frame **5** and press the F7 key to insert a blank keyframe. Next, type the following script in the **Actions** panel:

```
return_btn.addEventListener(MouseEvent.CLICK, gotoundercons);

function gotoundercons(event:MouseEvent):void
{
    gotoAndStop("Under Construction");
}
```

In these lines, **return_btn** is the instance name of the **return** button instance. The **gotoundercons** is a function created to command flash to go to the frame that is labeled as **Under Construction**. **MouseEvent.CLICK** executes the function when the **return** button instance is clicked. The **addEventListener** essentially subscribes the function to the specified event. When the mouse click event occurs, the function **gotoundercons** is executed. In this set of code, you have defined a function **gotoundercons** that will be executed when the event will occur. When the user will click **return** button instance, the Playhead will to go to frame that has a label name **"Under Construction"** .

3. In the **actions** layer, select frame **10** and press the F7 key to insert a blank keyframe. Next, type the following script in the **Actions** panel:

```
back_btn.addEventListener(MouseEvent.CLICK, goto);
function goto(event:MouseEvent):void
{
    gotoAndStop("Home");
}
```

This code defines a function **goto** to go to frame with the label name **Home** when the *back_btn* symbol instance is clicked.

4.  Save the flash file with the name *c05tut4* at the location *Documents\Flash_Projects\c05_tut\ c05_tut_04*.

5.  Press CTRL+ENTER to view the final output of the tutorial in the preview window. In this window, click the *Home* button instance; the **Home** page is displayed. You can also view the final rendered file of the tutorial by downloading the file *c05_flash_cc_rndr.zip* from *www.cadcim.com*. The path of the file is mentioned at the beginning of the TUTORIALS section.

## Tutorial 5

In this tutorial, you will create an XML photo gallery, as shown in Figure 5-58.

**(Expected time: 40 min)**

***Figure 5-58*** *The XML photo gallery*

The following steps are required to complete this tutorial:

a.  Download the images.
b.  Edit the images using Adobe Photoshop.
c.  Create an XML file.
d.  Create a new Flash document.
e.  Create a Movie Clip.
f.  Create ActionScript to load the XML file in Flash.

## Downloading the Images

In this section, you will download the images.

1.  Download the images used in this tutorial from the links listed below.

    *http://www.rgbstock.com/download/Ayla87/mQWjM9i.jpg,  http://www.rgbstock.com/download/ Ayla87/mfjLs5O.jpg, http://www.rgbstock.com/download/Ayla87/n1uUf1K.jpg, http://www.rgbstock. com/download/Ayla87/ndoDJIC.jpg, and http://www.sxc.hu/photo/337328*

**Note**

*Footage Courtesy: **Ayla87** (http://www.rgbstock.com/gallery/Ayla87), and **Supachai Panyaviwat** (http://www.sxc.hu/profile/mrsoop)*

2.  Save them with the names; *1.jpg, 2.jpg, 3.jpg, 4.jpg, and 5.jpg,* respectively at the location */Documents/Flash_Projects/c05_tut/c05_tut_05.*

## Editing the Images Using Adobe Photoshop

In this section, you will edit the images using Adobe Photoshop.

1.  Start Adobe Photoshop; the Adobe Photoshop screen is displayed, as shown in Figure 5-59.

*Figure 5-59  The Adobe Photoshop screen*

2.  Choose **File > Open** from the menubar; the **Open** dialog box is displayed. In this dialog box, choose **Documents > Flash_Projects > c05_tut > Resources > 1.jpg**; the *1.jpg* is displayed, as shown in Figure 5-60.

*Figure 5-60  The 1.jpg displayed*

3.  Choose **Image > Image Size** from the menubar; the **Image Size** dialog box is displayed, as shown in Figure 5-61.

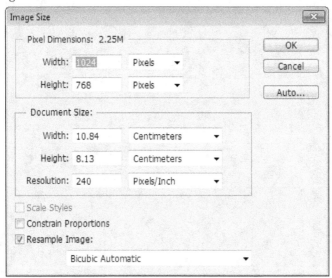

*Figure 5-61  The **Image Size** dialog box*

4.  In this dialog box, make sure the **Constrain Proportions** check box is cleared.

5.  In the **Pixel Dimensions** area, make sure the value of **Width** and **Height** is set to **1024** and **768,** respectively.

6.  Choose the **OK** button; the size of the image is set according to the values entered in the **Pixel dimensions** area.

7.  Press CTRL+S to save the image.

8. Repeat the procedure followed in Step 2 to import the images *2.jpg*, *3.jpg*, *4.jpg*, and *5.jpg*.

9. Repeat Steps 3 through 7 for the remaining images.

10. Choose the **Close** button to close Photoshop.

## Creating an XML File
In this section, you will create the XML file.

1. Open the Notepad application.

2. In Notepad, type the following codes:

```xml
<?xml version="1.0" encoding=@utf-8"?>

<imageFolder>

        <image>
                <imgURL>1.jpg</imgURL>
                <imgW>1024</imgW>
                <imgH>768</imgH>
        </image>
        <image>
                <imgURL>2.jpg</imgURL>
                <imgW>1024</imgW>
                <imgH>768
    </imgH>
        </image>
        <image>
                <imgURL>3.jpg</imgURL>
                <imgW>1024</imgW>
                <imgH>768</imgH>
        </image>
        <image>
                <imgURL>4.jpg</imgURL>
                <imgW>1024</imgW>
                <imgH>768</imgH>
        </image>
        <image>
                <imgURL>5.jpg</imgURL>
                <imgW>1024</imgW>
                <imgH>768</imgH>
        </image>

</imageFolder>
```

**Explanation**

**<?xml version="1.0" encoding=@utf-8"?>**
This is a document type definition.

```
<image>
        <imgURL>1.jpg</imgURL>
        <imgW>1024</imgW>
        <imgH>768</imgH>
</image>
```

In the above set of codes, **<image> </image>** is a container for the images and **<imgURL>1.jpg</imgURL>**, **<imgW>1024</imgW>**, and **<imgH>768</imgH>** are its children. The image container consists of the image URL, image width, and image height information. Note that the address of the image file within the **imgURL** tag is not mentioned as you have saved the XML file in the same folder where rest of the images are saved. The image **imgW** and **imgH** tags are used to retrieve image width and height of the image from the **Properties** panel.

XML is a set of rules for encoding documents in computer-readable form. The advantage of XML-based photo gallery is that instead of editing the FLA file manually to add an extra image, you can just edit the XML file.

3. Save this file with the file name *imagegallery.xml* in *\Documents\Flash_Projects\c05_tut\ c05_tut_05*.

## Creating a New Flash Document
In this section, you will create a new Flash document.

1. Choose **File > New** from the menubar; the **New Document** dialog box is displayed. In this dialog box, choose **ActionScript 3.0** from the **General** tab; a new Flash document is displayed.

2. Choose the Workspace switcher button in the application bar; a flyout is displayed. In this flyout, make sure the **Essentials** workspace is chosen.

## Creating a Movie Clip
In this section, you will create a movie clip.

1. In the **Timeline** panel, rename **Layer 1** as **background**.

2. Click on the stage; the **Document** properties panel is displayed. In the **Properties** area of the **Properties** panel, choose the **Edit document properties** button; the **Document Settings** dialog box is displayed. In this dialog box, enter **1024** and **768** in the **Stage size** edit box to set the dimensions of the Stage.

3.  Choose the **Background color** swatch; a flyout is displayed. In this flyout, enter **#000000** in the Hex edit box and press the ENTER key. Then, choose the **OK** button to close the dialog box.

4.  Choose **Rectangle Tool** from the **Tools** panel; the properties of this tool are displayed in the **Properties** panel.

5.  In the **Fill and Stroke** area of the **Properties** panel, choose the **Stroke color** swatch; a flyout is displayed. In this flyout, enter **#000000** in the Hex edit box and press the ENTER key. Next, choose the **Fill color** swatch; a flyout is displayed. In this flyout, enter **#000000** in the Hex edit box and press the ENTER key. Next, create a rectangle in the Stage.

6.  Choose **Selection Tool** from the **Tools** panel and marquee select the rectangle. In the **Position and Size** area of the **Properties** panel, set the value of **W** to **1024** and **H** to **768**.

7.  Press the F8 key; the **Convert to Symbol** dialog box is displayed. In this dialog box, type **imagebox** in the **Name** text box and make sure **Movie Clip** from the **Type** drop-down list is selected. Next, for specifying the registration point of the symbol, select the top left square of the **Registration** grid and choose the **OK** button; the rectangle is converted to a movie clip symbol and its instance is created in the Stage.

8.  Next, select the **imagebox** button symbol in the Stage, if it is not selected; the properties of this symbol are displayed in the **Properties** panel. Next, type **imagebox** in the **Instance name** text box.

9.  Align the *imagebox* instance exactly in the Stage using the **Align vertical center** and **Align horizontal center** buttons in the **Align** area of the **Align** panel.

## Creating ActionScript to Load XML File in Flash

In this section, you will create ActionScript to load the XML image gallery.

1.  Create a new layer above the **background** layer using the **New Layer** button and rename it as **actions**.

2.  Select frame **1**, if it is not selected and press the F9 key; the **Actions** panel is displayed. In this panel, type the following code:

```
1  var xmlReq:URLRequest = new URLRequest ("imagegallery.xml");
2  var xmlLoad:URLLoader = new URLLoader (xmlReq);
3  var Data:XML;
4  var imageLoad:Loader;
5  var Image:String;
6  var imgH:String;
7  var imgW:String;
8
9  var imageNum:Number = 0;
10 var Time:Timer = new Timer(100);
11 var Childnumber:Number;
```

```
12
13 xmlLoad.addEventListener(Event.COMPLETE, xmlLoadedF);
14 imagebox.addEventListener(MouseEvent.CLICK, nextImgF);
15 imagebox.buttonMode = true;
16
17 function xmlLoadedF(event:Event):void{
18 Time.start();
19 Time.addEventListener(TimerEvent.TIMER, checkF);
20 Data = new XML(event.target.data);
21 }
22
23 function checkF(event:TimerEvent):void{
24     if(imageNum ==0){
25         packetF();
26     }else if(imageNum < Childnumber){
27         imageLoad.unload();
28         packetF();
29     }else{
30         imageLoad.unload();
31         imageNum = 0;
32         packetF();
33     }
34 }
35
36     function packetF():void{
37     Time.removeEventListener(TimerEvent.TIMER, checkF);
38     Image = Data.image[imageNum].imgURL;
39     Childnumber = Data.*.length();
40     imgW = Data.image[imageNum].imgW;
41     imgH = Data.image[imageNum].imgH;
42     imageLoad = new Loader;
43     imageLoad.load(new URLRequest(Image));
44     imagebox.addChild(imageLoad);
45     imageLoad.x = (stage.stageWidth - Number(imgW)) /2;
46     imageLoad.y = (stage.stageHeight - Number(imgH))/2;
47
48 }
49
50 function nextImgF(event:MouseEvent):void{
51     Time.addEventListener(TimerEvent.TIMER, checkF);
52     imageNum++;
53 }
```

### Explanation

Line 1
**var xmlReq:URLRequest = new URLRequest("imagegallery.xml");**
In this code, a variable **xmlReq** is declared and the variable type is **URLRequest**. To associate a variable with a data type, you must declare the variable type along with the variable. **URLRequest("imagegallery.xml")** is an XML loading request.

Line 2
**var xmlLoad:URLLoader = new URLLoader (xmlReq);**
In this code, a variable **xmlLoad** is declared and the variable type is **URLLoader**. The **URLLoader** variable is loading the XML file.

Lines 3-11
**var Data:XML;**
**var imageLoad:Loader;**
**var Image:String;**
**var imgH:String;**
**var imgW:String;**
**var imageNum:Number = 0;**
**var Time:Timer = new Timer(100);**
**var Childnumber:Number;**
In these lines, variables are declared.

**var imageLoad:Loader;**
In this line, variable **imageLoad** is declared with the data type **Loader**. The **Loader** is an ActionScript 3.0 class responsible for loading an object.

**var Image:String;**
In this line, a variable is declared with the name **Image**. Declaring a variable without variable's type will generate a compiler warning in strict mode. You assign a variable's type by appending the variable name with a colon (:), followed by the variable's type. For example, the following code declares a variable **Image** that is of type String: This is a String type variable, containing some text data.

**var imageNumber:Number = 0;**
In this line, a variable is declared with the name **imageNumber** and type **Number**. Variable of **Number** type contain numerical values.

**var Time:Timer = new Timer(100);**
In this line, a variable is declared with the name **Time** and type **Timer**. This variable contains information about the timer that will continuously check the number of an image to let the program know when the image is clicked and it has to go ahead. In this case, the timer will cycle every one tenth of a second infinitely.

**var Childnumber:Number;**

In this line, a variable is declared with the name **Childnumber** and type **Number**. This variable of a number type contains the number of children in the XML document. Flash only recognizes one child, **var imageNum:Number = 0**. Here, you have defined what **Childnumber** should be equal to.

Line 13

**xmlLoader.addEventListener(Event.COMPLETE, xmlLoadedF);**

In these lines, an event listener is added to the URL loader which commands Flash to load the XML data after the XML file is loaded. When the file **imagegallery.xml** is loaded, the function **xmlLoadedF** will be executed. The function **xmlLoadedF** starts on the line 17.

Lines 14 and 15

**imagebox.addEventListener(MouseEvent.CLICK, nextImgF);**
**imagebox.buttonMode = true;**

In this set of codes, **imagebox** is a movie clip instance. When you move the cursor over it, **buttonMode = true** enables the users to know the area that is clickable. Here, you have applied a button mode to the Movie clip in Line 15.

Line 18

**Time.start();**

In this set of code, the timer is set to start and execute every tenth of a second. To inform the timer what is to be executed one tenth of a second, you will add an event listener, **checkTime.addEventListener(TimerEvent.TIMER, checkF).** In this line, every tenth of a second the timer will call the function **checkF**.

Lines 23 to 32

**if(imageNum ==0){**
     **packetF();**

In this code, the first condition is defined, if the **imageNum** equals **0**, the function **packetF** is executed.

**else if(imageNum < Childnumber){**
     **imageLoad.unload();**
     **packetF();**

Here, another condition is that if the image number is less than the number of children in the XML file, **imageLoad** object unloads to avoid the appearance of the stack of image in the Stage.

**else**
     **imageLoad.unload();**
     **imageNum = 0;**
     **packetF();**

Here, the program unloads the **imageload** and set the **imgNum** to **0**, and executes function **packetF**.

Line 38
**Image = imgData.image[imgNum].imgURL;**
In the above line, you have declared the **Image** variable of the String type. This line defines the value of **Image**.

Lines 40 and 41
**imgW = Data.image[imageNum].imgW;**
**imgH = Data.image[imageNum].imgH;**
In these lines of code, Flash gets the information of the image width and height with reference to the XML file.

Line 42
**imageLoad = new Loader;**
In this line, another variable that you have declared is **imageLoad**. Next, you have to initialize this object as a Loader.

Line 43
**imageLoad.load(new URLRequest(Image));**
In this line, you have defined the loading method of **imageLoad**. The load method takes the **URLRequest** object as its argument so that you can create a new **URLRequest** object. Since its constructor accepts a string to create the Image request, you pass the Image argument that the function **xmlLoadedF** accepts.

Line 44
**imagebox.addChild(imageLoad);**
This line of code adds the **imageLoad** object that holds a loaded image in the Stage.

Lines 45 and 46
**imageLoad.x = (stage.stageWidth – Number(imgW)) /2;**
**imageLoad.y = (stage.stageHeight – Number(imgH)) /2;**
The above code is used to align image to the center of the Stage.

Line 50-52
**function nextImgF(event:MouseEvent):void{**
**checkTime.addEventListener(TimerEvent.TIMER, checkF);**
**imageNum++;**
In this code, you have defined the **nextImgF** function. Here, you recover an event listener for the timer so that it can start calling the conditional function **packetF**.

**imgNum++**
In this line, you have set the function to take the **imgNum** and add one number to it.

3.  Save the flash file with the name *c05tut5* at the location *Documents\Flash_Projects\c05_tut\ c05_tut_05*.

4.   Press CTRL+ENTER to view the final output of the tutorial in the preview window. Note that in this window, the first image is displayed. Next, click on the image to display the next image. You can also view the final rendered file of the tutorial by downloading the file *c05_flash_cc_rndr.zip* from *http://www.cadcim.com*. The path of the file is mentioned at the beginning of the TUTORIALS section.

## Tutorial 6

In this tutorial, you will create external ActionScript file and use the most basic class, the Document class, to generate instances randomly, as shown in Figure 5-62.

**(Expected time: 40 min)**

*Figure 5-62  Instances generated randomly*

The following steps are required to complete this tutorial:

a.   Open the Flash document.
b.   Create a movie clip.
c.   Create an ActionScript file.

### Opening the Flash Document

In this section, you will open the Flash document.

1.   Choose **File > Open** from the menubar; the **Open** dialog box is displayed.

2.   Choose **Documents > Flash_Projects > c05_tut > c05_tut_06 > c05_tut_06_start.fla**. Next, choose the **Open** button from the dialog box; the Flash document is displayed.

## Creating a Movie clip

In this section, you will create a movie clip.

1. In the **Publish** area of the **Properties** panel, type **docClass** in the **Class** text box, as shown in Figure 5-63.

*Figure 5-63  The **Publish** area in the **Properties** panel*

2. The **Library** panel of this document contains a movie clip named **Bubble**. Right-click on the **Bubble** movie clip; a flyout is displayed. In this flyout, choose **Properties**; the **Symbol Properties** dialog box is displayed.

3. In the **Symbol Properties** dialog box, expand the **Advanced** area. In the **ActionScript Linkage** section of the **Advanced** area, select the **Export for ActionScrip**t check box; the **Class** and **Base Class** text boxes are automatically defined by Flash, as shown in Figure 5-64.

4. Next, choose the **OK** button; the **ActionScript Class Warning** message box is displayed, as shown in Figure 5-65, with message that the definition of this class could not be found. This is because the external class file has not been created yet. Choose the **OK** button to close the message box; the linkage information to attach it on the run time is created.

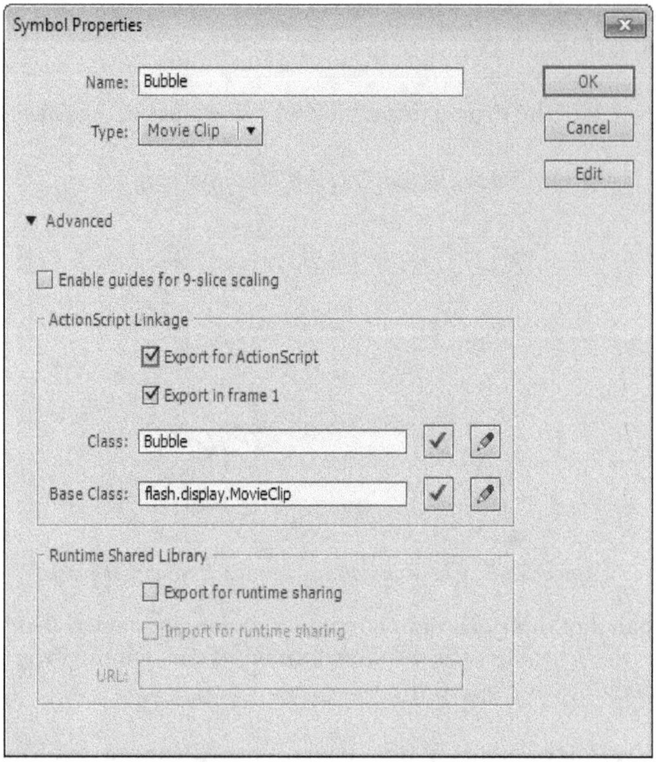

*Figure 5-64  The **Advanced** area of the **Symbol Properties** dialog box*

*Figure 5-65  The **ActionScript Class Warning** message box*

Next, you will create a Document class in the external ActionScript file that will represent the main movie.

## Creating an External ActionScript File

In this section, you will create an ActionScript file and link it to the Flash file.

1. Choose **File > New** from the menubar; the **New Document** dialog box is displayed. Double-click on the **ActionScript File** in the **General** tab of this dialog box; the **Script-1** document is displayed.

2. In the **Script-1** document, type the following code:

```
1  package
2  {
3      import flash.display.MovieClip;
4      import flash.utils.Timer;
5      import flash.events.TimerEvent;
6
7      public class docClass extends MovieClip
8          {
9                  private var timer:Timer = new Timer(100);
10
11                 public function docClass():void
12                 {
13          timer.addEventListener(TimerEvent.TIMER, createBubble);
14                 timer.start();
15                 }
16         private function createBubble(e:TimerEvent):void
17         {
18                 var bubble:Bubble = new Bubble();
19                 bubble.scaleX = bubble.scaleY = Math.random();
20                 bubble.x = Math.random() * this.stage.stageWidth
21                 bubble.y = Math.random() * this.stage.stageHeight
22                 this.addChild(bubble);
23         }
24     }
25 }
```

**Explanation**

Line 1
**package**
The **package** is a keyword. Notice that the name of the package is not mentioned in the script as here the ActionScript file is in the same directory as of the FLA file. The package keyword tells Flash that all of the code between its curly braces is part of a single group.

Line 3
**flash.display.MovieClip**
The **flash.display.MovieClip** is an external class file. These external class files are imported to the package to access functions that they contain.

Line 4
**import flash.utils.Timer;**
Here, you have imported the Timer.

Line 5
**import flash.events.TimerEvent;**
Here, you have imported the Timer class due to which the shape bubble is generated.

Line 7
**public class docClass extends MovieClip**
Here, you have declared a document class named **docClass extends MovieClip**, represents the main Timeline. **Public** means that other classes in your code will be able to see this class.

Line 11
**public function docClass():void**
Every class contains a function with the same name as the class. It is called the constructor function. The code inside this function executes when an object of this type of class is created. Code between the curly braces will be run when the SWF is loaded. Constructor functions do not need the **:void** because they cannot return a value.

Line 13
**timer.addEventListener(TimerEvent.TIMER, createBubble);**
**private var timer:Timer = new Timer(100);**
Here **timer** is the class property and as you will be using the timer within this class, it will be private. **:Timer** is the data type of the **timer**. You need to mention only the delay parameter inside the **Timer** parenthesis. This means how often you want the timer to call the function that will create the bubbles. The value inside the **Timer** parenthesis is entered in milliseconds, that means one tenth of a second.

Line 14
**timer.start();**
In this line, you have started the Timer.

Line 16
**private function createBubble(e:TimerEvent):void**
Here, you are declaring the **create Bubble** method as a private function as you will be calling it within this class. The object that will be called here is **TimerEvent**. **Void**, as the function does not return any value.

Lines 18
**var bubble:Bubble = new Bubble();**
Here, you have created a new instance of the *Bubble* movie clip.

Lines 19
**bubble.scaleX = bubble.scaleY = Math.random();**
In this code, adjust and randomize the scale of the *Bubble* movie clip. **Math.random** will return a number between 0 and 1. In ActionScript 3.0, numbers in the scale are between 0 and 1.

Lines 20 and 21
**bubble.x = Math.random() * this.stage.stageWidth**
**bubble.y = Math.random() * this.stage.stageHeight**
In the above lines, the position of the *Bubble* movie clip randomizes once it hits the Stage. The term **this** is referred to as the **docClass** that is controlling the main movie

(**c05_tut_06_start.fla**). The term **stage** refer to the main Timeline and **stageWidth** is responsible for getting any random number between 0 and the width of Stage.

Line 22
**this.addChild(bubble);**
In this line, a new child is added to the Stage (main Timeline). The new child is the instance of the **bubble** class.

3. Choose **File > Save As** from the menubar; the **Save As** dialog box is displayed. In this dialog box, type **docClass.as** in the **File** name text box and save it in \*Documents*\ *Flash_Projects\c05_tut\c05_tut_06*.

4. Close the *docClass.as* document and switch to *c05_tut_06_start.fla*.

5. In *c05_tut_06_start.fla*, press CTRL+ENTER to preview the random generation of the *Bubble* movie clip. You can also view the final rendered tutorial by downloading the file *c05_flash_cc_rndr.zip* from *http://www.cadcim.com*. The path of the file is mentioned at the beginning of the TUTORIALS section.

## Self-Evaluation Test

**Answer the following questions and then compare them to those given at the end of this chapter:**

1. Which of the following is an object-oriented programming language used in Flash?

    (a) C++                          (b) ActionScript
    (c) HTML                         (d) Java

2. The ActionScript 3.0 language is based on _____.

3. The _____ area is used to type the ActionScript code in the **Actions** panel.

4. The _____ tool is used to set an absolute or relative target path for an action in the script.

5. The **Help** tool is used to display the information for the selected ActionScript element in the Script pane. (T/F)

6. The keyword for variables is varb. (T/F)

## *Review Questions*

**Answer the following questions:**

1. Which of the following tools is used to find and replace an element or text in the script?

   (a) Toggle Fold             (b) Code Snippets
   (c) Toggle Breakpoint       (d) Find

2. The _____ tool is used to set and remove the breakpoints.

3. The _____ is the way to specify the actions that are to be performed in response to the event.

4. In ActionScript 3.0, the _____ keyword is used to store different values or data.

5. The **Insert a target path** tool is used to set an absolute or relative target path for an action in the script. (T/F)

6. The **Apply block comment** tool is used to add comment markers at the beginning and end of the selected code. (T/F)

# EXERCISES

## Exercise 1

In a Flash document, create a cube and convert it into a movie clip symbol. Next, in the movie clip Timeline, assign different colors to it on different frames. Then, create an AS file and use this movie clip to generate random instances, refer to Figure 5-66. You can view the final output of this exercise by downloading *c05_flash_cc_exr.zip* file from *www.cadcim.com*. The path of the file is as follows: *Textbooks > Animation and Visual Effects > Flash > The Adobe Flash Professional CC: A Tutorial Approach*.                    (**Expected time: 40 min**)

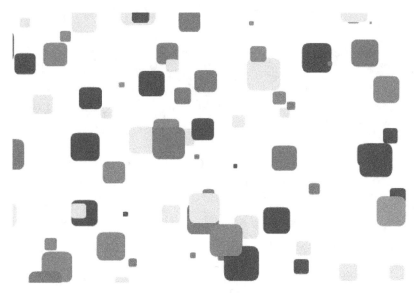

*Figure 5-66* *Randomly placed instances of movie clip symbol*

## Exercise 2

Using ActionScript 3.0, create the XML photo gallery, as shown in Figure 5-67. You can view the final output of this exercise by downloading the *c05_flash_cc_exr.zip* file from *www.cadcim.com*. The path of the file is mentioned in Exercise 1.

**(Expected time: 30 min)**

You can download the images to be used in this exercise from the following links:

*http://www.sxc.hu/photo/1354628  Courtesy:* **Chemtec** *(http://www.sxc.hu/profile/Chemtec)*
*http://www.sxc.hu/photo/1356877  Courtesy:* **Jamie Peabody** *(http://www.sxc.hu/profile/jpeabody)*
*http://www.sxc.hu/photo/1348808  Courtesy:* **bubblefish** *(http://www.sxc.hu/profile/bubblefish)*
*http://www.sxc.hu/photo/1327554  Courtesy:* **Michael Faes** *(http://www.sxc.hu/profile/rolve)*
*http://www.sxc.hu/photo/1327584  Courtesy:* **Alex Rauch** *(http://www.sxc.hu/profile/vocappella)*

*Figure 5-67*   *The XML photo gallery*

# Chapter 6

# Creating Interactive Applications

## Learning Objectives

**After completing this chapter, you will be able to:**
- *Add sound to the instances of buttons*
- *Add and edit the Dynamic Text*
- *Create text with multiple columns*
- *Add hyperlink to the text*
- *Add and edit components*
- *Create external links using components*
- *Add ActionScript to the components*

# INTRODUCTION

In Flash, you can create interactive applications using ActionScript. For example, when a user clicks on a movie clip or button, a graphic, text, or web page is displayed.

In this chapter, you will learn to add the Dynamic Text to a document. Dynamic Text supports a wider array of rich text layout features and sophisticated controls of text attributes. It allows greater control on text as compared to the Static Text. Moreover, it provides additional character styles. It also includes additional paragraph styles, including Margins, Format, Spacing, and Behavior. You can also add hyperlink to the text in your Flash document.

In Flash, you can use the ActionScript to create links to display external webpages. There are many ways to create links. One of the methods is to use components to create links. Components in Flash are generally the user interface widgets, such as button, check box, or menu bar. Instead of writing the codes for creating the art for these widgets, you can simply drag the components into your FLA file. You can manipulate a component using the ActionScript, but in some cases it is possible to modify components by setting parameters in the **Properties** panel.

# TUTORIALS

Before you start the tutorials, you need to download the *c06_flash_cc_tut.zip* file from *www.cadcim.com*. The path of the file is as follows: *Textbooks > Animation and Visual Effects > Flash > The Adobe Flash Professional CC: A Tutorial Approach*

Next, extract the contents of the zipped file to *\Documents\Flash_Projects*.

## Tutorial 1

In this tutorial, you will add sound to the button instances. You will also add TLF text to the Flash document using **Text Tool**.                              **(Expected time: 30 min)**

The following steps are required to complete this tutorial:

a.   Open the Flash document.
b.   Add sound to button instances.
c.   Add the Dynamic Text.
d.   Save the Flash document.

### Opening the New Flash Document

In this section, you will open the Flash document.

1.   Choose **File > Open** from the menubar; the **Open** dialog box is displayed.

2.   In this dialog box, choose **Documents > Flash_Projects > c06_tut > c06_tut_01 > c06_tut_01_start.fla** and then choose the **Open** button; the Flash document is displayed, as shown in Figure 6-1.

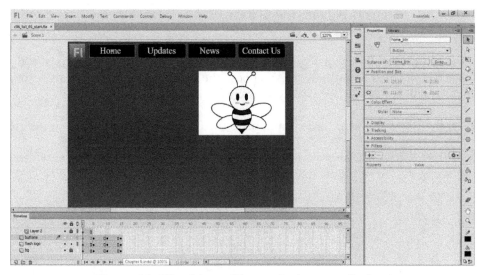

*Figure 6-1* *The c06_tut_01_start.fla document displayed*

## Adding Sound to Button Instances

In this section, you will add sound to button instances.

1. Double-click on the *home_btn* instance in the Stage to enter the symbol-editing mode, refer to Figure 6-2.

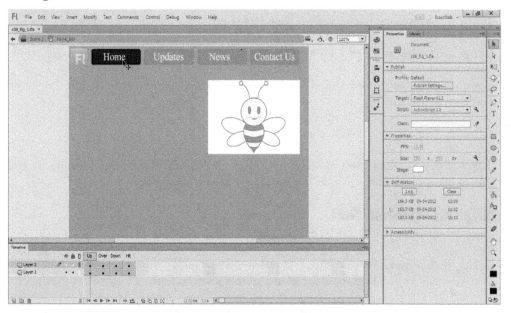

*Figure 6-2* *The symbol-editing mode of the home_btn instance*

2. In the **Timeline** panel, choose the **New Layer** button; a new layer is created.

3. Choose **File > Import > Import to Library** from the menubar; the **Import to Library** dialog box is displayed.

4. In the **Import to Library** dialog box, choose **Documents > Flash_Projects > c06_tut > Resources > Click Sound.wav**. Next, choose the **Open** button from the dialog box; the **Click Sound.wav** is displayed in the **Library** panel.

5. Select the **Down** frame of **Layer 3** and press the F7 key; a blank keyframe is inserted.

6. Drag the *Click Sound.wav* sound file from the **Library** panel to the Stage; the sound is inserted in the **Down** frame, refer to Figure 6-3.

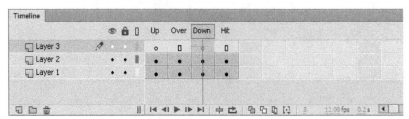

*Figure 6-3* *The sound inserted in the* **Down** *frame*

7. Click on **Scene 1** to return to the main Timeline.

8. Double-click on the *updates_btn* instance in the Stage to enter the symbol-editing mode.

9. In the **Timeline** panel, choose the **New Layer** button; a new layer is created.

10. Select the **Down** frame of **Layer 3** and press the F7 key; a blank keyframe is inserted.

11. Drag the *Click Sound.wav* sound file from the **Library** panel to the Stage; the sound is inserted in the **Down** frame.

12. Click on **Scene 1** to return to the main Timeline.

13. Follow the procedure used in Steps 7 to 11 to add the *Click Sound.wav* sound file to the **Down** frame of the *news_btn* and *contact us_btn* button instances.

## Adding the Dynamic Text

In this section, you will add the **Dynamic Text** to the document.

1. Select the **buttons** layer and choose the **New Layer** button in the **Timeline** panel; a layer is created above the **buttons** layer. Rename this layer to **text**.

2. Make sure the Playhead is on frame **1**. Choose **Text Tool** from the **Tools** panel; the tool properties are displayed in the **Properties** panel.

3. In the **Properties** panel, select **Dynamic Text** from the **Text type** drop-down list, refer to Figure 6-4.

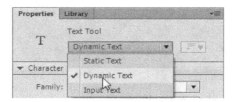

**Figure 6-4** *Selecting* **Dynamic Text** *from the* **Text type** *drop-down list*

4.  In the **Character** area of the **Properties** panel, select **Arial** from the **Family** drop-down list. Next, select **Narrow** from the **Style** drop-down list.

5.  Set the value of **Size** to **16**. Choose the **Color** swatch; a flyout is displayed. In this flyout, enter **#CCCCCC** in the Hex edit box.

6.  Now, expand the **Paragraph** area, choose the **Align left** button from the **Format** area and select **Multiline** from the **Line type** drop-down list of the **Behavior** area.

7.  Press and hold the left mouse button and drag the cursor in the Stage; the **Dynamic Text** box is displayed, as shown in Figure 6-5.

**Figure 6-5** *The* **Dynamic Text** *box*

8.  Open the *home_1.docx* file from **Documents > Flash_Projects > c06_tut > c06_tut_01 > Resources** folder. Next, copy the text from the file and paste it in the **Dynamic Text** box.

9.  Choose **Selection Tool** to view the text properly, refer to Figure 6-6. Make sure the text box is selected. In the **Position and Size** area of the **Properties** panel, make sure that the **Lock width and height values together** button is off (⊗). Next, set the value of **W** to **285** and **H** to **165**. Now, set the value of **X** to **21** and **Y** to **58**; the text box is positioned and resized, as shown in Figure 6-6.

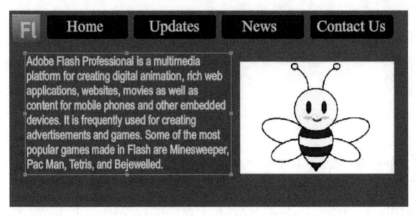

*Figure 6-6 The text box is positioned and resized*

10. Choose **Text Tool** from the **Tools** panel. Next, press and hold the left mouse button and drag the cursor in the Stage; the second **Dynamic Text** box is displayed, as shown in Figure 6-7.

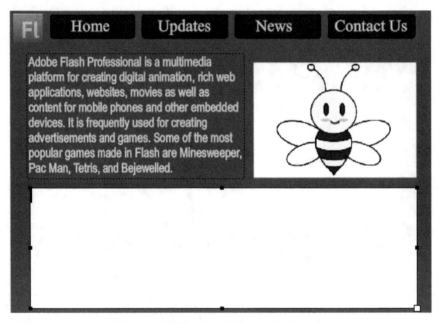

*Figure 6-7 The second **Dynamic Text** box*

11. Open the *home_2.docx* file from **Documents > Flash_Projects > c06_tut > c06_tut_01 > Resources** folder. Next, copy the text from the file and paste it in the second **Dynamic Text** box.

12. Choose **Selection Tool**, to view the text properly, refer to Figure 6-8. Make sure the text box is selected. In the **Position and Size** area of the **Properties** panel, make sure that the **Lock width and height values together** button is deactivated ( ). Next, set the value of **W** to **513** and **H** to **144**. Now, set the value of **X** to **21** and **Y** to **235**; the text box is positioned and resized, as shown in Figure 6-8.

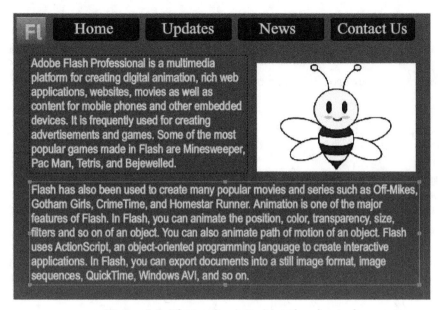

*Figure 6-8* *The text box is positioned and resized*

**Note**
*It is recommended not to resize a text box using **Transform Tool**. When the text box is resized using **Transform Tool**, the content gets distorted as the text is either stretched or squashed.*

13. Select frame **2** of the text layer and press the F7 key to insert a blank keyframe.

## Saving the Flash Document
In this section, you will save the Flash document. This document will be used in Tutorial 2.

1. Choose **File > Save As** from the menubar; the **Save As** dialog box is displayed. In this dialog box, browse to the location **Documents > Flash_Projects > c06_tut > c06_tut_01** folder.

2. Type **c06tut1** in the **File name** text box and select **Flash CC Document (*.fla)** from the **Save as type** drop-down list. Next, choose the **Save** button to save the document. Close the document.

3. Press CTRL+ENTER to view the final output of the tutorial. You can also view the final rendered file of the tutorial by downloading the file *c06_flash_cc_rndr.zip* from *http://www.cadcim.com*. The path of the zip file is mentioned at the beginning of the **TUTORIALS** section.

## Tutorial 2

In this tutorial, you will hyperlink the text.                                   **(Expected time: 15 min)**

The following steps are required to complete this tutorial:

a.   Open the Flash document.
b.   Hyperlink the text.
c.   Test the Flash document.

### Opening the New Flash Document

In this section, you will open the Flash document.

1.   Choose **File > Open** from the menubar; the **Open** dialog box is displayed.

2.   In this dialog box, choose **Documents > Flash_Projects > c06_tut > c06_tut_02 > c06_tut_02_start.fla** and then choose the **Open** button; the Flash document is displayed, as shown in Figure 6-9.

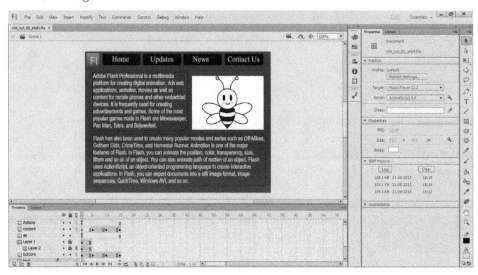

*Figure 6-9  The c06_tut_02_start.fla document displayed*

### Hyperlinking the Text

In this section, you will add hyperlink to the text.

1.   Choose **Selection Tool** and double-click on the first text box to make it active. Next, select the word **Adobe**. In the **Options** area of the **Properties** panel, enter **http://www.adobe.com/** in the **Link** text box and press the ENTER key.

2.   Place the Playhead on frame **5**. Choose **Selection Tool** and select the **Updates** text in the Stage.

3. In the **Options** area of the **Properties** panel, enter **http://www.flashmagazine.com/news/detail/adobe_announcing_cc_update/** in the **Link** text box.

4. Place the Playhead on frame **10**. Next, select the **Buying Guide** text. In the **Options** area of the **Properties** panel, enter **http://www.adobe.com/products/flash/buying-guide-upgrades.html** in the **Link** text box.

5. Select the **Customer Reviews** text. In the **Options** area of the **Properties** panel, enter **http://www.adobe.com/products/flash/reviews.html#customer-reviews** in the **Link** text box.

6. Select the **Industry Reviews** text. In the **Options** area of the **Properties** panel, enter **http://www.adobe.com/products/flash/reviews.html#industry-reviews** in the **Link** text box.

7. Select the **About Flash** text. In the **Options** area of the **Properties** panel, enter **http://www.adobe.com/products/flash.html** in the **Link** text box.

8. Place the Playhead on frame **15**. Next, select the **Contact Us** text in the Stage. In the **Options** area of the **Properties** panel, enter **http://www.adobe.com/aboutadobe/contact.html** in the **Link** text box.

9. Save the flash file with the name *c06tut2* at the location *Documents\Flash_Projects\c06_tut\c06_tut_02*.

## Testing the Flash Document

In this section, you will test the Flash document. To test the Flash document, first you need to open the preview window.

1. Press CTRL+ENTER to display the preview window, as shown in Figure 6-10. Hover the cursor on the upper text; the cursor will change into to a hand cursor, refer to Figure 6-10. Click on the upper text to check the hyperlink of the text; a browser window is displayed opening the specified website that is www.adobe.com.

2. One by one, choose the **Updates**, **News**, **Contact Us** buttons in the preview window and check the functionality of the hyperlinked text. You can also view the final rendered file of the tutorial by downloading the file *c06_flash_cc_rndr.zip* from *www.cadcim.com*. The path of the zip file is mentioned at the beginning of the **TUTORIALS** section.

*Figure 6-10* *The preview window displaying the output*

## Tutorial 3

In this tutorial, you will create external links of a website using components and ActionScript.                                                    **(Expected time: 30 min)**

The following steps are required to complete this tutorial:

a.  Open the Flash document.
b.  Open and edit a component.
c.  Add ActionScript to the component.
d.  Test the component.

### Opening the Flash Document

In this section, you will open the Flash document.

1.  Choose **File > Open** from the menubar; the **Open** dialog box is displayed.

2.  In this dialog box, browse to **Documents > Flash_Projects > c06_tut > c06_tut_03 > c06_tut_03_start.fla**. Next, choose the **Open** button from the dialog box; the Flash document is displayed, as shown in Figure 6-11.

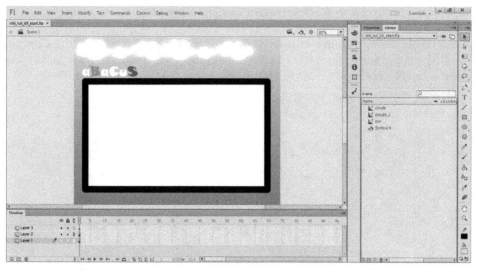

*Figure 6-11*  *The c06_tut_03_start.fla document displayed*

## Opening and Editing a Component

In this section, you will open a component from the **Components** panel and then edit it using the **Properties** panel.

1.   Make sure that the **Essentials** workspace is active. Choose **Window > Components** from the menubar; the **Components** panel is displayed, as shown in Figure 6-12.

 **Note**
*Alternatively, press CTRL+F7 to activate the **Components** panel.*

*Figure 6-12*  *The **Components** panel*

2. Make sure that the **Layer 3** is selected in the **Timeline** panel.

3. Double-click on the **Button** component in the **User Interface** folder of the **Components** panel; the component is added to the Stage and saved in the **Library** panel with the **Component Assets** folder, refer to Figures 6-13 and 6-14.

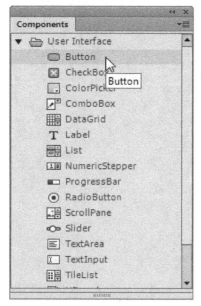

**Figure 6-13** *Choosing the* **Button** *component from the* **User Interface** *folder*

**Figure 6-14** *The* **Button** *component and the* **Component Assets** *folder*

4. Select the **Button** component in the Stage, if it is not selected; the component properties are displayed in the **Properties** panel.

5. In the **Component Parameters** area of the **Properties** panel, make sure that the **enabled** check box is selected. Next, in the **label** text box, type **Website**, refer to Figure 6-15.

6. In the **Properties** panel, type **website_btn** in the **Instance name** text box, refer to Figure 6-16.

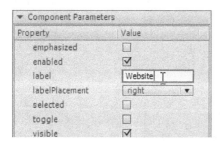

**Figure 6-15** *The* **Component Parameters** *area*

**Figure 6-16** *The instance name of the component*

7.  In the **Position and Size** area of the **Timeline** panel, set the value of **X** to **580** and **Y** to **170**; the component is positioned in the Stage.

## Adding ActionScript to the Component

In this section, you will add ActionScript to the component for linking it to the external web pages.

1.  Select the **Layer 3** in the **Timeline** panel and choose the **New Layer** button; a new layer is created. Rename this layer to **actionscript**.

2.  Make sure frame **1** of the **actionscript** layer is selected and press the F9 key; the **Actions** panel is displayed.

3.  In the Script pane, type the following script:

```
website_btn.addEventListener(MouseEvent.CLICK, onClick);
function onClick(event:MouseEvent):void{
navigateToURL(new URLRequest("http://www.cadcim.com/"), "_blank");
}
```

### Explanation

In the above line, **website_btn** is the instance name of the website component. **addEventListener(MouseEvent.CLICK, onClick)** is an event listener that will observe mouse clicks on **website_btn**. On clicking this component, the **onClick** function is executed invoking a URLRequest, **http://www.cadcim.com**. A **_blank** implies that the specified website will be loaded in a new window.

4.  Save the flash file with the name *c06tut3* at the location *Documents\Flash_Projects\c06_tut\ c06_tut_03*.

## Testing the Component

In this section, you will test the functionality of the component in the preview window.

1.  Press CTRL+ENTER to display the preview window, refer to Figure 6-17.

2.  In this window, click the **Website** button component; a browser window is displayed loading the specified website. You can also view the final rendered file of the tutorial by downloading the file *c06_flash_cc_rndr.zip* from *http://www.cadcim.com*. The path of the zip file is mentioned at the beginning of the **TUTORIALS** section.

*Figure 6-17*  *The button component displayed in the preview window*

## Self-Evaluation Test

**Answer the following questions and then compare them to those given at the end of this chapter:**

1. Which of the following shortcuts is used to display the **Components** panel?

   (a) CTRL+F3                          (b) CTRL+F7
   (c) CTRL+F6                          (d) CTRL+F9

2. There are _____ types of Paragraph Format in Flash CC.

3. The **Button** component is located in the _____ folder of the **Components** panel.

4. You can select a Selectable text type only when it has been published. (T/F)

## Review Questions

**Answer the following questions:**

1. Which of the following drop-down lists consists of the **Dynamic Text**?

   (a) Text type                        (b) Line type
   (c) Set the font style               (d) Set the font family

2.  The _____ folder is created in the **Library** panel when you add the **Button** component to the Stage.

3.  You can edit the parameters of a component using the _____ panel.

4.  The **Button** component is located in the **User Interface** folder of the **Components** panel. (T/F)

# EXERCISE

## Exercise 1

Using the ActionScript 3.0 code and the **Button** component, create a button on choosing which a website will be opened in a new browser window, refer to Figure 6-18. You can view the final output of this exercise by downloading *c06_flash_cc_exr.zip* file from *www.cadcim.com*. The path of the file is as follows: *Textbooks > Animation and Visual Effects > Flash > The Adobe Flash Professional CC: A Tutorial Approach*.                    **(Expected time: 40 min)**

*Figure 6-18*  *The external link website button*

**Answers to Self-Evaluation Test**
1. b, 2. Four, 3. User Interface, 4. T

# Chapter 7

# Working with Sound and Video

## Learning Objectives

**After completing this chapter, you will be able to:**
• *Import and edit sound files in Flash*
• *Import videos in Flash*
• *Play videos in Flash using the playback components*
• *Embed videos in a Flash document*
• *Edit videos using the Adobe Media Encoder*
• *Publish videos*

# INTRODUCTION

In Flash, you can import various types of sound files and use them in different ways. You can play the sound independent of Timeline or use Timeline to synchronize the sound. You can also control and edit sound, and add it to the button symbols. Flash supports many sound formats such as ASND, WAV, AIFF, mp3, and Sun AU.

**Note**
*The ASND (Adobe Sound Document) is the native sound format of Adobe Soundbooth.*

Flash is the most common platform to create videos for internet. There are two methods to display a video in Flash. The first one is to keep the videos as external files and use the ActionScript 3.0 FLVPlayback component to play the videos. ActionScript 3.0 FLVPlayback component is used to include a video player in the Flash document.

**Note**
*The components are inbuilt movies that you can add to your Flash documents. Each component has a specific function. You can use components with ActionScript to create complex applications. For example, rather than creating your own video player, you can simply drag a component from the **Components** panel into your document.*

The second method is used to embed the video in the Flash document. The appropriate video formats supported by Flash are FLV and F4V. FLV is the Flash video file format and uses On2VP6 codec. F4V is the latest Flash video format and uses H.264 codec (video compressing format). Flash can play any video encoded in H.264.

**Note**
*A codec is a video compression computer program that is used to compress a video file and then decompress it while playing or editing.*

# TUTORIALS

Before you start the tutorials, you need to download the *c07_flash_cc_tut.zip* file from *www.cadcim.com*. The path of the file is as follows: *Textbooks > Animation and Visual Effects > Flash > The Adobe Flash Professional CC: A Tutorial Approach.*

Next, extract the contents of the zip file to *\Documents\Flash_Projects*.

## Tutorial 1

In this tutorial, you will import sound files in Flash and then edit and place them in the Timeline.                                              **(Expected time: 45 min)**

The following steps are required to complete this tutorial:

a.   Create a new Flash document.
b.   Import the sound files.

    c.   Place the sound files in the Timeline.
    d.   Edit and control the sound files.
    e.   Set the quality of the sound.

## Creating a New Flash Document

In this section, you will create a new Flash document.

1.   Choose **File > New** from the menubar; the **New Document** dialog box is displayed.

2.   In this dialog box, choose **ActionScript 3.0** from the **General** tab and then choose the **OK** button; a new Flash document is created.

## Importing the Sound Files

In this section, you will import a sound file in the Flash document.

1.   Choose **File > Import > Import to Library** from the menubar; the **Import to Library** dialog box is displayed. In this dialog box, choose **Documents > Flash_Projects > c07_tut > Resources > animals.mp3**. Next, choose the **Open** button; the selected sound file is displayed in the **Library** panel.

    The sound files can be recognized with a unique icon located on the left of the file  name and the waveform of sound is displayed in the Item preview window when it is selected, refer to Figure 7-1. You can play the sound by choosing the **Play** button located at the top right of the Item preview window, refer to Figure 7-1.

2.   Choose **File > Import > Import to Library** from the menubar; the **Import to Library** dialog box is displayed. In this dialog box, choose **Documents > Flash_Projects > c07_tut > Resources > birds.mp3**. Next, choose the **Open** button; the selected sound is displayed in the **Library** panel.

**Note**

*Sound Courtesy:* **Dean Usher** *(http://www.freesounds.info)*

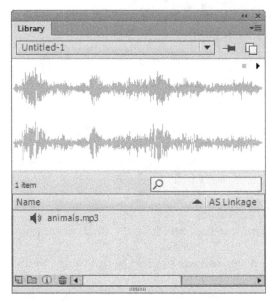

*Figure 7-1  The animals.mp3 sound file displayed in the **Library** panel*

## Placing the Sound Files in the Timeline

In this section, you will place the sound files in the Timeline.

1.  In the **Timeline** panel, choose the triangle located at the extreme right; a flyout is
    displayed. In this flyout, choose the **Large** option; the width of the frames increases
    in the **Timeline** panel, as shown in Figure 7-2.

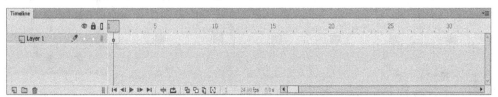

*Figure 7-2  The frames in the **Timeline** panel after choosing the **Large** option*

The options in the Frame View flyout are used to change the width of the frames in the
**Timeline** panel. The **Large** frame-width setting is useful for viewing the details of the
waveforms of sound.

2.  Choose **Insert > Timeline > Layer** from the menubar; a new layer is created in the
    **Timeline** panel. Alternatively, choose the **New Layer** button in the **Timeline** panel to
    create a new layer.

    **Note**
    *It is recommended that you place each sound file on a separate layer as each layer acts as a
    separate sound channel. When you play the SWF file, the sounds on all layers are combined.*

3.  Rename this layer to **Sound_1**.

4.  Drag *animals.mp3* from the **Library** panel to the Stage; a horizontal line is displayed on frame **1** of the **Sound_1** layer, as shown in Figure 7-3. This line represents the waveform of the sound.

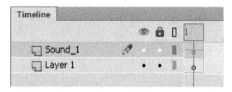

*Figure 7-3 Horizontal line on frame 1*

5.  In the **Timeline** panel, drag the slider to view frame **96**, refer to Figure 7-4. Next, select frame **96** of the **Sound_1** layer and press the F6 key to insert a keyframe; the waveform of sound is displayed in the Timeline, as shown in Figure 7-5.

*Figure 7-4 Dragging the slider*

*Figure 7-5 The waveform of the sound in the Timeline*

6.  Choose the **New Layer** button in the **Timeline** panel; a new layer is created. Rename this layer to **Sound_2**.

7.  In the **Sound_2** layer, select frame **16** and press the F6 key to insert a keyframe.

8.  In the **Sound_2** layer, select frame **1** and drag the *birds.mp3* from the **Library** panel to the Stage; the sound is inserted between frame **1** to **16** in the Timeline, refer to Figure 7-6.

*Figure 7-6 The layers containing sound files*

9.  In the **Timeline** panel, choose the **Play** button or press CTRL+ENTER to test the sound. You will notice that the sounds are overlapping.

Flash has two options to synchronize the sound: **Stream** and **Event**. The **Stream** option is used to synchronize the sound to play on a website. The **Event** option is used to synchronize the sound to the occurrence of an event. Event sounds get completely downloaded before they are played. They are stored in the memory and you can use them again with no download time. These sounds are used for short duration sounds like button clicks or looped sounds.

**Note**

*In the **Sound** area of the **Properties** panel, the **Sync** property of the sound is set to **Event** by default. To change the synchronization of the sound, select a frame in the sound layer; the **Frame** properties are displayed in the **Properties** panel. In the **Sound** area of the **Properties** panel, select the **Event** or **Stream** option from the **Sync** drop-down list to set the synchronization of the sound, refer to Figure 7-7. There are two other options, **Start** and **Stop** in the **Sync** drop-down list which are used to start and stop the specified sound, refer to Figure 7-7.*

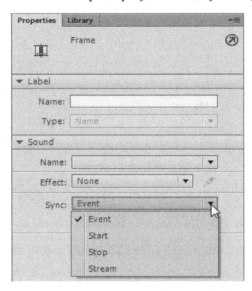

*Figure 7-7  The **Sync** drop-down list in the **Properties** panel*

## Editing and Controlling the Sound Files

In this section, you will edit and control the sound files using the **Edit Envelope** dialog box.

1. Select a frame in the **Sound_1** layer; the **Frame** properties are displayed in the **Properties** panel.

2. In the **Sound** area of the **Properties** panel, select **Stream** from the **Sync** drop-down list; the synchronization of the sound is set to the **Stream** sound and it stops at frame **96** with the Timeline (frame span).

3. Choose the **Play** button in the **Timeline** panel to play the sound. Notice that the sound plays with the Playhead till there are sufficient frames to play. The Playhead stops at frame **96** and so does the sound.

When the synchronization of the sound is set to **Stream**, Flash plays the sound as soon as it is loaded for the first few frames, without waiting for the complete sound to download. Stream sounds start and stop with the Playhead and stop completely as the frame span is over. Stream sounds are used for songs, sound tracks, voice files, and other longer sound files and they are synchronized to the Timeline.

4.   In the **Sound** area of the **Properties** panel, choose the **Edit sound envelope** button;  the **Edit Envelope** dialog box is displayed, as shown in Figure 7-8.

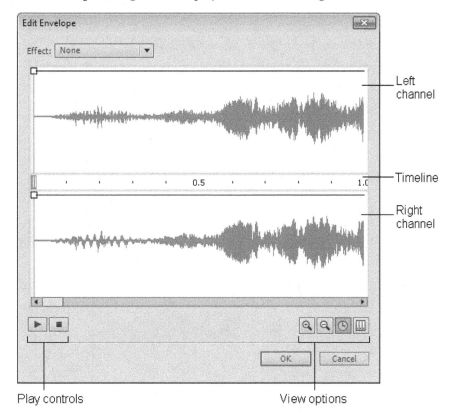

*Figure 7-8  The **Edit Envelope** dialog box*

5.   Choose the **Frames** button from the **View** option; the seconds view of the Timeline is changed to frame view.

Drag the slider at the bottom of the right channel to view the complete waveform of the sound. You will notice that a vertical line is displayed in the left and right channels on frame **95**, representing the ending point of the sound. The sound will play till frame **95** in the SWF file, refer to Figure 7-9.

6.   In the **Edit Envelope** dialog box, select the **Custom** option from the **Effect** drop-down list.

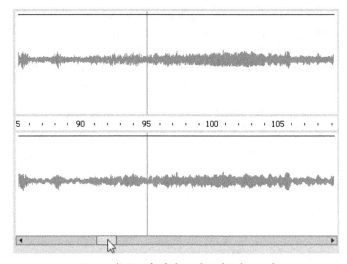

*Figure 7-9*  *The left and right channels*

**Note**
*The **Custom** option is used to edit the sound manually by creating handles.*

7.  Drag the slider located at the bottom of the right channel to frame **17**. Click on the envelope line in the left channel; a box is created in both channels representing the new handles on the envelope lines, refer to Figure 7-10.

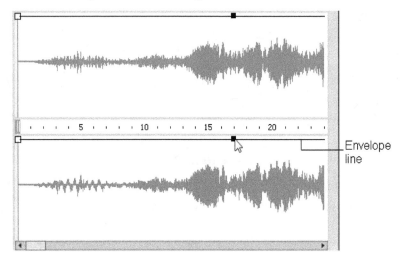

*Figure 7-10*  *Inserting a handle on frame **17***

Envelope lines represent the volume of the sound. They also display the approximate direction of the volume of the sound.

**Note**

*You can create and remove the handles to change the volume of the sound. To create a new handle, click on the envelope line. To remove an envelope handle, drag it out of the Edit Envelope dialog box.*

8. Drag the handle to the bottom of the left channel and place it on frame **17**, as shown in Figure 7-11. Placing the handle at the bottom indicates the decrease in the volume from 100% to 0%.

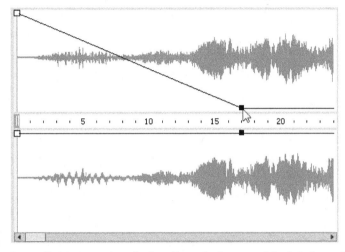

***Figure 7-11*** *Dragging the handle at the bottom of the left channel*

9. In the right channel, drag the handle located on frame **17** to the bottom of the channel, refer to Figure 7-12.

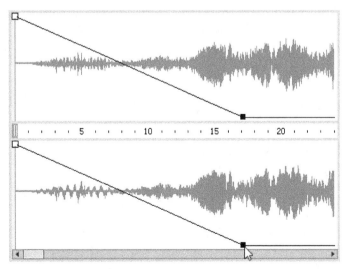

***Figure 7-12*** *Dragging the handle at the bottom of the right channel*

10. Drag the initial handles in both the channels to their bottom, refer to Figure 7-13.

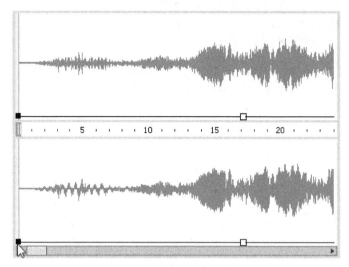

**Figure 7-13** *The initial handles placed at the bottom of their channels*

11. Drag the slider at the bottom of the right channel till frame **30** to view the waveform of sound till that frame.

12. In the left channel, place the cursor on the envelope line of frame **24** and drag it to the top of this channel, refer to Figure 7-14.

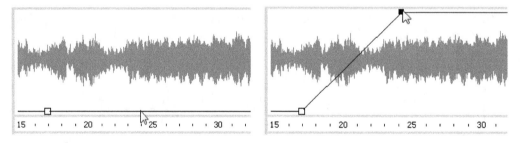

**Figure 7-14** *Creating and placing the handle on frame **24** of the left channel*

13. Repeat the same procedure as used in Step 12 for the right channel, refer to Figure 7-15. Choose the **OK** button.

The volume level in both the channels increases slowly. It starts from frame **17** and when it reaches frame **24**, it becomes 100%.

**Tip:** *You can also apply preset effects by choosing a suitable option from the **Effects** drop-down list.*

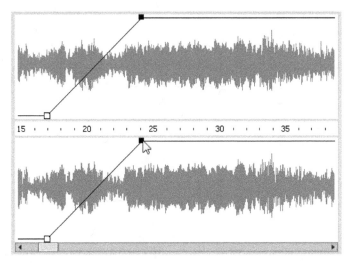

*Figure 7-15  Handle inserted and placed on frame 24 in the left and right channels*

14. In the **Sound_2** layer, select a frame between frame **1** and frame **15**; the frame properties are displayed in the **Properties** panel.

15. In the **Sound** area of the **Properties** panel, choose the **Edit sound envelope** button; the **Edit Envelope** dialog box is displayed. In this dialog box, the waveform of the *birds.mp3* sound is displayed.

16. In the **Edit Envelope** dialog box, choose the **Seconds** button.

17. Place the cursor on the left handle of the Timeline slider; the cursor changes into a double-headed arrow. Next, drag the Timeline slider to **0.6** second, refer to Figure 7-16. The sound is shortened as it has been clipped.

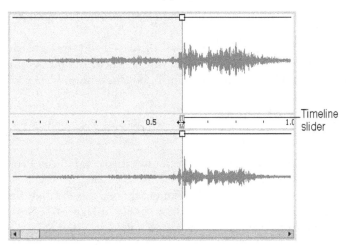

*Figure 7-16  Placing the left handle of the Timeline slider on **0.6** second*

18. Drag the panel slider located below the right channel to view the right end of the Timeline slider.

19. Drag the right end of the Timeline slider to **1.8** second, refer to Figure 7-17.

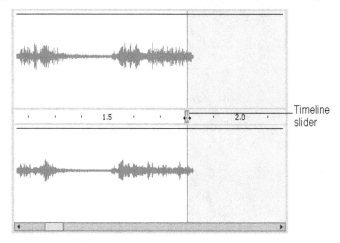

*Figure 7-17  Placing the Timeline slider on **1.8** second*

20. Choose the **OK** button; the appearance of the waveform in the **Sound_2** layer in the **Timeline** panel is changed, as shown in Figure 7-18.

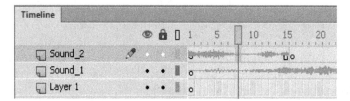

*Figure 7-18  The waveform changed in the Timeline of the **Sound_2** layer*

21. Press CTRL+ENTER; the preview window is displayed and you can hear the sound. Notice that for approximately half a second, you will first hear the birds sound followed by the animal sound but there will be no overlapping of these sounds.

## Setting the Quality of Sound
In this section, you will set the quality of the sound.

1. Click in the Stage; the **Document** properties are displayed in the **Properties** panel.

2. In the **Publish** area of the **Properties** panel, choose the **Publish Settings** button; the **Publish Settings** dialog box is displayed, as shown in Figure 7-19. Alternatively, choose **File > Publish Settings** from the menubar to invoke this dialog box.

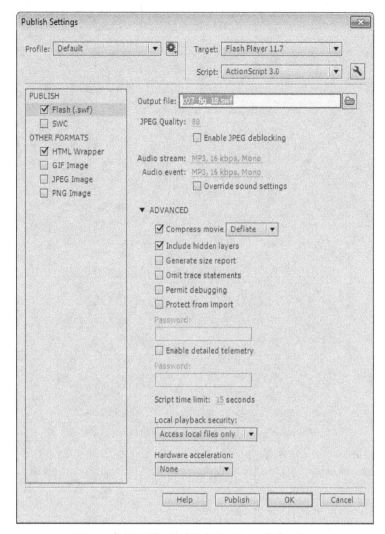

*Figure 7-19  The **Publish Settings** dialog box*

 **Tip:** *The keyboard shortcut to display the **Publish Settings** dialog box is CTRL+SHIFT+F12.*

3.  In this dialog box, click on the **Set Stream** (**MP3, 16 kbps, Mono**) text located on the right of the **Audio stream** option, as shown in Figure 7-20; the **Sound Settings** dialog box is displayed, as shown in Figure 7-21.

4.  In the **Sound Settings** dialog box, select **64 kbps** in the **Bit rate** drop-down list; the **Preprocessing** option is enabled in this dialog box.

 **Note**
*The **Preprocessing** option is displayed only if you select a bit rate of **20 kbps** or higher in the **Bit rate** drop-down list.*

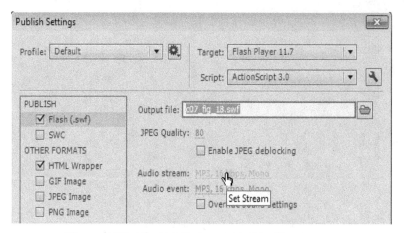

*Figure 7-20  The **Set Stream** text of **Audio stream***

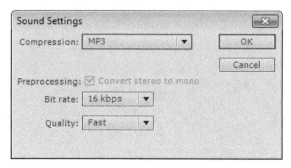

*Figure 7-21  The **Sound Settings** dialog box*

5.  Clear the **Convert stereo to mono** check box located on the right of the **Preprocessing** option. Select **Best** in the **Quality** drop-down list. Next, choose the **OK** button to return to the **Publish Settings** dialog box.

**Note**
*Stereo sound creates an illusion of direction and audible perspective. It gives an impression of sound coming from various directions, as in surround-sound. Mono sound is in the form of one channel.*

6.  Click on the **Set event** (**MP3, 16 kbps, Mono**) text located on the right of the **Audio event** option; the **Sound Settings** dialog box is displayed.

7.  In the **Sound Settings** dialog box of **Audio event**, select **64 kbps** in the **Bit rate** drop-down list; the **Preprocessing** option is displayed in this dialog box.

8.  Clear the **Convert stereo to mono** check box located on the right of the **Preprocessing** option and then select **Best** from the **Quality** drop-down list. Next, choose the **OK** button to return to the **Publish Settings** dialog box.

9.  In the **Publish Settings** dialog box, select the **Override sound settings** check box.

**Note**
*When you select the **Override sound settings** check box, Flash overrides the settings for individual sounds. If the **Override sound settings** check box is not selected, Flash publishes all stream sounds at the highest individual setting. This increases the size of the file.*

10. Choose the **OK** button to close this dialog box.

11. Save the flash file with the name *c07tut1* at the location *\Documents\Flash_Projects\c07_tut\ c07_tut_01*.

12. Press CTRL+ENTER to view the final output of the tutorial. You can also view the final rendered file of the tutorial by downloading the file *c07_flash_cc_rndr.zip* from *www.cadcim.com*. The path of the zip file is mentioned at the beginning of the TUTORIALS section.

**Note**
*You can delete and change the sound from the Timeline.*

*1. To delete the sound from the Timeline, select a frame in the Timeline of the sound layer; the **Frame** properties are displayed in the **Properties** panel. In the **Sound** area of this panel, select **None** in the **Name** drop-down list; the sound is removed from the Timeline.*

*2. To change the sound in the Timeline, select a frame in the Timeline of the sound layer; the **Frame** properties are displayed in the **Properties** panel. In the **Sound** area of the **Properties** panel, select the desired sound from the **Name** drop-down list.*

## Tutorial 2

In this tutorial, you will add sound to a button symbol. Figure 7-22 shows the waveform of the sound on the **Down** frame.

**(Expected time: 15 min)**

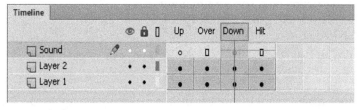

***Figure 7-22*** *Waveform of the sound on the **Down** frame of the button symbol*

The following steps are required to complete this tutorial:

a. Open the Flash document.
b. Open the Sound Library.
c. Place the sound on the Timeline.

## Opening the Flash Document

In this section, you will open the Flash document.

1. Choose **File > Open** from the menubar; the **Open** dialog box is displayed.

2. Choose **Documents > Flash_Projects > c07_tut > c07_tut_02 > c07_tut_02_start.fla** from the dialog box. Next, choose the **Open** button; the Flash document is displayed, as shown in Figure 7-23.

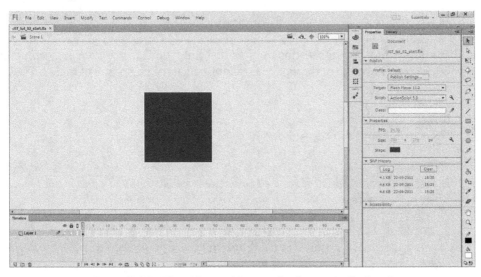

*Figure 7-23*  *The c07_tut_02_start.fla document displayed*

## Importing the Sound in the Library Panel

In this section, you will import sound files in the Flash document.

1. Choose **File > Import > Import to Library** from the menubar; the **Import to Library** dialog box is displayed. In this dialog box, choose **Documents > Flash_Projects > c07_tut > Resources > sword.mp3**. Next, choose the **Open** button; the selected sound file is displayed in the **Library** panel, as shown in Figure 7-24.

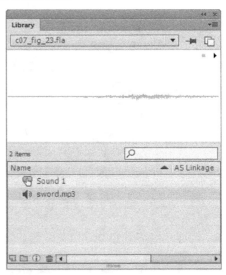

2. Select the **sword.mp3** to view the waveform in the Item preview window, refer to Figure 7-24. You can play the sound by choosing the **Play** button located at the top right of the Item preview window, refer to Figure 7-24.

*Figure 7-24*  *Sound file displayed in the* ***Library*** *panel*

## Adding Sound to the Button

In this section, you will place the sound on the button symbol's Timeline.

1. Double-click on the icon of the **Sound 1** button in the **Library** panel; the symbol-editing mode is displayed in the Scene area.

2. Choose the **New Layer** button in the **Timeline** panel; a new layer is created. Rename this layer as **Sound**.

3. In the **Sound** layer, select the **Down** frame and press the F6 key to insert a keyframe.

4. In the **Sound** area of the **Properties** panel, select **sword.mp3** from the **Name** drop-down list; the sound file is added and displayed in the **Down** and **Hit** frame in the Timeline, as shown in Figure 7-25.

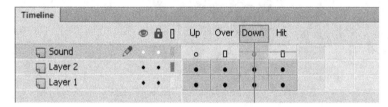

*Figure 7-25  The waveform of the sound displayed in the **Down** and **Hit** frame*

5. Click on **Scene 1** to return to the main Timeline.

6. Drag the **Sound 1** button symbol from the **Library** panel to the Stage.

7. Save the flash file with the name *c07tut2* at the location *\Documents\Flash_Projects\c07_tut\ c07_tut_02*.

8. Press CTRL+ENTER to view the final output of the tutorial in the preview window. In this window, click on the button symbol to play the sound. You can also view the final rendered file of the tutorial by downloading the file *c07_flash_cc_rndr.zip* from *www.cadcim.com*. The path of the zip file is mentioned at the beginning of the TUTORIALS section.

**Note**
*You can also add sound to the **Over** frame of the button symbol.*

# Tutorial 3

In this tutorial, you will encode the video in Adobe Media Encoder CC and use that video in your Flash document, as shown in Figure 7-26.                              **(Expected time: 45 min)**

*Figure 7-26* *The encoded video in Flash*

The following steps are required to complete this tutorial:

a.  Create a new Flash document.
b.  Launch Adobe Media Encoder.
c.  Convert the video file into F4V file.
d.  Crop the video and change the video length.
e.  Export the video.
f.  Import the encoded video in Flash.
g.  Import an image.
h.  Convert the video into a movie clip.

## Creating a New Flash Document

In this section, you will create a new Flash document.

1.  Choose **File > New** from the menubar; the **New Document** dialog box is displayed.

2.  In this dialog box, choose **ActionScript 3.0** from the **General** tab and then choose the **OK** button; a new Flash document is created.

## Launching Adobe Media Encoder

In this section, you will encode a video file using Adobe Media Encoder.

1.  To launch Adobe Media Encoder CC, choose the **Start** button on the taskbar; the **Start** menu will be displayed. Next, choose **All Programs > Adobe Media Encoder CC** from the **Start** menu, as shown in Figure 7-27; the **Adobe Media Encoder CC** is launched, as shown in Figure 7-28.

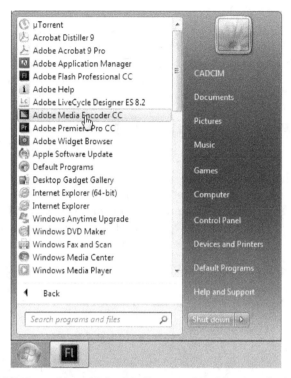

*Figure 7-27  Launching **Adobe Media Encoder CC** using the **Start** menu*

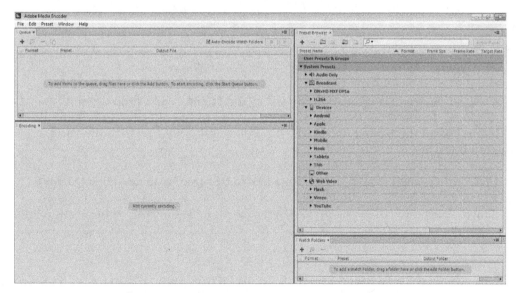

*Figure 7-28  The **Adobe Media Encoder CC** interface*

**Note**
*Adobe Media Encoder CC is a stand-alone video encoding application that is used to encode audio and video in formats such as FLV encoded with the On2 VP6 codec, F4V encoded with the H.264 codec, and H.264 video encoded with the H.264 codec. The video export formats provided by Adobe Media Encoder depend on the software with which it is installed. When installed with Flash, the video export formats available are Adobe FLV/F4V and H.264 video.*

## Converting the Video File into the F4V File
In this section, you will convert the MPG video file into F4V file using the Adobe Media Encoder.

1.  Choose **File > Add Source** from the menubar; the **Open** dialog box is displayed.

2.  In the **Open** dialog box, choose **Documents > Flash_Projects > c07_tut > Resources > road drive 1.MPG**. Next, choose the **Open** button from the dialog box; the *road drive 1.AVI* video file is displayed in the **Queue** area, as shown in Figure 7-29.

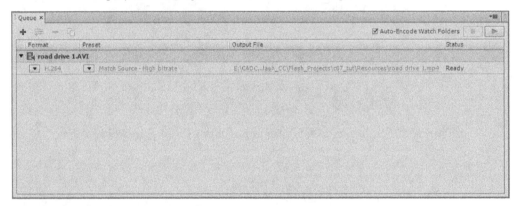

*Figure 7-29  The road drive 1.AVI displayed in the **Queue** area*

3.  Click on the triangle located on the left of the **H.264** text; a drop-down list is displayed. In this drop-down list, select **F4V**, refer to Figure 7-30. As the arrow is located below the **Format** option, the drop-down list is referred to as the **Format** drop-down list.

4.  Click on the triangle located on the left of the **Match Source Attributes (High Quality)** text; a drop-down list is displayed. In this drop-down list, make sure that **Match Source Attributes (High Quality)** is selected, refer to Figure 7-31. As the arrow is located below the **Preset** option, the drop-down list is referred to as the **Preset** drop-down list.

**Note**
*You can choose the desired location to save the encoded videos. Click on the text located below the **Output File** option; the **Save As** dialog box is displayed. In this dialog box, you can choose the desired location. Saving the video at the location where the original video is saved will not affect the original video.*

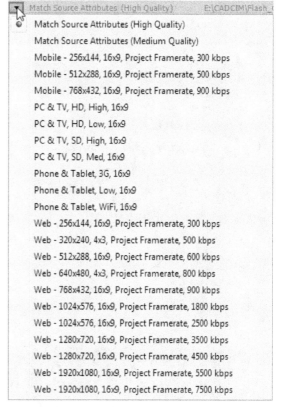

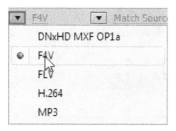

*Figure 7-30* *The* ***Format*** *drop-down list*        *Figure 7-31* *The* ***Preset*** *drop-down list*

5.  Select the **road drive 1.AVI**. Next, choose the **Start Queue (Return)** button located  at the top right corner of the **Queue** area; the encoding process starts, and the progress and preview of the video is displayed in the **Encoding** panel, refer to Figure 7-32.

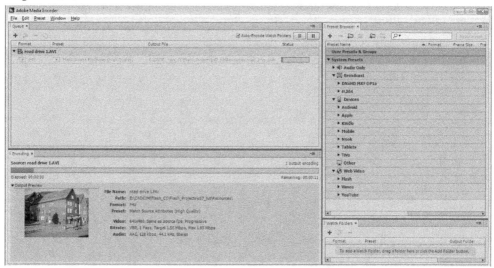

*Figure 7-32* *Encoding the MPG into F4V*

When the encoding process is completed, the text **Done** and a green check mark are displayed in the **Status** area, as shown in Figure 7-33. This status represents that the video file is successfully encoded and saved with the original video, as shown in Figure 7-34.

*Figure 7-33  The green check mark displayed in the **Status** area*

*Figure 7-34  The road drive 1.f4v video clip*

## Cropping the Video and Changing the Video Length

In this section, you will crop the video and shorten its length in Adobe Media Encoder.

1.  Select the *road drive 1.AVI* in the **Queue** area. Next, choose **Edit > Reset Status** from the menubar to reset the settings of *road drive 1.AVI* file, refer to Figure 7-35.

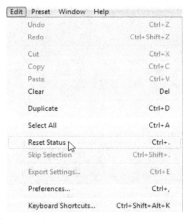

*Figure 7-35  Choosing **Reset Status** from menubar*

2.  Click on the **Match Source Attributes (High Quality)** text located below the **Preset** option, refer to Figure 7-36; the **Export Settings** dialog box is displayed, as shown in Figure 7-37. Alternatively, choose the default settings (text) in the **Preset** area to display the **Export Settings** dialog box.

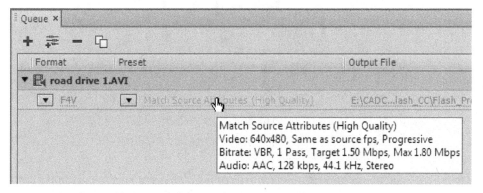

*Figure 7-36  Clicking on the* **Match Source Attributes (High Quality)** *text*

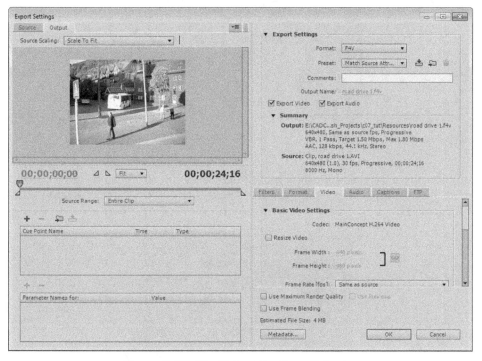

*Figure 7-37  The* **Export Settings** *dialog box*

3.  Choose the **Crop the output video** button located on the upper left corner of the **Source** area; the cropping bounding box is displayed on the video in the preview window, as shown in Figure 7-38.

**Figure 7-38**  *The cropping bounding box displayed over the video in the preview window*

4.  Place the cursor on the top right transform point; the shape of the cursor is changed to a double-headed arrow with a tool tip displaying the dimensions of the video, as shown in Figure 7-39.

**Figure 7-39**  *The dimensions of the video displayed in the tool tip*

5.  Drag the cursor inward to set the dimensions of the video to 565 x 368 pixels, as shown in Figure 7-40. Alternatively, set the value of **Top** to 112 and the value of **Right** to 75, refer to Figure 7-41.

**Figure 7-40**  *Cropping the video*

**Figure 7-41**  *Setting the **Top** and **Right** values*

**Note**
*You can also set the crop area in standard proportion. To do so, click on the triangle located on the right of **None**; a drop-down list is displayed. In this drop-down list, select the desired ratio, refer to Figure 7-42. The ratio will be applied to the selected portion.*

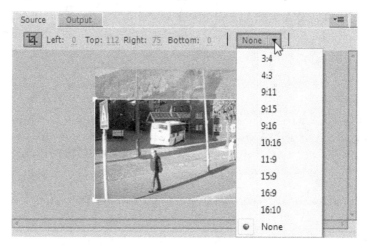

***Figure 7-42** The drop-down list displaying the ratios*

6.  Choose the **Output** tab; the output of the cropped video is displayed in the preview window. Next, choose the **Source** tab.

7.  Drag the Playhead in the Timeline to preview the footage, refer to Figure 7-43.

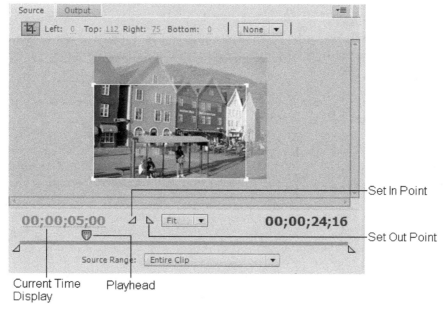

***Figure 7-43** Dragging the Playhead in the Timeline*

8.  Click on the **Current Time Display** edit box; it is activated. In this edit box, enter
    **00;00;02;26** and then choose the **Set In Point** button; the In point is placed at the
    time entered in the **Current Time Display**, as shown in Figure 7-44.

*Figure 7-44  Setting the In point of the footage*

9.  Again, click on the **Current Time Display** edit box; it is activated. In this edit box,
    enter **00;00;16;10** and then choose the **Set Out Point** button; the Out point is
    placed at the current time entered in the **Current Time Display**, as shown in
    Figure 7-45.

    The highlighted footage between the In and Out point markers is the portion of the video
    clip that will be encoded.

*Figure 7-45  Setting the Out point of the footage*

## Exporting the Video

In this section, you will export the video. The right area of the **Export Settings** dialog box
consists of the **Export Settings** area and various tabs that are used to modify video export
settings, refer to Figure 7-46.

1.  From the **Format** drop-down list, select the required format for the video output. For this
    video output, select **F4V**, refer to Figure 7-47.

    F4V is the latest Flash video format and uses H.264 codec (video compression format).
    As you have customized the cropping dimensions for the video, the **Custom** option is
    displayed as a default option in the **Preset** drop-down list, refer to Figure 7-48.

    **Note**
    *The availability of the preset options in the **Preset** drop-down list depends on the format you
    select in the **Format** drop-down list.*

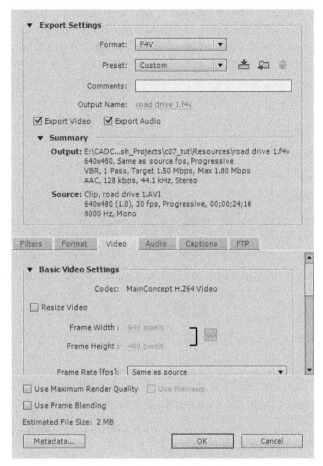

**Figure 7-46** *The **Export Settings** area*

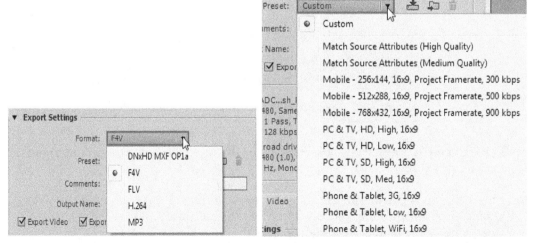

**Figure 7-47** *Partial view of the **Format** drop-down list*

**Figure 7-48** *Partial view of the **Preset** drop-down list*

2. Click on the text on the right of **Output Name**; the **Save As** dialog box is displayed. In this dialog box, choose **Documents > Flash_Projects > c07_tut > Resources** and save the file with the name *road drive 1.f4v;* the **Confirm Save As** message box is displayed, as shown in Figure 7-49. Choose the **Yes** button to close the dialog box.

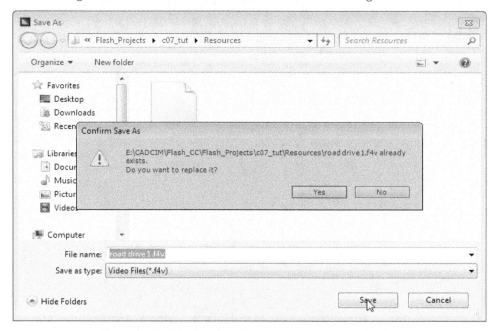

*Figure 7-49  The **Confirm Save As** message box is displayed*

3. In the **Export Settings** area, make sure the **Export Video** and **Export Audio** check boxes are selected, as shown in Figure 7-50.

*Figure 7-50  The **Export Video** and **Export Audio** check boxes selected*

4. In the **Export Settings** dialog box, choose the **OK** button located at the bottom right; the dialog box is closed.

5. Choose the **Start Queue (Return)** button located at the top right corner of the **Queue** area; the encoding process starts, and the progress and preview of the video is displayed in the **Encoding** panel, as shown in Figure 7-51.

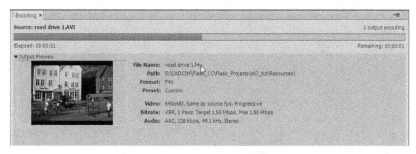

*Figure 7-51  The Encoding area*

When the encoding process is completed, the text **Done** and a green check mark are displayed in the **Status** area. This status represents that the video file is successfully encoded and saved with the original video.

6.   Choose the **Close** button; the Adobe Media Encoder is closed, refer to Figure 7-52.

*Figure 7-52  Closing the Media Encoder by choosing the Close button*

## Importing the Encoded Video in Flash
In this section, you will import the encoded video in Flash.

1.   Choose **File > Import Video** from the menubar, the **Import Video** dialog box is displayed.

2.   In the **Select Video** area of the **Import Video** dialog box, choose the **Browse** button, refer to Figure 7-53; the **Open** dialog box is displayed.

*Figure 7-53  The Browse button in the Import Video dialog box*

3.   In the **Open** dialog box, choose **Documents > Flash_Projects > c07_tut > Resources > road drive 1.f4v**. Next, choose the **Open** button; the path is displayed below the **Browse** button, as shown in Figure 7-54.

*Figure 7-54  The path displayed below the Browse button*

4.  In the **Select Video** area of the **Import Video** dialog box, choose the **Next** button; the **Skinning** area is displayed in this dialog box, as shown in Figure 7-55.

5.  In the **Skinning** area, make sure **None** is selected in the **Skin** drop-down list and then choose the **Next** button; the **Finish Video Import** area is displayed, as shown in Figure 7-56. This area shows the summary of the video import. Next, choose the **Finish** button; the video is displayed in the Stage, as shown in Figure 7-57, and the parameters of this video are displayed in the **Properties** panel.

6.  Rename **Layer 1** to **Video**.

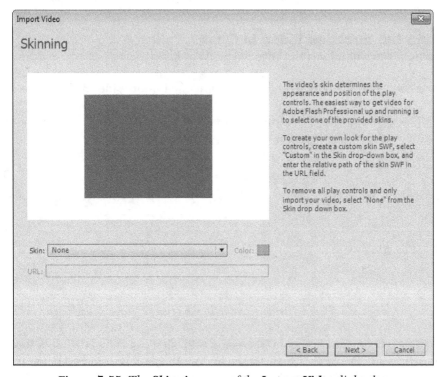

*Figure 7-55  The **Skinning** area of the **Import Video** dialog box*

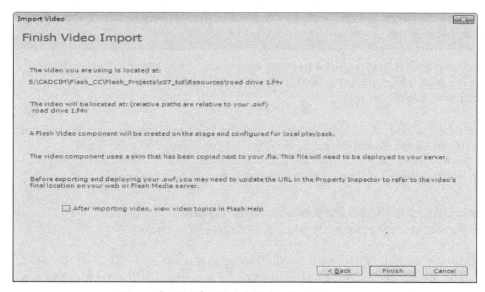

*Figure 7-56  The Finish Video Import area*

*Figure 7-57  The video displayed in the Stage*

## Importing an Image

In this section, you will import an image.

1.  Choose the **New Layer** button; a new layer is created. Rename this layer as **Image**.

2.  Make sure the **Image** Layer in the **Timeline** panel is selected. Next, choose **File > Import > Import to Stage** from the menubar; the **Import** dialog box is displayed. In this dialog box, choose **Documents > Flash_Projects > c07_tut > Resources > room.png**. Next, choose the **Open** button; the image is displayed in the Stage.

3.  Choose the **Align** button located on the left of the **Properties** panel; the **Align** panel is displayed.

4.  In this panel, select the **Align to Stage** check box, if it is not selected by default. In the **Match Size** area, choose the **Match width and height** button; the image is set to the size of the Stage.

5.  In the **Align** area of the **Align** panel, choose the **Align horizontal center** button and then the **Align vertical center** button; the image is aligned to the Stage.

6.  In the **Timeline** panel, drag the **Image** layer below the **Video** layer.

## Converting the Video into Movie Clip Symbol

In this section, you will convert the video into a movie clip symbol.

1.  Make sure the **Selection Tool** from the **Tools** panel is selected and select the video. Next, choose **Modify > Convert to Symbol** from the menubar; the **Convert to Symbol** dialog box is displayed.

2.  In this dialog box, type **video_mc** in the **Name** text box and make sure the **Movie Clip** in the **Type** drop-down list is selected. Next, choose the **OK** button; the video is converted into a movie clip symbol with the name *video_mc*.

3.  Select the *video_mc* instance in the Stage; the properties of this instance are displayed in the **Properties** panel.

4.  In the **Position and Size** area of the **Properties** panel, set the value of **W** to **212** and **H** to **110**. Set the value of **X** to **390** and **Y** to **225**; the *video_mc* instance is positioned in the Stage, as shown in Figure 7-58.

*Figure 7-58  The video positioned in the Stage*

5.   Choose the **3D Rotation Tool** from the **Tools** panel; the 3D rotation gizmo is displayed on the *video_mc* instance, as shown in Figure 7-59.

The **3D Rotation Tool** is used to create the visual impression of 3D. With the help of this tool, you can position the object at an angle and rotate it about any axis, refer to Figure 7-60. Note that the **3D Rotation Tool** works only on a movie clip symbol.

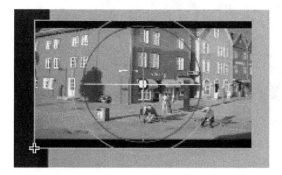

*Figure 7-59* *The 3D rotation gizmo displayed on the video_mc instance*

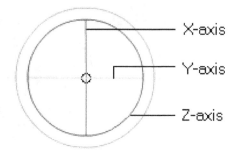

*Figure 7-60* *The 3D rotation gizmo*

6.   Place the cursor on Y-axis, as shown in Figure 7-61 and drag the cursor downward to align the *video_mc* instance to the wall of the room, as shown in Figure 7-62.

*Figure 7-61* *Y-axis of the gizmo*

7.   In the **Timeline** panel, place the **Image** layer above the **Video** layer; the *video_mc* is shifted behind the image, as shown in Figure 7-63.

8.   Save the flash file with the name *c07tut3* at the location *\Documents\Flash_Projects\c07_tut\ c07_tut_03*.

9.   Press CTRL+ENTER to view the final output of the tutorial. You can also view the final rendered file of the tutorial by downloading the file *c07_flash_cc_rndr.zip* from *www.cadcim.com*. The path of the zip file is mentioned at the beginning of the TUTORIALS section.

*Figure 7-62*  *Aligning the video_mc to the wall of the room*

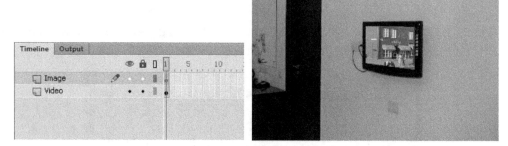

*Figure 7-63*  *The video_mc shifted behind the image*

## Tutorial 4

In this tutorial, you will embed videos in a Flash document, as shown in Figure 7-64.

**(Expected time: 45 min)**

The following steps are required to complete this tutorial:

a.   Open the Flash document.
b.   Convert video files into FLV files.
c.   Import the encoded videos in Flash.
d.   Place the videos in the Timeline.

*Figure 7-64* *The videos embedded in the Flash document*

## Opening the Flash Document

In this section, you will open the Flash document.

1. Choose **File > Open** from the menubar; the **Open** dialog box is displayed.

2. Choose **Documents > Flash_Projects > c07_tut > c07_tut_04 > c07_tut_04_start.fla**. Next, choose the **Open** button from the dialog box; the Flash document is displayed, as shown in Figure 7-65.

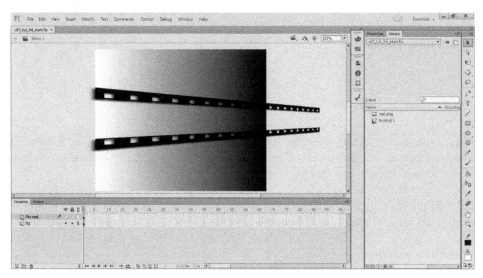

*Figure 7-65* *The c07_tut_04_start.fla document displayed*

## Converting Video Files into FLV Files in Media Encoder

In this section, you will convert video AVI files into FLV files.

1. Open **Adobe Media Encoder CC** from the start menu, as discussed earlier in the previous tutorial of this chapter.

2. Choose **File > Add Source** from the menubar; the **Open** dialog box is displayed. Alternatively, choose the **Add Source** button to display the **Open** dialog box, refer to Figure 7-66.

*Figure 7-66 Choosing the **Add Source** button*

3. In the **Open** dialog box, choose **Documents > Flash_Projects > c07_tut > Resources > sea view.avi**. Next, choose the **Open** button; the *sea view.avi* video file is displayed in the **Queue** area.

4. Repeat the same procedure as used in Step 2 and add *road drive.AVI* and *water fall.AVI* video files in the **Queue** area, refer to Figure 7-67.

*Figure 7-67 The video files in the **Queue** area*

5. In the **Queue** area, select the **road drive.AVI** video file and then choose **Edit > Export settings** from the menubar; the **Export Settings** dialog box is displayed. Alternatively, select the video file in the **Queue** area and press CTRL+E.

6. In the **Export Settings** area of the **Export Settings** dialog box, select **FLV** from the **Format** drop-down list and clear the **Export Audio** check box.

7. Choose the **Video** tab.

8. In the **Basic Video Settings** area of this tab, select the **Resize Video** check box to activate the width and height settings of the video, refer to Figure 7-68.

9. Set the value of **Frame Width** to **160** and **Frame Height** set to **120**.

*Figure 7-68  The **Resize Video** check box in the **Basic Video Settings** area*

10. Select **24** from the **Frame Rate [fps]** drop-down list.

**Note**
*It is recommended that the FLV file should have the same frame rate as that of the Flash docu-ment. This is because the embedded FLV is played in the Flash document itself.*

11. Click on the **Current Time Display** edit box; it is activated, as shown in Figure 7-69.
    In this edit box, enter **00;00;04;00** and choose the **Set In Point** button; the In point
    is placed at the time entered in the **Current Time Display**, as shown in Figure 7-70.

*Figure 7-69  The **Current Time Display** edit box activated*

*Figure 7-70  Setting the In point of the footage*

12. Click on the **Current Time Display** edit box; it is activated. In this edit box, enter
    **00;00;13;00** and choose the **Set Out Point** button; the Out point is placed at the
    current time entered in the **Current Time Display**, as shown in Figure 7-71.

    The highlighted footage between the In and Out point markers is the portion of the video
    clip that will be encoded.

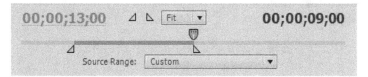

*Figure 7-71  Setting the Out point of the footage*

13. Choose the **OK** button to close the dialog box.

14. Repeat the procedure used in Steps 5 through 12 for other two videos in the **Queue** area.

15. Choose the **Start Queue (Return)** button located at the top right corner of the **Queue** area; Media Encoder begins the encoding process. Also, the progress and preview of the videos are displayed one by one in the **Encoding** area, refer to Figures 7-72, 7-73, and 7-74.

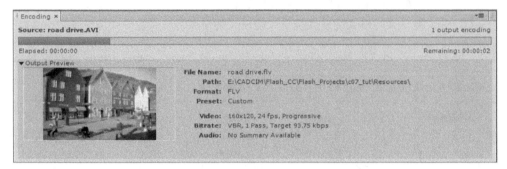

*Figure 7-72  Encoding road drive.AVI footage*

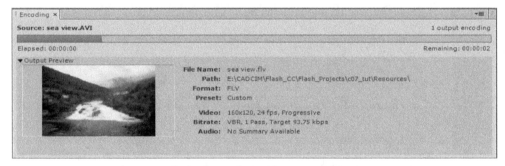

*Figure 7-73  Encoding sea view.AVI footage*

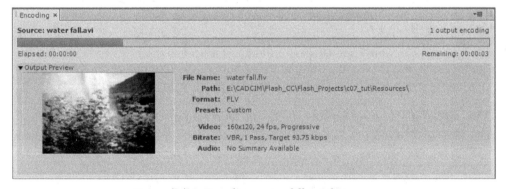

*Figure 7-74  Encoding water fall.avi footage*

These FLV files are saved at the same location as their original files.

16. Choose the **Close** button to close the Media Encoder.

## Importing the Encoded Files in Flash

In this section, you will import the FLV video files in Flash.

1.  Choose **File > Import > Import Video** from the menubar; the **Import Video** dialog box is displayed.

2.  In the **Select Video** area of this dialog box, select the **Embed FLV in SWF and play in timeline** radio button.

**Note**

*For embedding videos in Flash document, the videos must be in the FLV format. Embedding is best suited for short video clips.*

3.  In the **Select Video** area of the **Import Video** dialog box, choose the **Browse** button; the **Open** dialog box is displayed.

4.  In this dialog box, choose **Documents > Flash_Projects > c07_tut > Resources > road drive.flv**; the path is displayed below the **Browse** button, as shown in Figure 7-75.

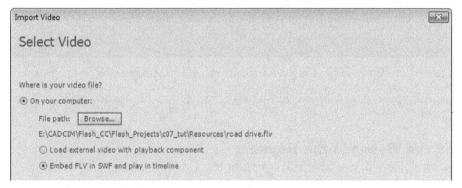

*Figure 7-75  The path displayed below the **Browse** button*

5.  Choose the **Next** button; the **Embedding** area is displayed in this dialog box, as shown in Figure 7-76.

*Figure 7-76  The **Embedding** area of the **Import Video** dialog box*

6.  Clear the **Place instance on stage** check box and then choose the **Next** button; the **Finish Video Import** area is displayed. This area displays the summary of settings of the imported video. Next, choose the **Finish** button; the video is displayed in the **Library** panel, as shown in Figure 7-77. In the **Library** panel, video files are displayed with a unique icon, located on the left of their names, refer to Figure 7-77.

*Figure 7-77  The road drive.flv file in the **Library** panel*

7.  Repeat the procedure followed in Steps 1 through 4 to import the *sea view.fla* and *water fall.fla* video files.

## Placing the Videos in the Timeline
In this section, you will place the video files on the Timeline and animate them.

1.  In the **Timeline** panel, choose the **New Layer** button; a new layer is created. Rename this layer to **Videos**.

2.  Drag the **road drive.flv** file from the **Library** panel to the Stage; the **Adding frames for media** message box is displayed, as shown in Figure 7-78 with the message that the *road drive.flv* file requires 216 frames to display its length but the Timeline consists of only one frame, which is not enough to display the entire length. Flash prompts you whether you want to increase the number of frames to display the length of the video or not.

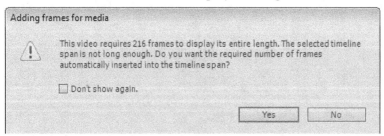

*Figure 7-78  The **Adding frames for media** message box*

3. In this message box, choose the **No** button; the video is displayed in the Stage and is placed on frame **1** in the Timeline.

4. Repeat Steps 2 and 3. Drag *sea view.flv* and *water fall.flv* video files from the **Library** panel to the Stage, refer to Figure 7-79.

*Figure 7-79  All the videos displayed in the Stage*

5. In the **Timeline** panel, select the **Videos** layer and right-click on a video in the Stage; a flyout is displayed. In this flyout, choose **Distribute to Layers**; the **Adding frames for media** message box is displayed.

   The **Distribute to Layers** is used to distribute the objects (symbols, images, video files, shapes) on a layer to different layers. The number of layers created for distribution depends on the number of objects on a layer. The naming of the distributed layer depends on the name of the objects.

6. In this message box, choose the **No** button to close it; the **Adding frames for media** message box is displayed again for the second video.

   **Note**
   *The **Adding frames for media** message box is displayed again because you are distributing three video files. In this case, the message box will be displayed thrice.*

7. Choose the **No** button in both the message boxes; the video files are distributed in layers with each layer consisting of a single video file. Also, the **Videos** layer becomes empty, as shown in Figure 7-80.

8. Click in the Pasteboard to deselect the videos.

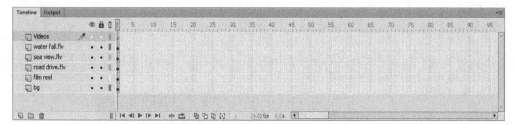

*Figure 7-80  The empty **Videos** layer*

9.  Select the **road drive.flv** video file in the Stage; the **Embedded Video** properties are displayed in the **Properties** panel. In the **Position and Size** area of the **Properties** panel, set the value of **H** to **112**.

10. Select the **sea view.flv** video file in the Stage; the **Embedded Video** properties are displayed in the **Properties** panel. In the **Position and Size** area of this panel, set the value of **H** to **104**.

11. Select the **road drive.flv** layer and then holding the SHIFT key, select the **water fall.flv** layer; the videos are selected in the Stage.

12. Choose the **Align** button located on the left of the **Properties** panel; the **Align** panel is displayed. Next, clear the **Align to stage** check box, if it is not cleared.

13. In the **Align** area of this panel, choose the **Align vertical center** button. Next, choose the **Space evenly horizontally** button from the **Space** area; the videos are aligned to each other, refer to Figures 7-81.

*Figure 7-81  The videos aligned to each other*

14. Press the F8 key; the **Convert to Symbol** dialog box is displayed. In this dialog box, type **videos_3** in the **Name** text box and select **Movie Clip** from the **Type** drop-down list. Select the bottom left square in the registration grid. Next, choose the **OK** button; the **Adding frames for media** message box is displayed. In this message box, choose the **Yes** button; all videos are converted into a symbol with the name **videos_3** and placed on the **water fall.flv** layer.

15. Select the *videos_3* instance in the stage; the properties of this instance are displayed in the **Properties** panel. Next, in the **Position and Size** area of the **Properties** panel, set the value of **X** to **26** and **Y** to **257**; the *videos_3* instance is positioned.

16. Choose **3D Rotation Tool** from the **Tools** panel; the rotation gizmo is displayed in the Stage.

17. Place the cursor on the Y axis of the gizmo and drag the cursor upward, as shown in Figure 7-82.

*Figure 7-82  Rotating the instance on the Y axis*

18. In the **Timeline** panel, select **waterfall.flv** layer and place it below the **film reel** layer; the *videos_3* instance is placed behind the reel instance, as shown in Figure 7-83.

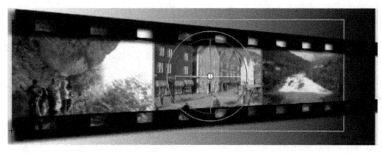

*Figure 7-83  The videos_3 instance placed behind the reel instance*

19. Save the flash file with the name *c07tut4* at the location *\Documents\Flash_Projects\c07_tut\ c07_tut_04*.

20. Press CTRL+ENTER to view the final output of the tutorial. You can also view the final rendered file of the tutorial by downloading the file *c07_flash_cc_rndr.zip* from *www.cadcim.com*. The path of the zip file is mentioned at the beginning of the TUTORIALS section.

## Self-Evaluation Test

**Answer the following questions and then compare them to those given at the end of this chapter:**

1.  Which of the following shortcuts is used to display the **Publish Settings** dialog box?

(a) CTRL+ALT+F12                                    (b) CTRL+SHIFT+F12
(c) ALT+SHIFT+F2                                      (d) CTRL+SHIFT+F10

2.  The _____ is the Flash video format that uses On2VP6 codec.

3.  The _____ and _____ are two types of sounds in Flash.

4.  The _____ button is used to display the **Edit Envelope** dialog box.

5.  The _____ sound creates an illusion of surround-sound.

6.  The **Stream** sound is played as soon as it is loaded for the first few frames, without waiting for the complete sound to download. (T/F)

## Review Questions

**Answer the following questions:**

1.  Which of the following sound gets completely downloaded before it is played?

    (a) **Stream**                    (b) **Event**
    (c) **Start**                     (d) All of the above

2.  _____ is the latest Flash video format that uses H.264 codec.

3.  In the **Edit Envelope** dialog box, the _____ button is used to change the Timeline view from seconds to frames.

4.  The _____ represents the volume of the sound and also displays approximate direction of the volume of the sound.

5.  The **Set In Point** button is used to set the In point of the video file in the **Export Settings** dialog box. (T/F)

# EXERCISES

## Exercise 1

Import any mp3 sound file in Flash and place it in the Timeline.    **(Expected time: 15 min)**

## Exercise 2

Encode any video file with MPG format into F4V using Adobe Media Encoder. Then, import and embed the encoded video in your Flash document.    **(Expected time: 30 min)**

**Answers to Self-Evaluation Test**
**1.** b, **2.** FLV, **3. Stream** and **Event, 4. Edit sound envelope, 5.** Stereo, **6.** T

# Chapter *8*

# Working with External Content

## Learning Objectives

*After completing this chapter, you will be able to:*
- *Load the external SWF file*
- *Unload the external SWF file*
- *Position the loaded content*

# INTRODUCTION

One of the most important features of ActionScript is to load the external Flash content into a single SWF file during runtime and to establish interactivity with the loaded content. There are several benefits of loading the external content during runtime. If you place various SWF files in a project, it makes the project heavier and takes more time to publish on web. Whereas, by using ActionScript, you can keep SWF files separately and load them during runtime. As a result, the file size of the project will be smaller and it will load faster on web. Also, it helps in managing the memory more efficiently. Using ActionScript, you can also load only the file with which you need to interact instead of loading the entire project. You can play multiple SWF files in succession without making the browser load another HTML page.

Using ActionScript, you can also create complex user interface by combining multiple SWF files. You can edit an individual SWF file without affecting the other files of the interface. As a result, multiple artists can work on separate FLA files in the same project. Therefore, you have better flexibility of organizing your project assets.

In Flash, you can import the external content using the Loader class. The Loader class is used to load external content in Flash such as SWF, JPG, PNG, GIF, and so on. It uses the **Load()** method to initiate loading of external content during runtime. The loaded object is added as a child of the Loader object. Some of the commonly used methods of loading external files are listed next.

1.  **Loader()**
    Creates a Loader object that is used to load files, such as SWF, JPEG, GIF, or PNG.

2.  **load(request:URLRequest, context:LoaderContext = null):void**
    Loads an SWF, JPEG, progressive JPEG, unanimated GIF, or PNG file into an object that is a child of the Loader object.

3.  **removeChild()**
    Removes a child of the Loader object that was loaded by using the **Load()** method.

# TUTORIALS

Before you start the tutorials, you need to download the *c08_flash_cc_tut.zip* file from *www.cadcim.com*. The path of the file is as follows: *Textbooks > Animation and Visual Effects > Flash > The Adobe Flash Professional CC: A Tutorial Approach*

Next, extract the contents of the zipped file to *\Documents\Flash_Projects*.

## Tutorial 1

In this tutorial, you will load the external SWF during runtime.

**(Expected time: 30 min)**

The following steps are required to complete this tutorial:

a. Open the Flash document.
b. Load the external SWF file.
c. Preview the content.
d. Position the SWF file.

### Opening the Flash Document

In this section, you will open the Flash document.

1. Choose **File > Open** from the menubar; the **Open** dialog box is displayed.

2. In this dialog box, choose **Documents > Flash_Projects > c08_tut > c08_tut_01 > c08_tut_01_start.fla**. Next, choose the **Open** button; the Flash document is displayed, as shown in Figure 8-1.

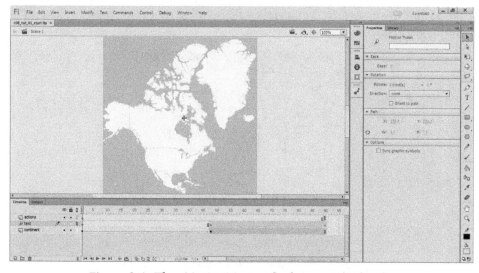

*Figure 8-1* *The c08_tut_01_start.fla document displayed*

This document consists of three layers in the **Timeline** panel namely, **continent**, **text**, and **actions**. The **text** layer consists of the **text** movie clip instance that is visible only on frame **90**, as shown in Figure 8-2.

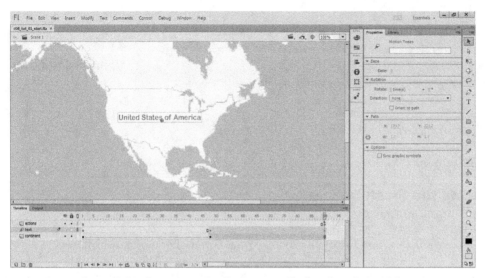

*Figure 8-2* The **text** *movie clip instance displayed on frame* **90**

3.  Select the *text* movie clip instance in the Stage; the properties of the movie clip are displayed in the **Properties** panel. In the **Instance name** text box of this panel, type **text_mc**, as shown in Figure 8-3.

*Figure 8-3* *Assigning a name to the text movie clip instance*

## Loading the External SWF File

In this section, you will create the ActionScript code to load the external SWF file.

1.  In the **actions** layer, select frame **90**.

2.  Choose **Window > Actions** from the menubar; the **Actions** panel is displayed with the **stop()** function already written in it, as shown in Figure 8-4. Alternatively, press the F9 key to display the **Actions** panel.

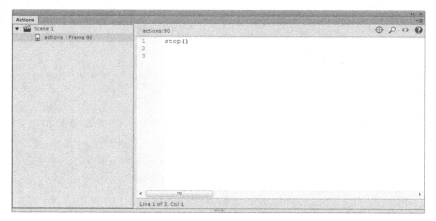

*Figure 8-4  The **Stop()** function displayed in the **Actions** panel*

3.   In this panel, type the following script:

```
var oneLoader:Loader=new Loader();
text_mc.addEventListener(MouseEvent.CLICK, page1Load);
function page1Load(myevent:MouseEvent):void {
var oneURL:URLRequest= new URLRequest("c08_tut_01_page1.swf");
oneLoader.load(oneURL);
addChild(oneLoader);
}
```

**Explanation**

**var oneLoader:Loader=new Loader();**
This ActionScript code creates a new Loader object with the name oneLoader.

**text_mc.addEventListener(MouseEvent.CLICK, page1Load);**
In the above line, a listener is created that will observe a mouse click on **text_mc**. The **text_mc** is the name of the **text** movie clip instance in the Stage. On clicking this instance, the **page1Load** content is executed.

**function page1Load(myevent:MouseEvent):void {**
**var oneURL:URLRequest= new URLRequest("c08_tut_01_page1.swf");**
**oneLoader.load(oneURL);**
**addChild(oneLoader);**
These lines consist of a function named **page1Load**. In this function, a URLRequest object is created with the SWF file name that is to be loaded. Next, it loads the URLRequest object into a Loader object and then adds the Loader object to the Stage.

**Note**
*When you add an event listener to the movie clips, you can make them respond to the mouse clicks. You can also change the shape of the mouse to the hand icon. To do so, set the property button mode to true for the movie clip using the ActionScript code.*

4.  Close the **Actions** panel.

## Previewing the Content

In this section, you will preview the external loaded content in the preview window to test the content.

1.  Press CTRL+ENTER; the preview window is displayed, as shown in Figure 8-5.

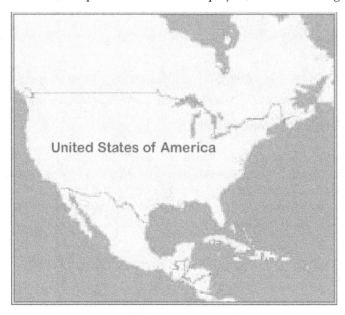

*Figure 8-5*  *The preview window*

2.  In the preview window, click on the **text** movie clip instance in the Stage; the *c08_tut_01_page1.swf* file is displayed, as shown in Figure 8-6.

3.  Close the preview window to return to the Flash document.

**Note**
*The external file to be loaded should always be at the same location at which the SWF file on which it has to be loaded is placed.*

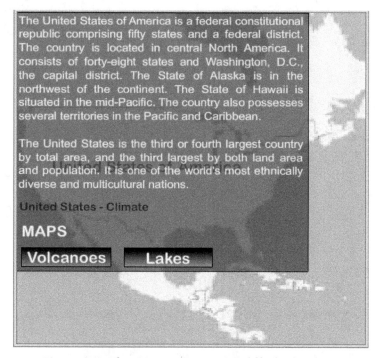

***Figure 8-6*** *The c08_tut_01_page1.swf file displayed*

## Positioning the SWF File

In this section, you will create the ActionScript code to assign a position to the external SWF file in the main SWF file.

1. In the **actions** layer, select frame **90** and then press the F9 key; the **Actions** panel is displayed.

2. Type the script listed below after "**var oneLoader:Loader=new Loader();**" line of code, refer to Figure 8-7.

```
oneLoader.x=10;
oneLoader.y=10;
```

3. Close the **Actions** panel. Next, save the flash file with the name *c08tut1* at the location *\Documents\Flash_Projects\c08_tut\c08_tut_01*. Press CTRL+ENTER; the preview window is displayed. In this window, click on **United States of America** (*text* movie clip instance); the *c08_tut_01_page1.swf* file is positioned 10 pixels right to the x axis and 10 pixels down to the y axis, as shown in Figure 8-8.

   You can also view the final rendered file of the tutorial by downloading the file *c08_flash_cc_rndr.zip* from *www.cadcim.com*. The path of the zipped file is mentioned at the beginning of the TUTORIALS section.

```
Actions
▼ Scene 1                    actions:90                                    ⊕ ₽ <>  ❼
  ⬚ actions : Frame 90    1    stop()
                          2    var oneLoader:Loader=new Loader();
                          3    oneLoader.x=10;
                          4    oneLoader.y=10;
                          5        text_mc.addEventListener(MouseEvent.CLICK, page1Load);
                          6        function page1Load(myevent:MouseEvent):void {
                          7        var oneURL:URLRequest= new URLRequest("c08_tut_01_page1.sw
                          8        oneLoader.load(oneURL);
                          9        addChild(oneLoader);
                          10       }
                          11
                          12
                                ◄               III                    ►
                               Line 4 of 12, Col 16
```

*Figure 8-7*  *The ActionScript code for positioning the loaded SWF file*

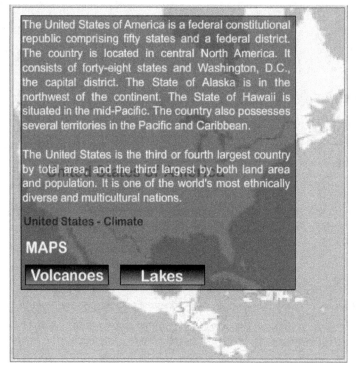

*Figure 8-8*  *The c08_tut_01_page1.swf file displayed after positioning*

## Tutorial 2

In this tutorial, you will load and unload the multiple SWF files into a single SWF file to create an online magazine, as shown in Figure 8-9. **(Expected time: 30 min)**

*Figure 8-9* *The online magazine*

The following steps are required to complete this tutorial:

a. Open the Flash document.
b. Load the external SWF files.
c. Unload the loaded content.
d. Position the loaded content.

## Opening the Flash Document

In this section, you will open the Flash document.

1.  Choose **File > Open** from the menubar; the **Open** dialog box is displayed.

2.  In this dialog box, choose **Documents > Flash_Projects > c08_tut > c08_tut_02 > c08_tut_02_start.fla**. Next, choose the **Open** button from the dialog box; the Flash document is displayed, as shown in Figure 8-10.

    This document consists of six instances in the Stage in the outline mode.

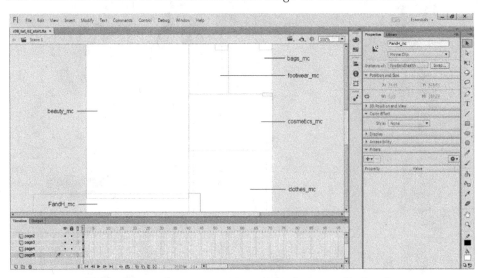

**Figure 8-10**  *The c08_tut_02_start.fla document displayed*

**Note**
*The outline mode is used to display all objects on a layer as colored outlines. To display all objects on a layer as outlines, choose the **Show All Layers as Outlines** button on the right of the layer's name. To turn off the outline display, choose the button again. To view all objects on all layers as outlines, choose the **Show All Layers as Outlines** button in the Timeline Header, as shown in Figure 8-11.*

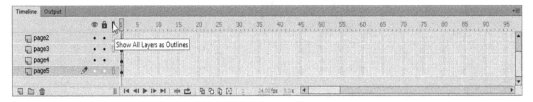

**Figure 8-11**  *Choosing the **Show All Layers as Outlines** button in the Timeline Header*

## Loading the External SWF Files

In this section, you will load six external SWF files using a single SWF file.

1. In the **Timeline** panel, select the **mag name** layer and then choose the **New Layer** button; a new layer is created above the **mag name** layer. Rename the new layer as **AS3**.

2. Select frame **1** in **AS3** layer and press the F9 key; the **Actions** panel is displayed. In this panel, type the following script:

```
1   var magLoader:Loader=new Loader ();
2   beauty_mc.addEventListener(MouseEvent.CLICK, pagecontent1);
3   function pagecontent1(myevent:MouseEvent):void{
4      var myURL:URLRequest=new URLRequest("beauty_content.swf")
5      magLoader.load(myURL);
6      addChild(magLoader);
7   }
8   FandH_mc.addEventListener(MouseEvent.CLICK, pagecontent2);
9   function pagecontent2(myevent:MouseEvent):void{
10     var myURL:URLRequest=new URLRequest("foodandhealth_content.swf")
11     magLoader.load(myURL);
12     addChild(magLoader);
13  }
14  clothes_mc.addEventListener(MouseEvent.CLICK, pagecontent3);
15  function pagecontent3(myevent:MouseEvent):void{
16     var myURL:URLRequest=new URLRequest("clothes_content.swf")
17     magLoader.load(myURL);
18     addChild(magLoader);
19  }
20  cosmetics_mc.addEventListener(MouseEvent.CLICK, pagecontent4);
21  function pagecontent4(myevent:MouseEvent):void{
22     var myURL:URLRequest=new URLRequest("cosmetics_content.swf")
23     magLoader.load(myURL);
24     addChild(magLoader);
25  }
26  bags_mc.addEventListener(MouseEvent.CLICK, pagecontent5);
27  function pagecontent5(myevent:MouseEvent):void{
28     var myURL:URLRequest=new URLRequest("bags_content.swf")
29     magLoader.load(myURL);
30     addChild(magLoader);
31  }
32  footwear_mc.addEventListener(MouseEvent.CLICK, pagecontent6);
33  function pagecontent6(myevent:MouseEvent):void{
34     var myURL:URLRequest=new URLRequest("footwear_content.swf")
35     magLoader.load(myURL);
36     addChild(magLoader);
37  }
```

**Explanation**

Line 1
**var magLoader:Loader=new Loader ();**
This ActionScript code creates a new Loader object with the name magLoader.

Line 2
**beauty_mc.addEventListener(MouseEvent.CLICK, pagecontent1);**
On typing the above code, an event listener is created. It will observe a mouse click event on the object named **beauty_mc**. Here, **beauty_mc** is the name of the **beauty** movie clip instance in the Stage. On clicking this instance, the **pagecontent1** function is executed.

Lines 3 to 6
**function pagecontent1(myevent:MouseEvent):void{**
**var myURL:URLRequest=new URLRequest("beauty_content.swf")**
**magLoader.load(myURL);**
**addChild(magLoader);**
These lines consist of a function named **pagecontent1**. In this function, a URLRequest object is created with the SWF file name to be loaded. Next, it loads the URLRequest object into the Loader object and then adds the Loader object to the Stage.

Lines 8 to 37
**FandH_mc.addEventListener(MouseEvent.CLICK, pagecontent2);**
**function pagecontent2(myevent:MouseEvent):void{**
**var myURL:URLRequest=new URLRequest("foodandhealth_content.swf")**
**magLoader.load(myURL);**
**addChild(magLoader);**
-------------------------------------------------------------------------------------
**footwear_mc.addEventListener(MouseEvent.CLICK, pagecontent6);**
**function pagecontent6(myevent:MouseEvent):void{**
**var myURL:URLRequest=new URLRequest("footwear_content.swf")**
**magLoader.load(myURL);**
**addChild(magLoader);**
**}**

**Explanation**
By typing the above set of codes, five different event listeners are created for each of the other five instances in the Stage.

3.   Close the **Actions** panel.

4.   Press CTRL+ENTER; the preview window is displayed. In this window, click on the **beauty_mc** instance; the **beauty_content** SWF file is displayed, as shown in Figure 8-12. Note that the **beauty_content** SWF file is not aligned in the center and there is no option available to return to the main (initial SWF file).

**Note**
*The loaded content is aligned with the registration point of the loader object. By default, the loader object is positioned at the top left corner of the Stage, which is the origin of Stage.*

5.  Close the preview window to return to the Flash document.

    Next, you will unload the loaded content.

*Figure 8-12  The **beauty_content** SWF file displayed in the preview window*

## Unloading the Loaded Content
In this section, you will create the ActionScript code to unload the loaded content and go back to the main SWF to play the animation of the initial SWF file.

1.  Select frame **1** in the **AS3** layer and press the F9 key; the **Actions** panel is displayed.

2.  In this panel, type the following script:

```
38 magLoader.addEventListener(MouseEvent.CLICK, removecontent);
39 function removecontent(myevent:MouseEvent):void {
40     removeChild(magLoader);
41 }
```

**Explanation**

In the above set of codes, the command **removeChild()** is used to specify the name of the loader between parentheses to remove it from the Stage.

3.  Press CTRL+ENTER to view the output in the preview window. Note that when you click on the loaded external content, the initial SWF file is displayed.

4.  Close the preview window.

5.  To play the animation in the initial SWF file, type the following script listed below after "**function removecontent(myevent:MouseEvent):void {**" line of code:

```
beauty_mc.gotoAndPlay(1);
FandH_mc.gotoAndPlay(1);
clothes_mc.gotoAndPlay(1);
cosmetics_mc.gotoAndPlay(1);
bags_mc.gotoAndPlay(1);
footwear_mc.gotoAndPlay(1);
```

**Explanation**

In the above set of codes, when the user clicks on the external loaded SWF file, the SWF is removed and the function **removecontent** is executed. When this function is executed, the Playhead of each instance in the Stage moves to the first frame and plays the animation of the initial SWF file.

6.  Close the **Actions** panel.

7.  Press CTRL+ENTER; the preview window is displayed. In this window, click on an instance; the SWF file is displayed. Next, click on the loaded external SWF file; the initial SWF is displayed with the animation.

## Positioning the Loaded Content

In this section, you will create the ActionScript code to position the loaded content.

1.  In the **AS3** layer of the **Timeline** panel, select frame **1** and press the F9 key; the **Actions** panel is displayed.

2.  Type the script listed below after "**var magLoader:Loader=new Loader();**" line of code.

```
magLoader.x=0;
magLoader.y=80;
```

3. Close the **Actions** panel. Next, save the flash file with the name *c08tut2* at the location *\Documents\Flash_Projects\c08_tut\c08_tut_02*.

4. Press CTRL+ENTER; the preview window is displayed. In this window, click on any instance; the respective SWF content is loaded, refer to Figure 8-13. You can also view the final rendered file of the tutorial by downloading the file *c08_flash_cc_rndr.zip* from *www.cadcim.com*. The path of the zipped file is mentioned at the beginning of the TUTORIALS section.

***Figure 8-13*** *The online magazine*

## Self-Evaluation Test

**Answer the following questions and then compare them to those given at the end of this chapter:**

1. Which of the following methods is used to add an event listner to observe mouse clicks?

    (a) var magLoader:Loader=new Loader ();
    (b) addEventListener(MouseEvent.CLICK, function name#)
    (c) var oneURL:URLRequest= new URLRequest
    (d) None of the above

2. The _____ method is used to create a loader object to load files.

3. The _____ method is used to remove the child of a loader object from the Stage.

4. The loader object is positioned at the registration point of the Stage by default. (T/F)

## Review Questions

**Answer the following questions:**

1. Which of the following codes represents the position of the loaded content in the Stage?

    (a) oneLoader.x=100;                  (b) Loader.x(100)
    (c) oneLoader.x(100);                  (d) None of the above

2. The _____ button is used to display objects in all layers as outlines.

3. The _____ method is used to load the external content into an object, which is the child of the loader object.

4. The location of the external content and the main SWF file must be the same. (T/F)

# EXERCISE

## Exercise 1

Using the **ActionScript 3.0** code, create an online gallery, as shown in Figure 8-14. You can view the final output of this file by downloading *c08_flash_cc_exr.zip* file from *www.cadcim.com*. The path of the file is as follows: *Textbooks > Animation and Visual Effects > Flash > The Adobe Flash Professional CC: A Tutorial Approach*                    **(Expected time: 40 min)**

You can download the images to create the gallery from the following link:
*www.rgbstock.com/searchgallery/Ayla87*

*Figure 8-14*  *The online gallery*

# Chapter 9

# Exporting and Publishing Flash Content

## Learning Objectives

**After completing this chapter, you will be able to:**

* *Export Flash content in the GIF, JPEG, and PNG formats*
* *Export Flash content as an image sequence*
* *Export Flash content to the QuickTime and AVI formats*
* *Publish Flash content for web*

# INTRODUCTION

In Flash, you can export artwork as a still image, image sequence, and video. You can also publish your Flash work for web. In this chapter, you will learn how to export and publish Flash document and artwork. Table 9-1 displays a list of formats in which a Flash file can be exported.

*Table 9-1* *Different file formats in which a Flash file can be exported*

| File | Extension |
|------|-----------|
| Animated GIF, GIF sequence, and GIF image | .gif |
| JPEG sequence and image | .jpg |
| PNG sequence and image | .png |
| Bitmap image | .bmp |
| Flash document | .swf |
| QuickTime | .mov |
| WAV audio | .wav |
| Windows AVI | .avi |

**Note**
*PNG is the only bitmap format that supports transparency.*

In this chapter, you will learn to export Flash content in various file formats. You will also learn to publish Flash content for web.

# TUTORIALS

Before you start the tutorials, you need to download the *c09_flash_cc_tut.zip* file from *www.cadcim.com*. The path of the file is as follows: *Textbooks > Animation and Visual Effects > Flash > The Adobe Flash Professional CC: A Tutorial Approach*

Next, extract the contents of the zipped file to *\Documents\Flash_Projects*.

## Tutorial 1

In this tutorial, you will export a flash document in PNG format. You will also export an object to the document in the PNG format.

**(Expected time: 10 min)**

The following steps are required to complete this tutorial:

a.  Open the Flash document.
b.  Export Flash document in the PNG format.
c.  Export an entity in the PNG format.

## Opening the Flash Document

In this section, you will open the Flash document.

1. Choose **File > Open** from the menubar; the **Open** dialog box is displayed.

2. Browse to **Documents > Flash_Projects > c09_tut > c09_tut_01 > c09_tut_01_start.fla**.
   Next, choose the **Open** button from the dialog box; the Flash document is displayed, as
   shown in Figure 9-1.

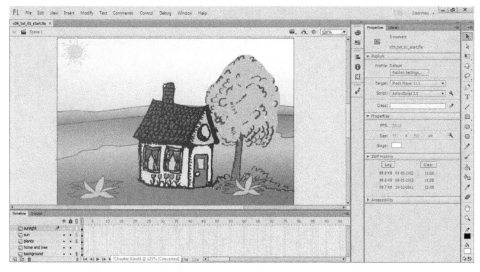

*Figure 9-1*  *The c09_tut_01_start.fla document displayed*

## Exporting the Flash Document in the PNG Format

In this section, you will export the entire Flash document in the PNG format.

1. Choose **File > Export > Export Image** from the menubar; the **Export Image** dialog box
   is displayed.

2. In this dialog box, select **PNG Image (*.png)** from the **Save as type** drop-down list and
   make sure **c09_tut_01_start.png** is written in the **File name** text box, as shown in Figure 9-2.

3. Choose **Documents > Flash_Projects > c09_tut > c09_tut_01** as the location for saving
   the file.

4. Choose the **Save** button; the **Export PNG** dialog box is displayed, as shown in Figure 9-3.
   Next, choose the **Export** button, refer to Figure 9-3; a *.png* file is created and saved.

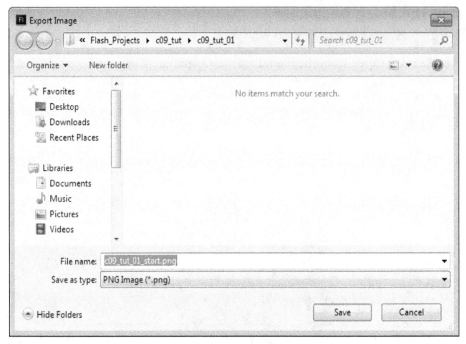

*Figure 9-2  The **Export Image** dialog box*

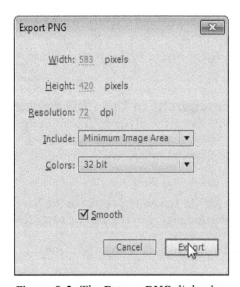

*Figure 9-3  The **Export PNG** dialog box*

## Exporting an Entity to the PNG Format

In this section, you will export an entity to the PNG format.

1.  In the *c09_tut_01_start.fla* document, select the **sun** layer in the **Timeline** panel; the sun is selected in the Stage. Next, right-click on the **sun** layer; a shortcut menu is displayed, as shown in Figure 9-4.

2.  In the shortcut menu, select the **Hide Others** option, refer to Figure 9-4; all other layers except the **sun** layer is hidden.

*Figure 9-4* *The shortcut menu displayed on clicking on the sun layer*

3.  Choose **File > Export > Export Image** from the menubar; the **Export Image** dialog box is displayed.

4.  In this dialog box, choose **Documents > Flash_Projects > c09_tut > c09_tut_01** as the location for saving the file and type **sun** in the **File name** text box.

5.  Select **PNG Image (\*.png)** from the **Save as type** drop-down list and then choose the **Save** button; the **Export PNG** dialog box is displayed. Next, choose the **Export** button; the *sun.png* file is created.

## Tutorial 2

In this tutorial, you will export a movie as an animated GIF and GIF sequence.

**(Expected time: 15 min)**

The following steps are required to complete this tutorial:

a.  Open the Flash document.
b.  Export Flash document as an animated GIF.
c.  Export Flash document as GIF sequence.

### Opening the Flash Document

In this section, you will open the Flash document.

1.  Choose **File > Open** from the menubar; the **Open** dialog box is displayed.

2.  Browse to **Documents > Flash_Projects > c09_tut > c09_tut_02 > c09_tut_02_start.fla**. Next, choose the **Open** button from the dialog box; the Flash document is displayed, as shown in Figure 9-5.

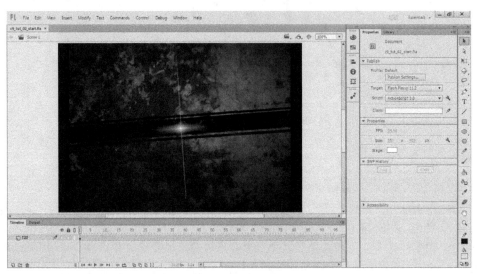

*Figure 9-5  The c09_tut_02_start.fla document displayed*

The Stage of this document displays an instance of *t20.flv* video file.

### Exporting Flash Document as an Animated GIF

In this section, you will export embedded FLV as an animated GIF.

1.  Choose **File > Export > Export Movie** from the menubar; the **Export Movie** dialog box is displayed, refer to Figure 9-6.

2.  In this dialog box, browse to the location **Documents > Flash_Projects > c09_tut > c09_tut_02**, refer to Figure 9-6.

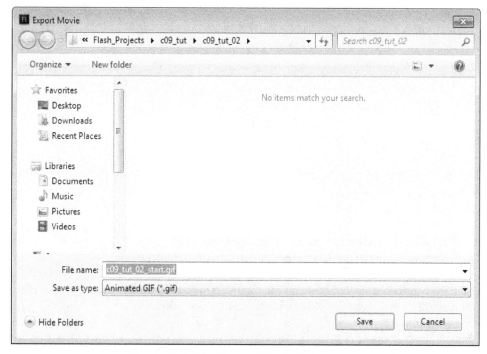

*Figure 9-6* *The **Export Movie** dialog box*

3.  In the **File name** text box, type the file name as **t20_ag** and select **Animated GIF (*.gif)** from the **Save as type** drop-down list. Next, choose the **Save** button; the **Export GIF** dialog box is displayed, refer to Figure 9-7.

4.  In this dialog box, make sure **550** and **400** are entered in the **Width** and **Height** edit boxes, respectively. Choose the **Match Screen** button to use the Stage resolution, as shown in Figure 9-7.

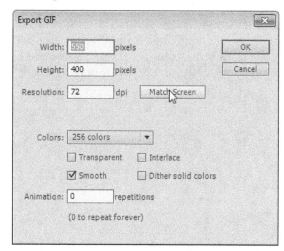

*Figure 9-7* *The **Export GIF** dialog box*

**Note**
*The **Animation** edit box in the **Export GIF** dialog box is available for the animated GIF export format only. You can enter the number of repetitions in this edit box, where 0 stands for endless repetitions.*

5.  Choose the **OK** button; the embedded FLV is exported as an animated GIF and is saved at the chosen location.

    Some of the programs that can open the animated GIF files are Microsoft Windows, Photo Viewer, Adobe Photoshop CS5, Adobe Photoshop Elements 10, Adobe Illustrator CS5, CorelDRAW Graphics Suite X5, Corel PaintShop Pro X4, ACD Systems Canvas 12, ACDSee Photo Manager 14, Laughingbird The Logo Creator, Nuance PaperPort 14, Nuance OmniPage 18, Roxio Creator 2012, and Web browser.

## Exporting Flash Document as GIF Sequence

In this section, you will export the embedded FLV as a GIF sequence.

1.  Open the window explorer, browse to the location **Documents > Flash_Projects > c09_tut > c09_tut_02**. Next, create a folder with the name **GIF_sequence**.

2.  Choose **File > Export > Export Movie** from the menubar; the **Export Movie** dialog box is displayed.

3.  In this dialog box, browse to the location **Documents > Flash_Projects > c09_tut > c09_tut_02 > GIF_sequence**.

4.  In the **File name** text box, type **t20_seq** and select **GIF Sequence (*.gif)** from the **Save as type** drop-down list. Next, choose the **Save** button; the **Export GIF** dialog box is displayed. In this dialog box, choose the **OK** button; the embedded FLV is saved as a GIF sequence, refer to Figure 9-8.

    Exporting images or videos as GIF, animated GIF, and GIF sequence has many advantages. Its small file size is compatible with internet. Another advantage of GIF files is transparency. A color within the color table can be selected as the transparent color. One of the disadvantages of GIF format is that it does not have a color palette of more than 256 colors.

**Note**
*The method explained in this tutorial can also be used to export PNG or JPEG sequences.*

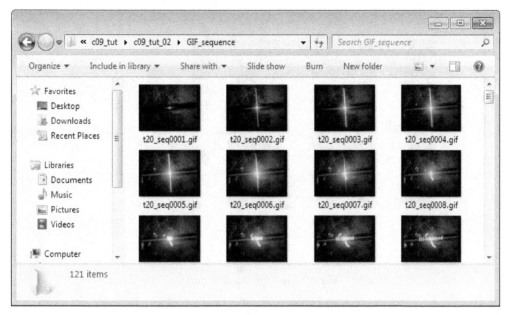

***Figure 9-8*** *The GIF sequence of t20 FLV*

## Tutorial 3

In this tutorial, you will export a copy of an embedded FLV to a standalone FLV file.

**(Expected time: 10 min)**

The following steps are required to complete this tutorial:

a. Open the Flash document.
b. Export an embedded FLV to a standalone FLV file.

### Opening the Flash Document

In this section, you will open the Flash document.

1. Choose **File > Open** from the menubar; the **Open** dialog box is displayed.

2. Browse to **Documents > Flash_Projects > c09_tut > c09_tut_03 > c09_tut_03_start.fla**. Next, choose the **Open** button from the dialog box; the Flash document is displayed, as shown in Figure 9-9.

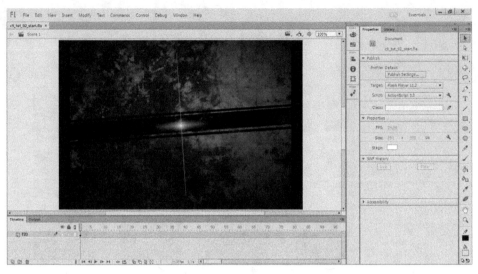

**Figure 9-9** *The c09_tut_03_start.fla document displayed*

The Stage of this document displays an instance of *t20.flv* video file.

## Exporting an Embedded FLV to a Standalone FLV File
In this section, you will export an embedded FLV to a standalone FLV file.

1.  Select **t20.flv** video file in the **Library** panel and right-click on it; a flyout is displayed. In this flyout, choose **Properties**; the **Video Properties** dialog box is displayed, as shown in Figure 9-10.

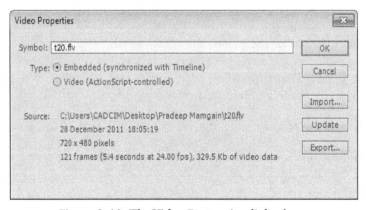

**Figure 9-10** *The **Video Properties** dialog box*

2.  In this dialog box, choose the **Export** button; the **Export FLV** dialog box is displayed, refer to Figure 9-11.

3.  In this dialog box, browse to the location **Documents > Flash_Projects > c09_tut > c09_tut_03.**

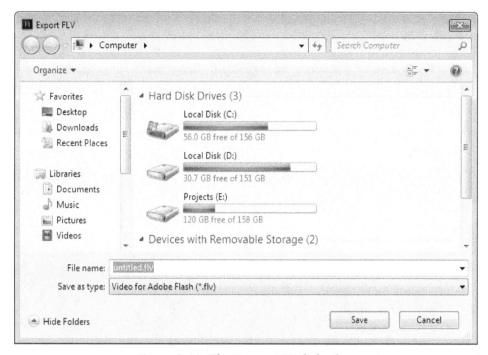

*Figure 9-11  The **Export FLV** dialog box*

4.  In the **File name** text box, type **t20_copy** and choose the **Save** button; a copy of the embedded FLV is created and the dialog box is closed.

5.  Choose the **OK** button in the **Video Properties** dialog box to close it.

## Tutorial 4

In this tutorial, you will export a Flash document as QuickTime movie.

**(Expected time: 10 min)**

The following steps are required to complete this tutorial:

a.  Open the Flash document.
b.  Export the QuickTime movie.

### Opening the Flash Document

In this section, you will open the Flash document.

1.  Choose **File > Open** from the menubar; the **Open** dialog box is displayed.

2.  Browse to **Documents > Flash_Projects > c09_tut > c09_tut_04 > c09_tut_04_start.fla**. Next, choose the **Open** button from the dialog box; the Flash document is displayed.

    The Stage of this document displays an instance of *t20.flv*.

## Exporting the QuickTime Movie

In this section, you will export the Flash document as QuickTime movie.

1.  Choose **File > Export > Export Video** from the menubar; the **Export Video** dialog box is displayed.

2.  In this dialog box, make sure the **Convert video in Adobe Media Encoder** check box is cleared. Next, choose the **Browse** option, refer to Figure 9-12; the **Select Export Destination** dialog box is displayed, as shown in Figure 9-13.

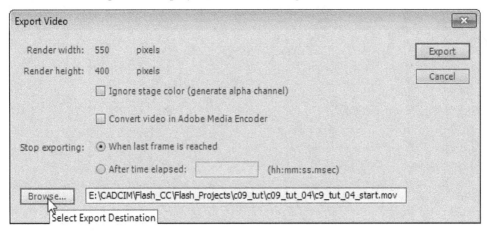

*Figure 9-12* *The **Export Video** dialog box*

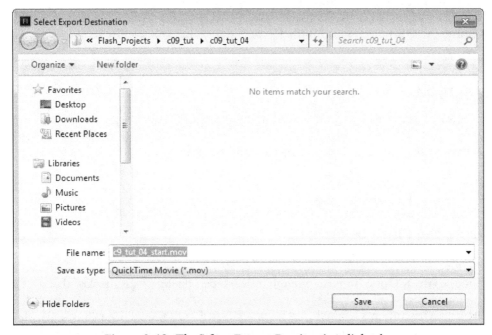

*Figure 9-13* *The **Select Export Destination** dialog box*

3. In this dialog box, browse to the location **Documents > Flash_Projects > c09_tut > c09_tut_04** and type **t20_qt** in the **File name** text box and make sure **QuickTime (*.mov)** from the **Save as type** drop-down list is selected. Next, choose the **Save** button; the **Export Video** dialog box is displayed again.

4. Choose the **Export** button; the embedded FLV is exported as QuickTime and is saved at the chosen location.

## Tutorial 5

In this tutorial, you will export a Flash document/project as HTML using the **Toolkit for CreateJS** extension.                                              **(Expected time: 15 min)**

The following steps are required to complete this tutorial:

a. Open the Flash document.
b. Export the JavaScript content using the **Toolkit for CreateJS** extension.
c. Export the content.

### Opening the Flash Document
In this section, you will open the Flash document.

1. Choose **File > Open** from the menubar; the **Open** dialog box is displayed.

2. Browse to **Documents > Flash_Projects > c09_tut > c09_tut_05 > c09_tut_05_start.fla**. Next, choose the **Open** button from the dialog box; the Flash document is displayed, as shown in Figure 9-14.

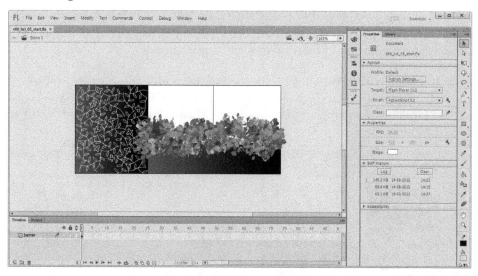

*Figure 9-14  The c09_tut_05_start.fla document displayed*

## Exporting the JavaScript using Toolkit for CreateJS Extension

In this section, you will export the JavaSript using **Toolkit for CreateJS** extension in Flash.

1. Choose **Window > Toolkit for CreateJS** from the menubar; the **Toolkit for CreateJS** panel is displayed, as shown in Figure 9-15.

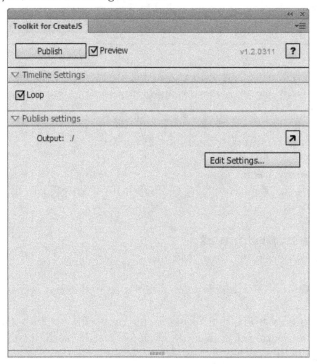

*Figure 9-15  The Toolkit for CreateJS panel*

**Toolkit for CreateJS** is an extension of Adobe Flash that makes it easier to create animation and interactive assets for HTML5 games and applications.

2. In the **Toolkit for CreateJS** panel, choose the **Publish** button; the browser window showing the Flash content is displayed, as shown in Figure 9-16 and a JavaScript file is created. To view the JavaScript file, browse to **Documents > Flash_Projects > c09_tut > c09_tut_05**, refer to Figure 9-17.

*Figure 9-16  The browser window showing the Flash content*

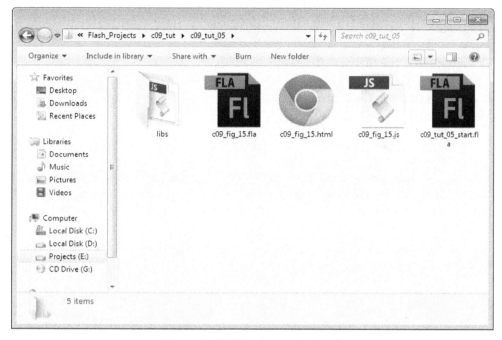

*Figure 9-17* *The .js JavaScript file*

## Tutorial 6

In this tutorial, you will generate sprite sheet of an animated symbol, as shown in Figure 9-18. **(Expected time: 15 min)**

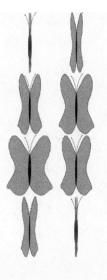

*Figure 9-18* *Sprite sheet of an animated symbol*

The following steps are required to complete this tutorial:

a.   Open the Flash document.
b.   Generate the sprite sheet.

## Opening the Flash Document

In this section, you will open the Flash document.

1.   Choose **File > Open** from the menubar; the **Open** dialog box is displayed.

2.   Browse to **Documents > Flash_Projects > c09_tut > c09_tut_06 > c09_tut_06_start.fla**.
     Next, choose the **Open** button from the dialog box; the Flash document is displayed, as
     shown in Figure 9-19.

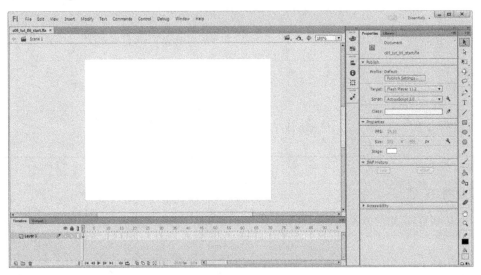

*Figure 9-19*   *The c09_tut_06_start.fla document displayed*

## Generating the Sprite Sheet

In this section, you will generate the sprite sheet of an animated symbol.

A sprite sheet is a portrayal of various sprites arranged in one image, detailing the exact
frames of animation for each character or object.

1.   In the **Library** panel, select the **butterfly** symbol and right-click on it; a flyout is displayed.
     In this flyout, choose **Generate Sprite Sheet**; the **Generate Sprite Sheet** dialog box is
     displayed, as shown in Figure 9-20.

2.   In the **Generate Sprite Sheet** dialog box, make sure that **Auto size** is selected in the **Image
     dimensions** drop-down list.

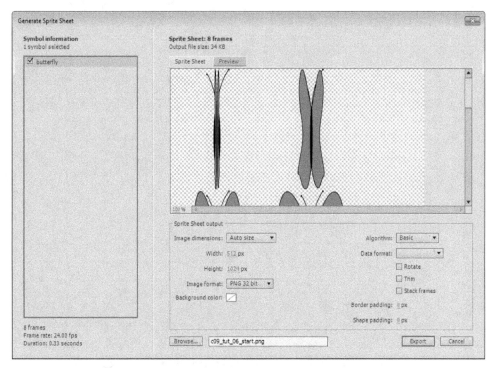

*Figure 9-20  The **Generate Sprite Sheet** dialog box*

3. Select **PNG 32 bit** from the **Image format** drop-down list, if it is not selected. Next, click on the **Background color** swatch; a flyout is displayed. In this flyout, make sure the No Color button is chosen.

4. In the **Sprite Sheet Filename** text box, type **butterfly_sprite sheet**, as shown in Figure 9-21. Next, choose the **Browse** button; the **Select destination folder** is displayed, as shown in Figure 9-22. In this folder, browse to the location **Documents > Flash_Projects > c09_tut > c09_tut_06** and choose the **Save** button; the dialog box is closed.

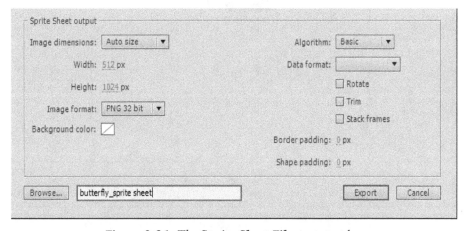

*Figure 9-21  The **Sprite Sheet Filename** text box*

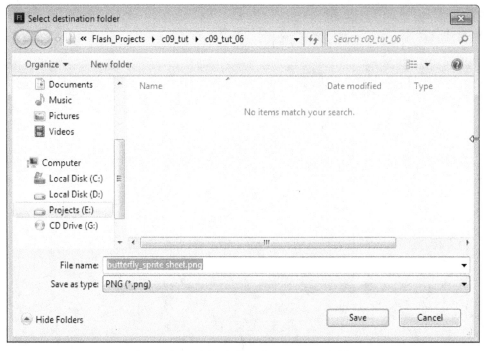

**Figure 9-22**  *The Select destination folder*

5.   Choose the **Export** button to close the **Generate Sprite Sheet** dialog box; the sprite sheet is created in the specified folder, refer to Figure 9-23.

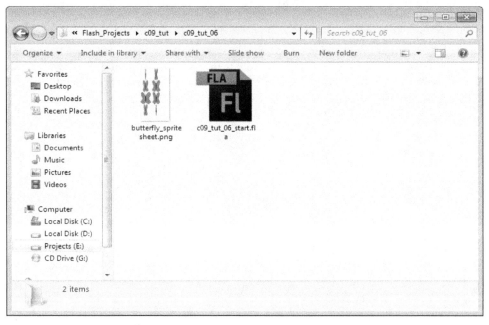

**Figure 9-23**  *The sprite sheet created in the specified folder*

## Tutorial 7

In this tutorial, you will publish a Flash document for web.    (**Expected time: 30 min**)

The following steps are required to complete this tutorial:

a.   Open the Flash document.
b.   Publish Flash document for the web.

### Opening the Flash Document

In this section, you will open the Flash document.

1.   Choose **File > Open** from the menubar; the **Open** dialog box is displayed.

2.   Browse to **Documents > Flash_Projects > c09_tut > c09_tut_07 > c09_tut_07_start.fla**.
     Next, choose the **Open** button from the dialog box; the Flash document is displayed, as
     shown in Figure 9-24.

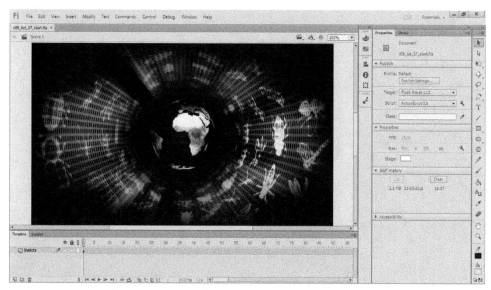

*Figure 9-24*  *The c09_tut_07_start.fla document displayed*

### Publishing for the Web

In this section, you will publish the Flash document for the web.

1.   Choose **File > Publish Settings** from the menubar; the **Publish Settings** dialog box is
     displayed.

2.  In this dialog box, choose the **Profile Options** button; a flyout is displayed. In this  flyout, choose **Create profile**; the **Create New Profile** dialog box is displayed, as shown in Figure 9-25.

*Figure 9-25  The **Create New Profile** dialog box*

3.  In this dialog box, type **Web** in the **Profile name** text box and choose the **OK** button to close the dialog box.

4.  In the **Publish Settings** dialog box, make sure the **Flash (.swf)** check box in the **PUBLISH** area and the **HTML Wrapper** check box in the **OTHER FORMATS** area are selected, refer to Figure 9-26.

**Note**
*When a Flash document is published for the web, Flash creates an SWF file along with an HTML document. The HTML document contains HTML script that is responsible for the layout of the Web page.*

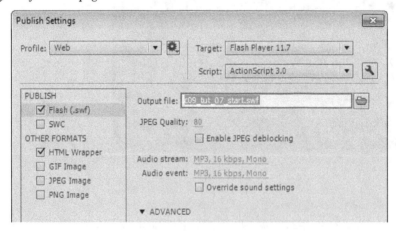

*Figure 9-26  The **Flash (.swf)** and **HTML Wrapper** check boxes*

5.  Select **Flash Player 11.7** as the version of Flash player from the **Target** drop-down list, refer to Figure 9-27. Make sure that **ActionScript 3.0** is selected in the **Script** drop-down list.

6.  Choose the **Set Stream** text button in the **Publish Settings** dialog box, refer to Figure 9-28; the **Sound Settings** dialog box is displayed for the **Audio stream** option, as shown in Figure 9-29.

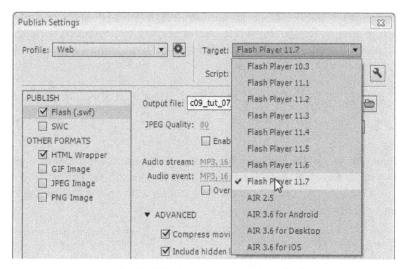

*Figure 9-27  Selecting a version of Flash player*

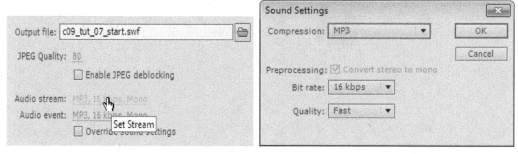

*Figure 9-28  Choosing the **Set Stream** text button*

*Figure 9-29  The **Sound Settings** dialog box*

7.  In this dialog box, select **128 kbps** from the **Bit rate** drop-down list and **Best** from the **Quality** drop-down list. Next, choose the **OK** button to close the dialog box.

8.  Choose the **Set Event** text button in the **Publish Setting** dialog box; the **Sound Settings** dialog box is displayed again for the **Audio event** option. In this dialog box, select **128 kbps** from the **Bit rate** drop-down list and **Best** from the **Quality** drop-down list. Next, choose the **OK** button to close the dialog box.

9.  Select the **HTML Wrapper** option in the **OTHER FORMATS** area of the **Publish Settings** dialog box; the **HTML** document settings are displayed on the right side.

10. Select **Flash Only** from the **Template** drop-down list, if not already selected and then select the **Detect Flash Version** check box.

    The **Detect Flash Version** check box is used to detect if the correct version of Flash Player is installed or not.

11. Choose the **Publish** button; Flash creates an SWF file, an HTML file, and an *swfobject.js* file, refer to Figure 9-30. The *swfobject.js* file contains the JavaScript code that will detect the Flash version specified in the **Publish Settings** dialog box. Choose the **OK** button to close the dialog box.

You need the HTML document of the SWF to play it in a web browser and to specify browser settings.

**Note**
*You can also change the way your Flash content is displayed in a web browser window. The options in the **Size** drop-down list and the **SCALE AND ALIGNMENT** area in the **Publish Settings** dialog box are used to change the display settings of the Flash content for the web browser, refer to Figures 9-31 and 9-32.*

*Figure 9-30  The HTML, SWF, and swfobject.js files*

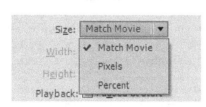

*Figure 9-31  The **Size** drop-down list*

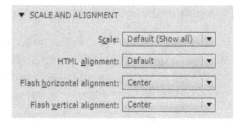

*Figure 9-32  The options in the **SCALE AND ALIGNMENT** area*

## Self-Evaluation Test

Answer the following questions and then compare them to those given at the end of this chapter:

1.  Which of the following formats supports transparency?

    (a) GIF                                    (b) JPEG
    (c) PNG                                    (d) All of the above

2.  The _____ option in the **Export GIF** dialog box is available for the animated GIF export format.

3.  The _____ mode displays the data in each frame.

4.  The _____ is the only bitmap format that supports transparency.

5.  The HTML document is used to insert the Flash content in a browser window. (T/F)

6.  A sprite sheet is a portrayal of various sprites arranged in one image, detailing the exact frames of animation for each character or object. (T/F)

## Review Questions

Answer the following questions:

1.  Which of the following is the file extension for a bitmap image?

    (a) .bmp                                   (b) .png
    (c) .swf                                   (d) .jpg

2.  The _____ check box is used to detect if the correct version of Flash Player is installed or not.

3.  _____ is an extension of Adobe Flash that makes it easier to create animation and interactive assets for HTML5 games and applications.

4.  The HTML document contains an HTML script which is responsible for the layout of the Web page. (T/F)

# EXERCISES

## Exercise 1

Create various graphics such as symbols and shapes on a layer. Also, import a bitmap to the Stage. Next, publish the entire Flash document for the web.          **(Expected time: 20 min)**

## Exercise 2

Convert an AVI into FLV using Adobe Media Encoder. Next, import the FLV to Flash. Then, export it as an animated GIF and as a PNG sequence. **(Expected time: 20 min)**

**Answers to Self-Evaluation Test**
**1.** c, **2. Animation**, **3.** Frame By Frame, **4.** PNG, **5.** T, **6.** T

# Chapter **10**

# **Working with Android Applications**

## *Learning Objectives*

**After completing this chapter, you will be able to:**
* *Create certificate to publish content*
* *Publish Android content for mobile*
* *Create Android application in Flash*
* *Run .apk file in android mobile phone*

# INTRODUCTION

In Flash, you can create various android mobile applications. You can also publish android content for your android mobile. In this chapter, you will learn to create and publish android mobile applications. The file extension for android applications is .apk.

# TUTORIALS

Before you start the tutorials, you need to download the *c10_flash_cc_tut.zip* file from *www.cadcim.com*. The path of the file is as follows: *Textbooks > Animation and Visual Effects > Flash > The Adobe Flash Professional CC: A Tutorial Approach*

Next, extract the contents of the zip file to *\Documents\Flash_Projects*.

## Tutorial 1

In this tutorial, you will learn to publish a flash document to an android application.

**(Expected time: 20 min)**

The following steps are required to complete this tutorial:

a.   Open the Flash document.
b.   Create certificate to publish content.
c.   Publish a flash document to an android application.
d.   Run the android file(.apk) in android mobile phone.

### Opening and Saving the Flash Document

In this section, you will open the Flash document.

1.   Choose **File > Open** from the menubar; the **Open** dialog box is displayed.

2.   Browse to **Documents > Flash_Projects > c10_tut > c10_tut_01 > c10_tut_01_start.fla**. Next, choose the **Open** button from the dialog box; the Flash document is displayed, as shown in Figure 10-1.

3.   Save the flash file with the name *c10tut1* at the location *\Documents\Flash_Projects\c10_tut\ c10_tut_01*

### Publishing the Flash Document to Android File (.apk)

In this section, you will publish the flash document to android file (.apk).

1.   Select **AIR 3.6 for Android** from the **Target** drop-down list in the **Publish** area of the **Properties** panel, refer to Figure 10-2.

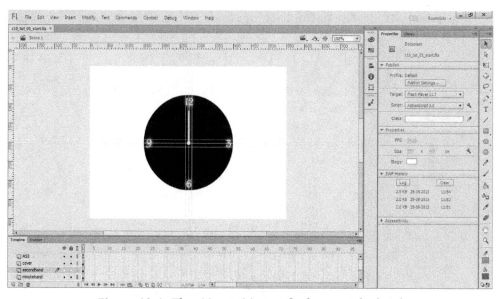

**Figure 10-1** *The c10_tut_01_start.fla document displayed*

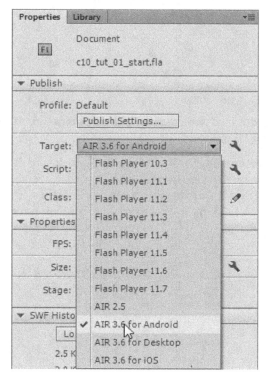

**Figure 10-2** *The **Properties** panel displayed*

2.  Choose **File > AIR 3.6 for Android Settings** from the menubar, as shown in Figure 10-3; the **AIR for Android Settings** dialog box is displayed, as shown in Figure 10-4.

*Figure 10-3* *Choosing* ***AIR 3.6 for Android Settings*** *from the menubar*

3.  Choose the **Deployment** tab from this dialog box. Next, choose the **Create** button located on the right of the **Certificate** drop-down list, as shown in Figure 10-5; the **Create Self-Signed Digital Certificate** dialog box is displayed, refer to Figure 10-6. In this dialog box, enter **12345** in the **Password** and **Confirm password** text boxes and also specify the text in other text boxes, as shown in Figure 10-6.

**Note**
*You can specify any password of your choice in the* ***Password*** *text box.*

*Figure 10-4  AIR for Android Settings dialog box displayed*

*Figure 10-5  Choosing the **Create** button*

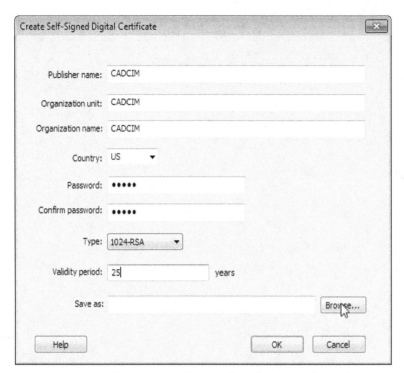

*Figure 10-6  The **Create Self-Signed Digital Certificate** dialog box with desired values specified in the text boxes*

4.   Choose the **Browse** button, refer to Figure 10-6; the **Select File Destination** dialog box is displayed, as shown in Figure 10-7.

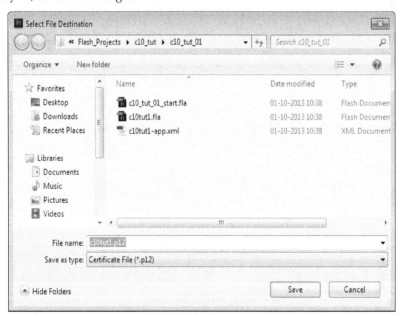

*Figure 10-7  The **Select File Destination** dialog box*

5. In this dialog box, browse to the location **Documents > Flash_Projects > c10_tut > Resources** and type **Certificate** in the **File name** edit box. Next, choose the **Save** button to save the document.

6. Choose the **OK** button from the **Create Self-Signed Digital Certificate** dialog box; the **Adobe Flash Professional** message box is displayed with the message **Self-signed certificate has been created**, as shown in Figure 10-8. Again, choose the **OK** button to close the message box. You will notice that the path of the file **Certificate.p12** is displayed in the **Certificate** drop-down list of the **Air for Android Settings** dialog box, refer to Figure 10-9.

*Figure 10-8 The **Adobe Flash Professional** message box*

*Figure 10-9 The path specified for the **Certificate.p12** file*

7. Type the password **12345** and select the **Embed AIR runtime with application** radio button in the **AIR runtime** area, refer to Figure 10-10.

8. Choose the **Icons** tab. Select **icon 72x72** for the icon size of the content, refer to Figure 10-11. Next, click on the **Browse** icon, as shown in Figure 10-11; the **Open** dialog box is displayed, as shown in Figure 10-12.

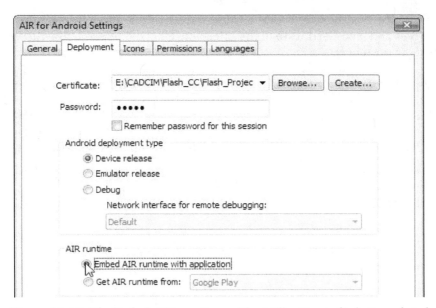

*Figure 10-10  The **Embed AIR runtime with application** radio button selected*

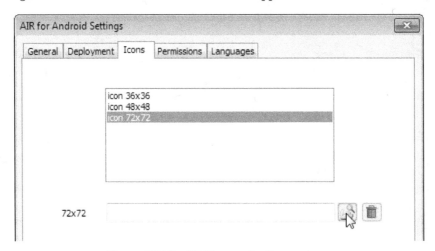

*Figure 10-11  Clicking on the Browse icon*

9.   Browse to **Documents > Flash_Projects > c10_tut > Resources**. Next, select
     **Clock.png** from the **Open** dialog box and then choose the **Open** button; the
     **Adobe Flash Professional** message box is displayed with the message **The icon
     must be copied to a folder relative to the root content folder so that it can be published.
     Do you want to proceed?**, as shown in Figure 10-13. Choose the **OK** button to close the
     dialog box.

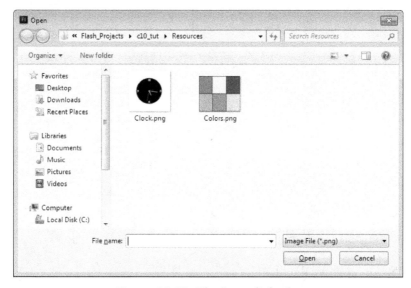

*Figure 10-12  The **Open** dialog box*

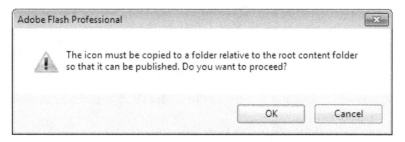

*Figure 10-13  The **Adobe Flash Professional** message box*

10.  Choose the **Publish** button at the bottom of the **Air 3.6 for Android Settings** dialog box; the **Publishing** progress bar is displayed, as shown in Figure 10-14.

*Figure 10-14  The **Publishing** progress bar*

11.  Once the publishing is completed, the **Adobe Flash Professional** message box is displayed with the message **The APK was packaged successfully, but a warning occurred. Warning: Application has not specified its permission requirements in application.xml**, as shown in Figure 10-15. Choose the **OK** button to close the message box.

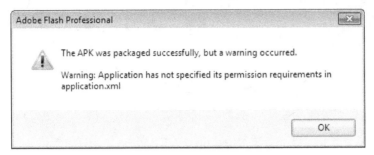

*Figure 10-15* *The Adobe Flash Professional* *message box*

You will notice that the *c10tut1.apk* and *c10tut1.swf* files are published at the location *\Documents\Flash Projects\c10_tut\c10_tut_01*.

12. Choose the **OK** button to close the **AIR for Android Settings** dialog box.

13. Press CTRL + S to save the file.

**Note**
*Android file (.apk) can be run only in the Android based devices. You must have an Android device to run this application.*

## Installing and Running the Android File(.apk) In Android Mobile Phone

In this section, you will install and run the android file(.apk) in an android mobile phone.

1. Connect your android mobile phone with the computer.

2. Browse to **Documents > Flash_Projects > c10_tut > c10_tut_01 > c10tut1.apk**. Next, copy the **c10tut1.apk** file to your android mobile phone.

3. Install **c10tut1.apk** in your android mobile phone and open it.

   Figure 10-16 shows the **c10tut1.apk** file opened in the android mobile phone.

*Figure 10-16* *The c10tut1.apk file opened in the android mobile phone*

## Tutorial 2

In this tutorial, you will create an android application. **(Expected time: 50 min)**

The following steps are required to complete this tutorial:

a. Create a new Flash document.
b. Create a rectangular shape with different colors applied on it.
c. Convert the colors into movie clip symbols.
d. Create the target movie clip symbol.
e. Swap and the move movie clip symbols.
f. Add the ActionScript Linkage property to it.
g. Create class files.
h. Publish a Flash document to an android application.
i. Running the android file (.apk) in android mobile phone.

### Creating a New Flash Document
In this section, you will create a new Flash document.

1. Choose **File > New** from the menubar; the **New Document** dialog box is displayed.

2.  In the **New Document** dialog box, choose **AIR for Android** from the **Type** area in the **General** tab, refer to Figure 10-17.

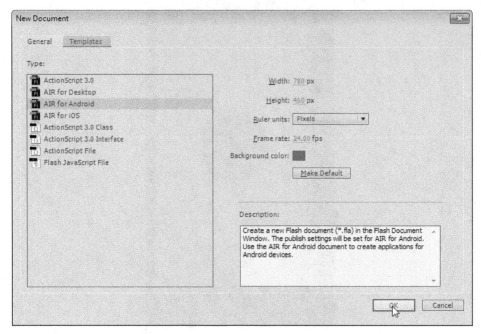

*Figure 10-17 The **New Document** dialog box displayed*

3.  In the **Width** and **Height** edit boxes, enter the values **780** and **460** respectively, refer to Figure 10-17. Next, choose the **Background color** swatch; a flyout is displayed. In this flyout, enter **#666666** in the Hex edit box and press the ENTER key.

4.  Choose the **OK** button; a new Flash document is displayed and the color of the Stage is changed according to the specified value, as shown in Figure 10-18.

 **Note**
*You can choose any color of your choice from the **Background color** swatch to change the color of the Stage.*

5.  Choose the **Center Stage** button on the upper right side of the Scene area to move the Stage to center, as shown in Figure 10-19.

6.  Choose **File > Save As** from the menubar; the **Save As** dialog box is displayed. In this dialog box, type **c10tut2** in the **File name** text box and save it in \*Documents\Flash_projects\ c10_tut\c10_tut_02*.

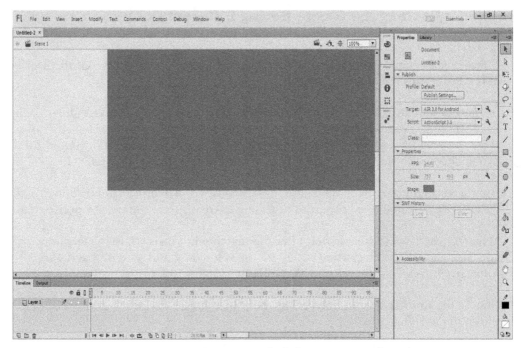

*Figure 10-18  A new Flash document opened*

*Figure 10-19  Stage in the center of the scene area*

## Creating a Rectangular Shape Having Different Colors

In this section, you will create a rectangular shape having different colors.

1. Choose the **Rectangle Tool** from the **Tools** panel; the properties of this tool are displayed in the **Properties** panel.

2. In the **Fill and stroke** area of the **Properties** panel, choose the **Stroke color** swatch; a flyout is displayed. In this flyout, make sure **#000000** is entered in the Hex edit box and press the ENTER key. Next, choose the **Fill color** swatch; a flyout is displayed. In this flyout, choose the No Color button. Next, enter **3** in the **Stroke** edit box.

3. Draw a rectangular frame in the Stage. Next, choose the **Selection Tool** and double-click on the frame created; the properties of rectangle are displayed in the **Properties** panel.

4. Make sure the **Lock width and height values together** button is off. In the **Position and Size** area of the **Properties** panel, set the value of **X** and **Y** to **428** and **106**, respectively. Next, set the value of **W** and **H** to **345** and **192**, respectively.

5. Choose the **Line Tool** from the **Tools** panel. Next, create partitions in the rectangle, as shown in the Figure 10-20.

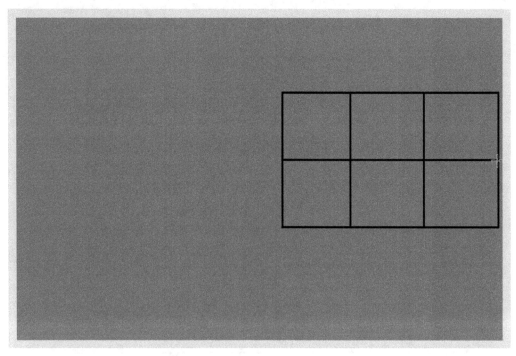

*Figure 10-20 Partitions created*

Next, you will fill the colors in the partitions.

6. Choose the **Paint Bucket Tool** from the **Tools** panel; the properties of this tool are displayed in the **Properties** panel.

7. In the **Fill and stroke** area of the **Properties** panel, choose the **Fill color** swatch; a flyout is displayed. Enter #FF0000 in the Hex edit box and press the ENTER key.

8. Click on the first partition of the rectangle; the red color is filled, as shown in Figure 10-21.

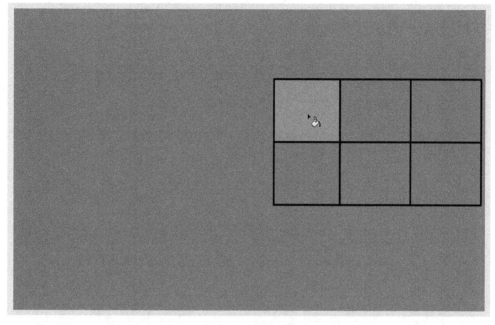

*Figure 10-21* *Red color filled in the first partition*

9. Similarly, fill other partitions with yellow, blue, orange, pink, and green colors, as shown in Figure 10-22.

*Figure 10-22* *Other partitions filled with different colors*

## Converting Colors into movie clip Symbols

In this section, you will convert the colors into Movie Clip symbols.

1. Select the red color in the Stage using the **Selection Tool** from the **Tools** panel. Next, choose **Modify > Convert to Symbol** from the menubar or press the F8 key; the **Convert to Symbol** dialog box is displayed.

2. In the **Convert to Symbol** dialog box, type **red** in the **Name** text box and make sure the **Movie clip** from the **Type** drop-down list is selected. Next, select the top left square of the **Registration** grid for specifying the registration point of the symbol. Choose the **OK** button; a movie clip with the name *red* is created and saved in the **Library** panel.

3. Similarly, convert all other colors into a movie clip symbol and name them **yellow**, **blue**, **orange**, **pink**, and **green**, respectively.

   You will notice that all the colors are converted into movie clip symbols and are listed in the **Library** panel.

   Next, you will convert the frame into a movie clip symbol.

4. Marquee select all the objects in the Stage, refer to Figure 10-23. Next, press the SHIFT key and deselect all the colors by clicking.

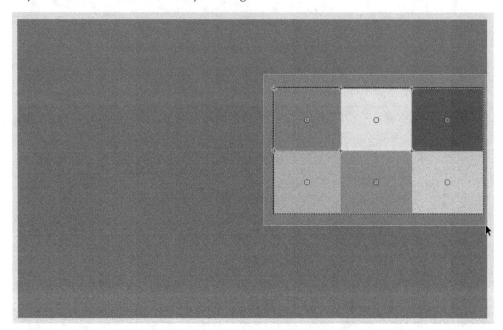

*Figure 10-23 All objects selected*

5. Make sure the frame is selected in the Stage. Next, choose **Modify > Convert to Symbol** from the menubar or press the F8 key; the **Convert to Symbol** dialog box is displayed.

6.  In the **Convert to Symbol** dialog box, type **frame** in the **Name** text box and make sure the **Movie clip** from the **Type** drop-down list is selected. Next, select the top left square of the **Registration** grid for specifying the registration point of the symbol. Choose the **OK** button; a movie clip with the name *frame* is created and saved in the **Library** panel.

## Creating Target Movie Clip Symbols

In this section, you will create the target movie clip symbols.

1.  Select *red* in the **Library** panel, choose the triangle located at the extreme right of the **Library** panel; the **Library** panel menu is displayed, as shown in Figure 10-24. In this menu, choose **Duplicate**; the **Duplicate Symbol** dialog box is displayed with the name of the symbol as *red copy*.

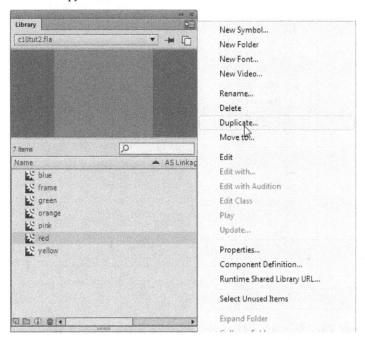

*Figure 10-24  Partial view of the **Library** panel menu*

2.  In the **Duplicate Symbol** dialog box, type **red2** in the **Name** text box and choose the **OK** button; a duplicate of the *red* movie clip symbol is created in the **Library** panel with the symbol name as *red2*.

3.  Similarly, create duplicate of all the other colors and name them **yellow2**, **blue2**, **orange2**, **pink2**, and **green2**, respectively.

    You will notice that duplicate of colors are created as the target movie clip symbols which are listed in the **Library** panel, as shown in Figure 10-25.

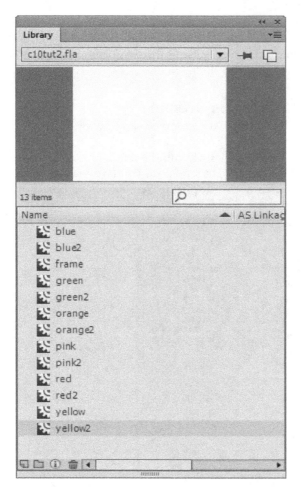

**Figure 10-25** *Target movie clip symbol of colors listed in the Library panel*

## Swapping and Moving the Colors Movie Clip Symbols

In this section, you will swap and move the colors movie clip symbols.

1.  Select the red instance in the Stage. Next, choose the **Swap** button in the **Properties** panel, refer to Figure 10-26; the **Swap Symbol** dialog box is displayed, as shown in Figure 10-27. Next, select **red2** from the list and choose the **OK** button, refer to Figure 10-27.

**Note**
*The **Swap** button is used to swap two symbols.*

2.  Similarly, select all the other color instances in the Stage and swap each one of them with **yellow2**, **blue2**, **orange2**, **pink2**, and **green2** instances, respectively.

*Figure 10-26* Choosing *Swap* button

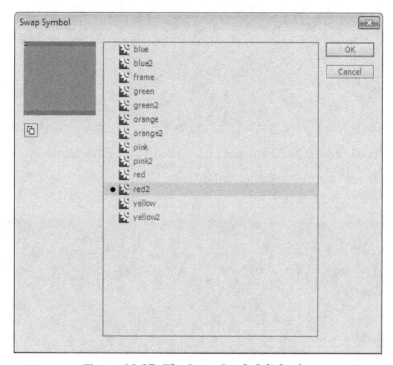

*Figure 10-27* The *Swap Symbol* dialog box

Next, you will move the color movie clip symbols to the left hand side.

3. Select all the color movie clip symbols on the Stage using the SHIFT key. Next, move them to the left hand side using the LEFT-ARROW key, refer to Figure 10-28.

4. In the **Color Effect** area of the **Properties** panel, choose **Alpha** from the **Color Styles** drop-down list. Next, set the value **40%** in the **Alpha amount** edit box.

 **Note**
*When the value in the **Alpha amount** is set to **40%**, you will notice that the opacity of the selected colors in the Stage is decreased, refer to Figure 10-28.*

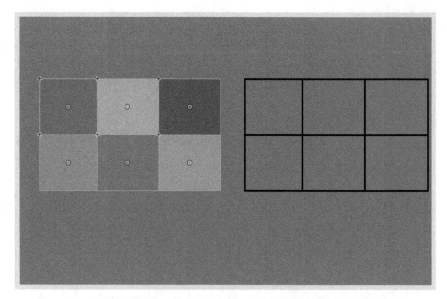

**Figure 10-28**  *Colors movie clip symbols moved to left hand side*

5.  Select the frame movie clip symbol in the Stage. Next, place it on the colors by moving it to the left hand side using the LEFT-ARROW key, refer to Figure 10-29.

**Figure 10-29**  *Frame placed on the colors*

Next, you will give instance name to the target colors.

6.  Select red2 on the Stage.

7.  In the **Properties** panel, type **R1T** in the **Instance name** text box, as shown in Figure 10-30.

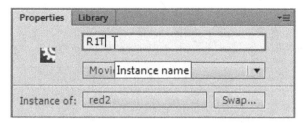

*Figure 10-30 R1T specified in the **Intance name** text box*

8. Similarly, select all the other target colors in the Stage and assign them the names as **Y1T**, **B1T**, **O1T**, **P1T**, and **G1T,** respectively.

## Adding ActionScript Linkage Properties to Colors
In this section, you will add ActionScript Linkage properties to colors.

1. Select the instance **blue** in the **Library** panel. Click on the **Properties** icon at the bottom of the **Library** panel; the **Symbol Properties** dialog box is displayed, refer to Figure 10-31.

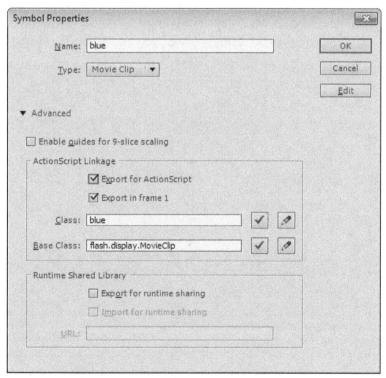

*Figure 10-31 The **Symbol Properties** dialog box*

2. In this dialog box, expand the Advanced node and select the check box on the left of the **Export for ActionScript**; you will notice that the options related to this check box get activated, refer to Figure 10-31. Next, choose the **OK** button; the **ActionScript Class Warning** message box is displayed, as shown in Figure 10-32. Choose the **OK** button to close the message box.

**Note**
*When choosing the **Export for ActionScript** check box, a Class name **blue** is automatically defined in the **Class** text box. You can manually change its name as per your requirement.*

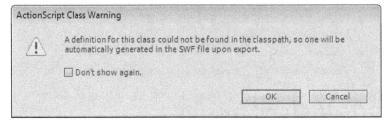

*Figure 10-32   The **ActionScript Class Warning** message box*

3.   Select the instance **yellow**. Next, press the CTRL key and select other instances **red**, **orange**, **pink**, and **green** and then choose the **Properties** icon at the bottom of the **Library** panel; the **Editing Properties for 5 Symbols** dialog box is displayed, refer to Figure 10-33.

4.   In this dialog box, select the **Export for ActionScript** and **Export in frame 1** check boxes, and also select **Yes** in the drop-down lists located on the right side of these check boxes, as shown in Figure 10-33. Next, choose the **OK** button; the ActionScript Linkage Properties are added to all the colors in the **Library** panel, refer to Figure 10-34.

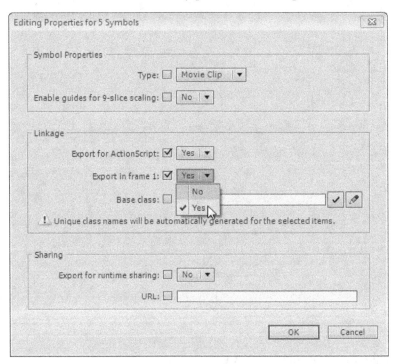

*Figure 10-33   The **Editing Properties for 5 Symbols** dialog box*

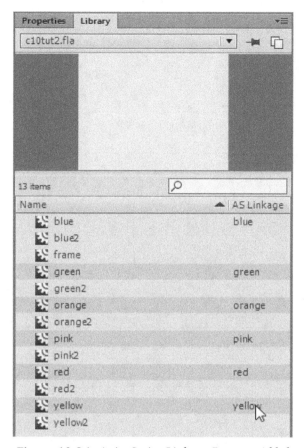

**Figure 10-34** *ActionScript Linkage Property Added to all colors*

## Creating Class File

In this section, you will create a class file which will control the functionality of scattering colors randomly on the stage.

1. Choose **File > New** from the menubar; the **New Document** dialog box is displayed, refer to Figure 10-35.

2. In the **New Document** dialog box, choose **ActionScript 3.0 Class** from the **Type** area in the **General** tab, and also type **Main** in the **Class name** text box, refer to Figure 10-35. Next, choose the **OK** button; the **Target** ActionScript document file is opened with script written in it, as shown in Figure 10-36. Next, delete the script.

3. Choose **File > Save As** from the menubar; the **Save As** dialog box is displayed. In this dialog box, type **Main.as** in the **File name** text box and save it in \*Documents\Flash_projects\ c10_tut\c10_tut_02*.

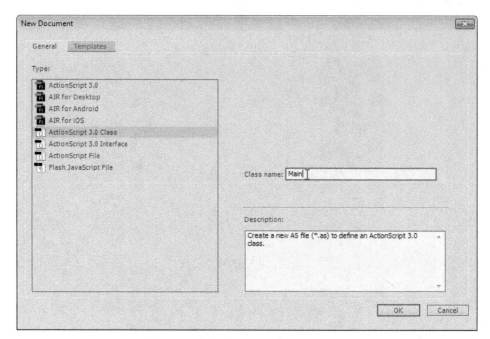

*Figure 10-35  The **New Document** dialog box*

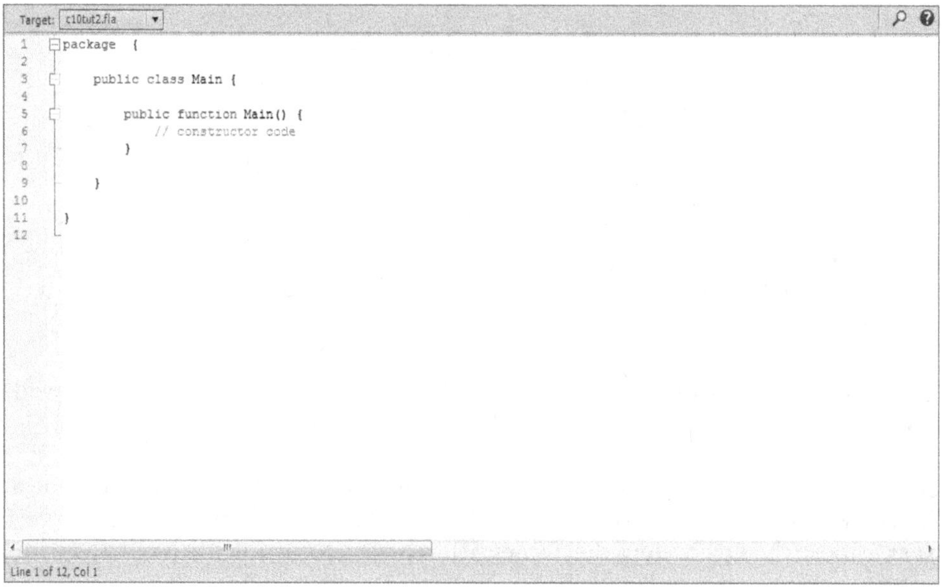

*Figure 10-36  The **Target** ActionScript document file*

4.  In the **Target** ActionScript document, type the following code:

```
1       package
2       {
3           import blue;
4           import green;
5           import orange;
6           import pink;
7           import red;
8           import yellow;
9           import flash.display.MovieClip;
10          import flash.events.TouchEvent;
11          import flash.ui.Multitouch;
12          import flash.ui.MultitouchInputMode;
13          import ColorDrag;
14
15          public class Main extends MovieClip
16          {
17                  private var blue_mc:blue;
18                  private var green_mc:green;
19                  private var orange_mc:orange;
20                  private var pink_mc:pink;
21                  private var red_mc:red;
22                  private var yellow_mc:yellow;
23
24
25                  public function Main()
26                  {
27                          Multitouch.inputMode = MultitouchInputMode.TOUCH_POINT;
28                          addPieces();
29                  }
30
31                  private function addPieces():void
32          {
33                  blue_mc = new blue();
34                  addChild(blue_mc);
35                  blue_mc.x = Math.random()* stage.stageWidth / 10;
36                  blue_mc.y = Math.random()* stage.stageHeight / 10;
37                  blue_mc._targetPiece = B1T;
38                  blue_mc.addEventListener(TouchEvent.TOUCH_END, CheckTarget);
39
40                  green_mc = new green();
41                  addChild(green_mc);
42                  green_mc.x = Math.random()* stage.stageWidth / 10;
43                  green_mc.y = Math.random()* stage.stageHeight / 10;
44                  green_mc._targetPiece = G1T;
45                  green_mc.addEventListener(TouchEvent.TOUCH_END, CheckTarget);
46
```

```
47          orange_mc = new orange();
48          addChild(orange_mc);
49          orange_mc.x = Math.random()* stage.stageWidth / 10;
50          orange_mc.y = Math.random()* stage.stageHeight / 10;
51          orange_mc._targetPiece = O1T;
52          orange_mc.addEventListener(TouchEvent.TOUCH_END, CheckTarget);
53
54          pink_mc = new pink();
55          addChild(pink_mc);
56          pink_mc.x = Math.random()* stage.stageWidth / 10;
57          pink_mc.y = Math.random()* stage.stageHeight / 10;
58          pink_mc._targetPiece = P1T;
59          pink_mc.addEventListener(TouchEvent.TOUCH_END, CheckTarget);
60
61          red_mc = new red();
62          addChild(red_mc);
63          red_mc.x = Math.random()* stage.stageWidth / 10;
64          red_mc.y = Math.random()* stage.stageHeight / 10;
65          red_mc._targetPiece = R1T;
66          red_mc.addEventListener(TouchEvent.TOUCH_END, CheckTarget);
67
68          yellow_mc = new yellow();
69          addChild(yellow_mc);
70          yellow_mc.x = Math.random()* stage.stageWidth / 2;
71          yellow_mc.y = Math.random()* stage.stageHeight / 10;
72          yellow_mc._targetPiece = Y1T;
73          yellow_mc.addEventListener(TouchEvent.TOUCH_END, CheckTarget);
74          }
75
76          private function CheckTarget(event:TouchEvent):void
77          {
78          if(event.currentTarget.hitTestObject(event.currentTarget._targetPiece))
79          {
80                  event.currentTarget.x = event.currentTarget._targetPiece.x;
81                  event.currentTarget.y = event.currentTarget._targetPiece.y;
82                  event.currentTarget.kill();
83          }else{
84                  event.currentTarget.x = event.currentTarget._xPos;
85                  event.currentTarget.y = event.currentTarget._yPos;
86                  }
87
88          }
89
90      }
91  }
```

**Explanation**

Line 1
**package**
The **package** is a keyword. Notice that the name of the package is not mentioned in the script as here the ActionScript file is in the same directory as that of the FLA file. The package
keyword tells Flash that all the codes between the curly braces is part of a single group.

Line 3 to 8
**import blue;**
**import green;**
**import orange;**
**import pink;**
**import red;**
**import yellow;**
Here, you have imported all the Colors.

Line 9
**flash.display.MovieClip;**
The **flash.display.MovieClip** is an external class file. These external class files are imported to the package to access functions that they contain.

Line 10
**flash.events.TouchEvent;**
Here, you have imported the Touch Event to apply the touch effects to all the colors.

Line 11
**import flash.ui.Multitouch;**
Here, you have imported the Multitouch to apply multiple touch effects to all the colors.

Line 12
**import flash.ui.MultitouchInputMode;**
Here, you have imported the MultitouchInputMode to provide values and to indentify the touch effects for different gestures.

Line 13
**import ColorDrag;**
Here, you have imported the ColorDrag to make the colors draggable.

Line 15
**public class Main extends MovieClip**
Here, you have declared a document class named **Main extends MovieClip**, which represents the main Timeline. **Public** means that other classes in your code will be able to see this class.

Line 17 to 22
**private var blue_mc:blue;**
**private var green_mc:green;**
**private var orange_mc:orange;**
**private var pink_mc:pink;**
**private var red_mc:red;**
**private var yellow_mc:yellow;**
Here, you are declaring all the colors as a private function as you will be calling it within this class.

Line 25
**public function Main()**
Here, you are declaring a function class named **Main**. **Public** means that other classes in your code will be able to see this class.

Line 27
**Multitouch.inputMode = MultitouchInputMode.TOUCH_POINT;**
Here, you will provide TOUCH_POINT using the Multitouch.inputMode to all the pieces including the target Pieces.

Line 28
**addPieces();**
In this line, new pieces are added to the Stage (main Timeline). The new pieces are the Target pieces.

Line 31
**private function addPieces():void**
Here, you are declaring a function **addPieces** method as a private function as you will be calling it within this class.

Line 33
**blue_mc = new blue();**
Here, you have created a new instance of the *blue* movie clip.

Line 34
**addChild(blue_mc);**
In this line, a new child is added to the Stage (main Timeline). The new child is the instance of the **blue_mc** class.

Line 35 to 37
**blue_mc.x = Math.random()* stage.stageWidth / 10;**
**blue_mc.y = Math.random()* stage.stageHeight / 10;**
**blue_mc._targetPiece = B1T;**
In the above lines, the position of the *blue_mc* Color movie clip randomizes once it hits the Stage. The term **stage** is referring to the main Timeline and **stageWidth** and **stageHeight** with the value 10 is responsible to place the targetPiece on the Stage.

Line 38

**blue_mc.addEventListener(TouchEvent.TOUCH_END, CheckTarget);**
Here **TOUCH_END** is the class property. As you will be using the **TouchEvent** within this class, it will be private. This means how often you want the **TouchEvent** to call the function that will check the target.

Line 40 to 45

**green_mc = new green();**
**addChild(green_mc);**
**green_mc.x = Math.random()* stage.stageWidth / 10;**
**green_mc.y = Math.random()* stage.stageHeight / 10;**
**green_mc._targetPiece = G1T;**
**green_mc.addEventListener(TouchEvent.TOUCH_END, CheckTarget);**
The explanation of these lines is similar to that of Line 33 to 38.

Line 47 to 52

**orange_mc = new orange();**
**addChild(orange_mc);**
**orange_mc.x = Math.random()* stage.stageWidth / 10;**
**orange_mc.y = Math.random()* stage.stageHeight / 10;**
**orange_mc._targetPiece = O1T;**
**orange_mc.addEventListener(TouchEvent.TOUCH_END, CheckTarget);**
The explanation of these lines is similar to that of Line 33 to 38.

Line 54 to 59

**pink_mc = new pink();**
**addChild(pink_mc);**
**pink_mc.x = Math.random()* stage.stageWidth / 10;**
**pink_mc.y = Math.random()* stage.stageHeight / 10;**
**pink_mc._targetPiece = P1T;**
**pink_mc.addEventListener(TouchEvent.TOUCH_END, CheckTarget);**
The explanation of these lines is similar to that of Line 33 to 38.

Line 61 to 66

**red_mc = new red();**
**addChild(red_mc);**
**red_mc.x = Math.random()* stage.stageWidth / 10;**
**red_mc.y = Math.random()* stage.stageHeight / 10;**
**red_mc._targetPiece = R1T;**
**red_mc.addEventListener(TouchEvent.TOUCH_END, CheckTarget);**
The explanation of these lines is similar to that of Line 33 to 38.

Line 68 to 73

**yellow_mc = new yellow();**
**addChild(yellow_mc);**
**yellow_mc.x = Math.random()* stage.stageWidth / 2;**

**yellow_mc.y = Math.random()\* stage.stageHeight / 10;**
**yellow_mc._targetPiece = Y1T;**
**yellow_mc.addEventListener(TouchEvent.TOUCH_END, CheckTarget);**
The explanation of these lines is similar to that of Line 33 to 38.

Line 76
**private function CheckTarget(event:TouchEvent):void**
Here, you are declaring a function **CheckTarget** method as a private function as you will be calling it within this class. The object that will be called here is TouchEvent, which is **void** as the function does not return any value.

Line 78 to 85
**if(event.currentTarget.hitTestObject(event.currentTarget._targetPiece))**
**{**
    **event.currentTarget.x = event.currentTarget._targetPiece.x;**
    **event.currentTarget.y = event.currentTarget._targetPiece.y;**
    **event.currentTarget.kill();**
**}else{**
    **event.currentTarget.x = event.currentTarget._xPos;**
    **event.currentTarget.y = event.currentTarget._yPos;**
By typing the above codes, you are checking whether the all Colors are at their original Target places or not. If they are at their original position; they will lock and if not; they will go back to their previous position.

5.   Press CTRL + S to save the file.

6.   Choose the **Properties** tab of the file **c10tut2**. Next, type **Main** in the **Document Class** text box of the **Publish** area, as shown in Figure 10-37.

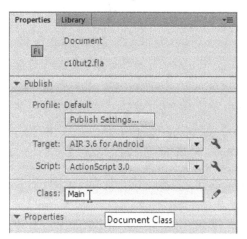

*Figure 10-37 The **Publish** area*

Now, you will move all the objects in the Stage to other location

7.  Marquee select all the objects in the Stage and set the value of **Y** to **240** in the **Position and Size** area of the **Properties** panel.

Next, you will create a new class file to make the colors draggable using the **TouchEvent** function.

### Creating a New Class File

In this section, you will create a new class file which will make the colors draggable using the **TouchEvent** function.

1.  Choose **File > New** from the menubar; the **New Document** dialog box is displayed, refer to Figure 10-38.

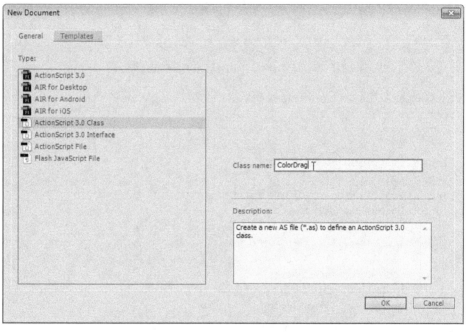

*Figure 10-38 The New Document dialog box*

2.  In the **New Document** dialog box, choose **ActionScript 3.0 Class** from the **Type** area in the **General** tab, and also type **ColorDrag** in the **Class name** text box, refer to Figure 10-38. Next, choose the **OK** button; a **Target** ActionScript document file is opened with scripts written in it, as shown in Figure 10-39. Next, delete those scripts.

3.  Choose **File > Save As** from the menubar; the **Save As** dialog box is displayed. In this dialog box, type **ColorDrag.as** in the **File name** text box and save it in *\Documents\Flash_projects\ c10_tut\c10_tut_02*.

*Figure 10-39  The **Target** ActionScript document file opened*

4.  In the **Target** ActionScript document, type the following code:

```
1   package
2   {
3       import flash.display.MovieClip;
4       import flash.ui.Multitouch;
5       import flash.ui.MultitouchInputMode;
6       import flash.events.TouchEvent;
7
8       public class ColorDrag extends MovieClip
9       {
10              public var _targetPiece:*;
11              public var _xPos:Number;
12              public var _yPos:Number;
13
14              public function ColorDrag()
15              {
16              Multitouch.inputMode = MultitouchInputMode.TOUCH_POINT;
17              this.addEventListener(TouchEvent.TOUCH_BEGIN, dragClip);
18              this.addEventListener(TouchEvent.TOUCH_END, dropClip);
19              }
20
21              private function dragClip(event:TouchEvent):void
22      {
23              parent.setChildIndex(this, parent.numChildren -1);
24              _xPos = this.x;
25              _yPos = this.y;
26              this.startDrag();
```

```
27
28      }
29
30      private function dropClip(event:TouchEvent):void
31              {
32              this.stopDrag();
33              }
34                      public function kill():void
35              {
36                      this.removeEventListener(TouchEvent.TOUCH_BEGIN, dragClip);
37                      this.removeEventListener(TouchEvent.TOUCH_END, dropClip);
38              }
39
40      }
41
42  }
```

**Explanation**

Line 1
**package**
The **package** is a keyword. Notice that the name of the package is not mentioned in the script as here the ActionScript file is in the same directory as that of the FLA file. The package keyword tells Flash that all of the code between its curly braces is part of a single group.

Line 3
**flash.display.MovieClip;**
The **flash.display.MovieClip** is an external class file. These external class files are imported to the package to access functions that they contain.

Line 4
**import flash.ui.Multitouch;**
Here, you have imported the Multitouch function.

Line 5
**import flash.ui.MultitouchInputMode;**
Here, you have imported the MultitouchInputMode function.

Line 6
**flash.events.TouchEvent;**
Here, you have imported the TouchEvent to apply the touch effects to all the Colors.

Line 8
**public class ColorDrag extends MovieClip**
Here, you have declared a document class named **ColorDrag extends MovieClip**, which represents the main Timeline. **Public** means that other classes in your code will be able to see this class.

Line 10
**public var _targetPiece:*;**
Here, you have to give instance name and the data type as wild card (*).

Line 12 and 13
**public var _xPos:Number;**
**public var _yPos:Number;**
Here, you are capturing the x and y position.

Line 14
**public function ColorDrag()**
In the above line, you are declaring a function class named **ColorDrag**. **Public** means that other classes in your code will be able to see this class.

Line 16
**Multitouch.inputMode = MultitouchInputMode.TOUCH_POINT;**
Here, you will provide TOUCH_POINT using the MULTItouch.inputMode to all the pieces including the target Pieces.

Line 17 and 18
**this.addEventListener(TouchEvent.TOUCH_BEGIN, dragClip);**
**this.addEventListener(TouchEvent.TOUCH_END, dropClip);**
Here, you will add two EventListners which will provide the TouchEvents to drag and drop the Colors.

Line 21
**private function dragClip(event:TouchEvent):void**
Here, you are declaring a function **dragClip** method as a private function as you will be calling it within this class. The object that will be called here is TouchEvent, which is **void** as the function does not return any value.

Line 23 to 26
**parent.setChildIndex(this, parent.numChildren -1);**
Here, you are setting the index number.

Line 24 and 25
**_xPos = this.x;**
**_yPos = this.y;**
Here, you are assigning values to x and y position.

Line 26
**this.startDrag();**
Here, you are declaring a method **startdrag** to control the dragging process. It will start the dragging process.

Line 30
**private function dropClip(event:TouchEvent):void**
Here, you are declaring a function **dropClip** method as a private function as you will be

calling it within this class. The object that will be called here is TouchEvent, which is **void** as the function does not return any value.

Line 32
**this.stopDrag();**
Here, you are declaring a method **stopdrag** to control the dragging process. It will stop the dragging process after dropping the colors to its specified places.

Line 34
**public function kill():void**
Here, you are declaring a public method which will kill the dragging funtion.

Line 36 and 37
**this.removeEventListener(TouchEvent.TOUCH_BEGIN, dragClip);**
**this.removeEventListener(TouchEvent.TOUCH_END, dropClip);**
Here, you will remove both EventListners which are providing the TouchEvents to drag and drop the colors.

5.  Press CTRL + S keys to save the file.

6.  In the file c10tut2, choose the **Library** tab and select the instance **blue** in the **Library** panel. Next, choose the **Properties** icon at the bottom of the **Library** panel; the **Symbol Properties** dialog box is displayed, refer to Figure 10-40.

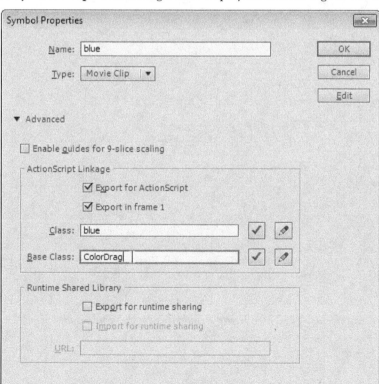

*Figure 10-40  The **Symbol Properties** dialog box*

7. In this dialog box, type **ColorDrag** in the **Base Class** text box, refer to Figure 10-40. Next, choose the **OK** button; the **ActionScript Class Warning** message box is displayed, as shown in Figure 10-41 and choose the **OK** button to close the message box.

*Figure 10-41  The **ActionScript Class Warning** message box*

8. Select the instance **green**. Next, press the CTRL key and select other instances namely **red**, **orange**, **pink**, and **yellow** and then choose the **Properties** icon at the bottom of the **Library** panel; the **Editing Properties for 5 Symbols** dialog box is displayed. Next, type **ColorDrag** in the **Base Class** text box, refer to Figure 10-42.

9. Next, choose the **OK** button to close the dialog box and press CTRL + S keys to save the file.

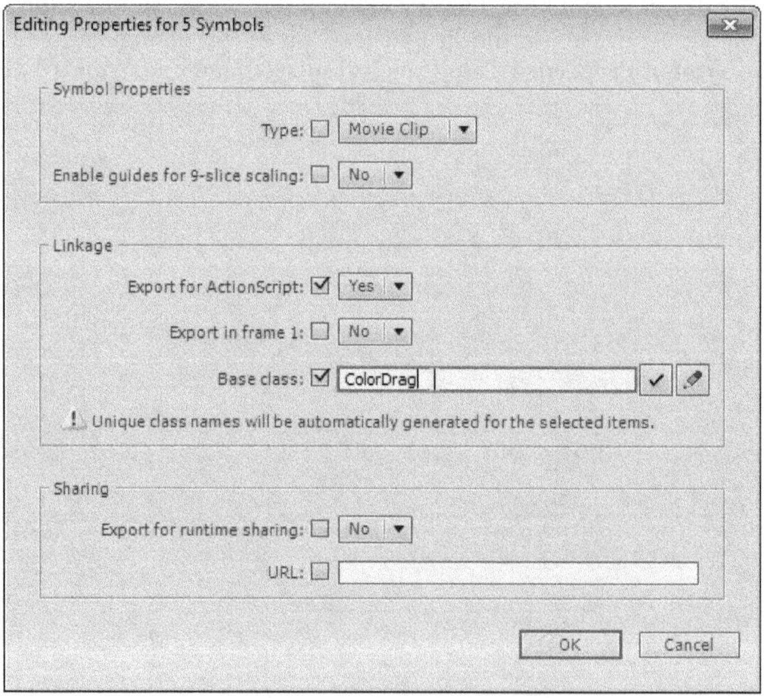

*Figure 10-42  The **Editing Properties for 5 Symbols** dialog box*

## Publishing the Flash Document to Android File(.apk)

In this section, you will publish the flash document to android file(.apk).

1.  In the **Properties** panel, make sure **AIR 3.6 for Android** is selected in the **Target** drop-down list of the **Publish** area, refer to Figure 10-43.

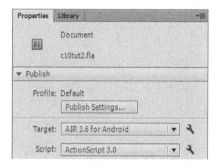

*Figure 10-43  The **Properties** panel*

2.  Choose **File > AIR 3.6 for Android Settings** from the menubar; the **AIR for Android Settings** dialog box is displayed, as shown in Figure 10-44.

3.  Choose the **Deployment** tab from this dialog box. Next, choose the **Browse** button, as shown in Figure 10-45; the **Open** dialog box is displayed. In this dialog box, browse to **Documents > Flash_Projects > c10_tut > Resources > 12345.p12**. Next, choose the **Open** button; the path of the file **12345.p12** is displayed in the **Certificate** drop-down list, refer to Figure 10-46.

4.  Type the password **12345** in the **Password** edit box and select the radio button **Embed AIR runtime with application** in the **AIR runtime** area, refer to Figure 10-46.

 **Note**
*You can set the password of your choice in the **Password** text box.*

5.  Choose the **Icons** tab. Select **icon 72x72** for the icon size of the content, refer to Figure 10-47. Next, click on the browse icon, as shown in Figure 10-47; the **Open** dialog box is displayed.

6.  Browse to **Documents > Flash_Projects > c10_tut > Resources**. Next, select **Colors.png** from this dialog box and choose the **Open** button; the **Adobe Flash Professional** message box is displayed asking "**The icon must be copied to a folder relative to the root content folder so that it can be published. Do you want to proceed?**", as shown in Figure 10-48. Choose the **OK** button to close the dialog box.

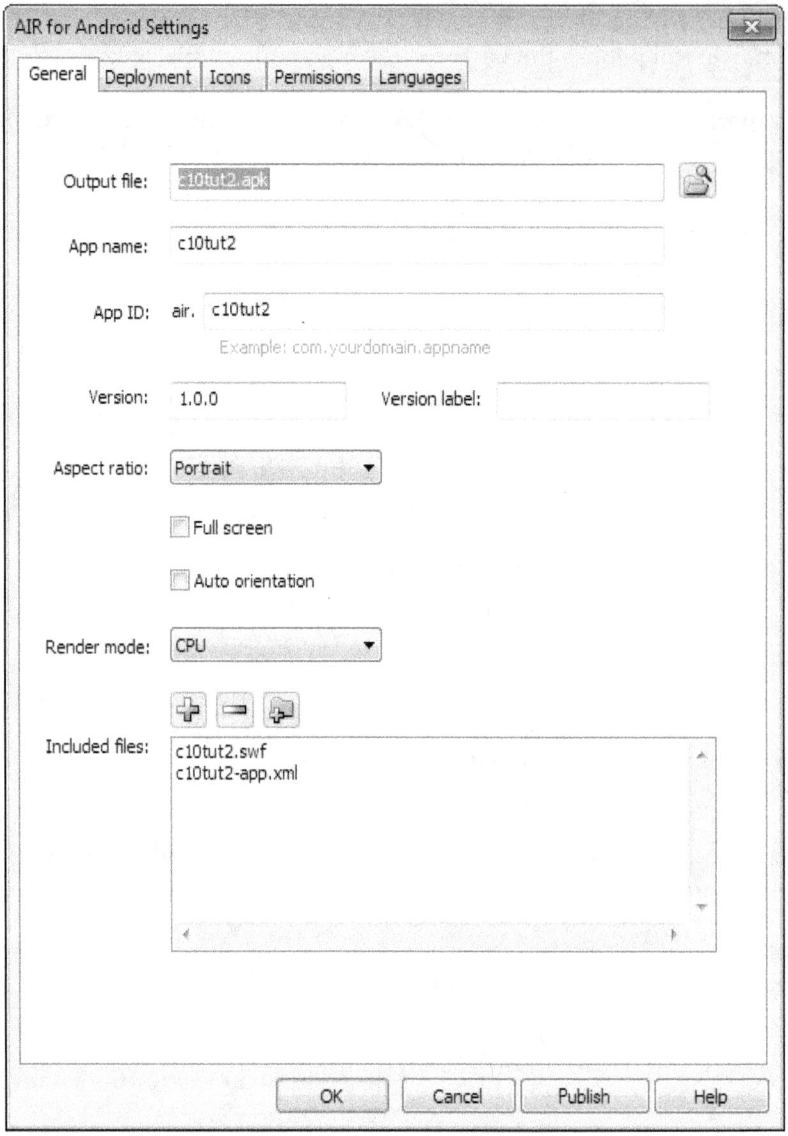

*Figure 10-44  The **AIR for Android Settings** dialog box*

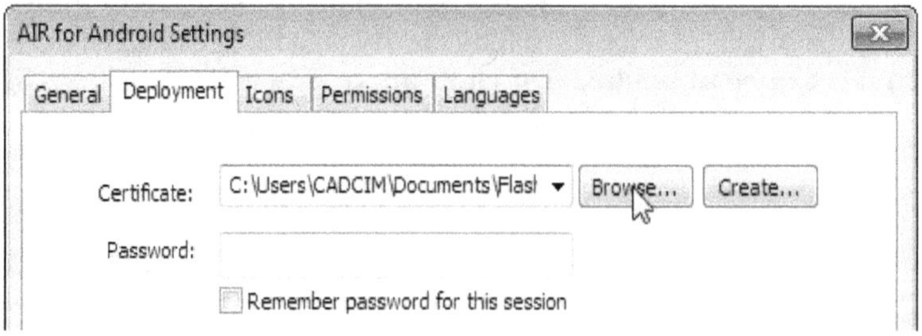

*Figure 10-45  Choosing the **Browse** button*

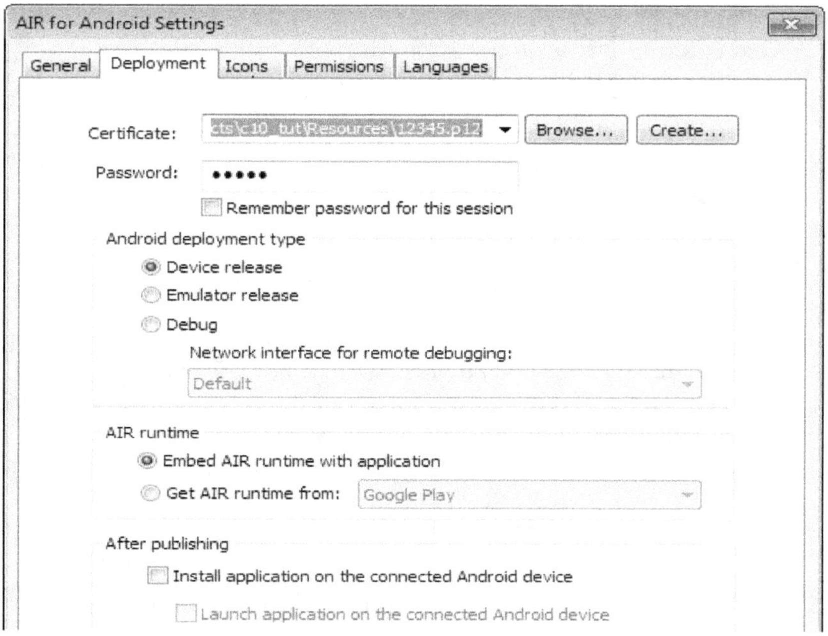

*Figure 10-46* The **Embed AIR runtime with application** *radio button selected*

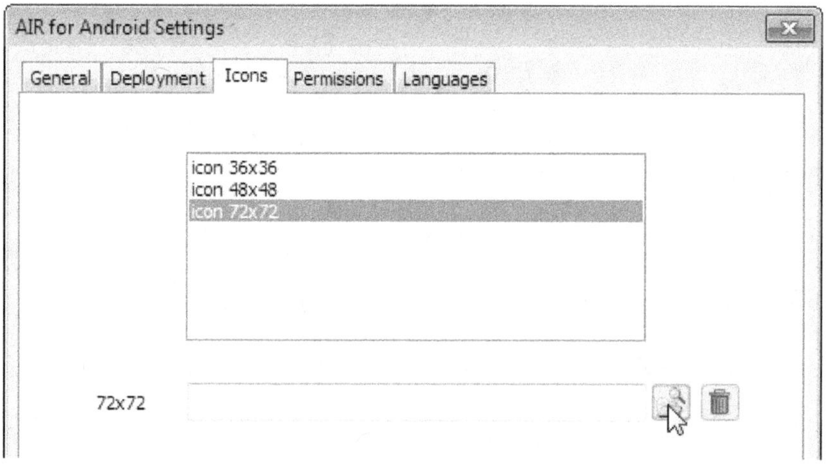

*Figure 10-47* *Clicking on the browse icon*

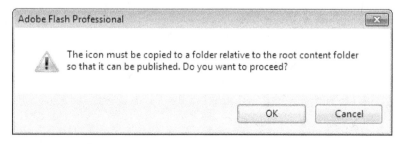

*Figure 10-48* **Adobe Flash Professional** *message box displayed*

7.  Choose the **Publish** button at the bottom of the **Air 3.6 for Android Settings** dialog box; a progress bar is displayed, as shown in Figure 10-49.

*Figure 10-49  Publishing progress bar displayed*

8.  When the publishing is over, the **Adobe Flash Professional** message box is displayed with the message **The APK was packaged successfully, but a warning occurred. Warning: Application has not specified its permission requirements in application.xml**, as shown in Figure 10-50. Choose the **OK** button to close the message box.

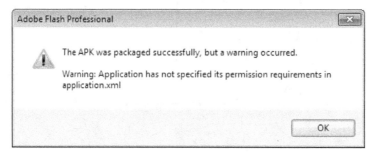

*Figure 10-50  Adobe Flash Professional message box*

You will notice that the *c10tut2.apk* and *c10tut2.swf* files are published at the location *\Documents\Flash Projects\c10_tut\c10_tut_02*.

9.  Choose the **OK** button to close the **AIR for Android Settings** dialog box.

10. Press CTRL + S to save the file.

## Installing and Running the Android File(.apk) In Android Mobile Phone

In this section, you will install and run the android file(.apk) in android mobile phone.

1.  Connect your android mobile phone with the computer.

2.  Browse to **Documents > Flash_Projects > c10_tut > c10_tut_02 > c10tut2.apk**. Next, copy the **c10tut2.apk** file to your android mobile phone.

3.  Install **c10tut2.apk** in your android mobile phone and open it.

    The final **.apk** file running in the android mobile phone, refer to Figure 10-51.

***Figure 10-51*** *Final .apk file running in the android mobile phone*

## Self-Evaluation Test

**Answer the following questions and then compare them to those given at the end of this chapter:**

1.  Which of the following is the extension of an android application?

    (a) .apk                          (b) .ma
    (c) .jar                          (d) .dat

2.  To create a certificate for Publishing a .apk file, you need to choose the _____ tab in the **AIR for Android Settings**.

3.  You can change the color of the Stage by choosing the color of your choice from the _____ color swatch.

4.  You can publish a file by choosing the _____ button from the **AIR 3.6 for Android Settings** dialog box.

5.  You can set the password of your choice in the **Password** text box of the **Create Self-Signed Digital Certificate** dialog box while creating the certificate to publish the content. (T/F)

## Review Questions

**Answer the following questions:**

1. Which of the following icon sizes are used for an android application?

    (a) icon 36x36                          (b) icon 48x48
    (c) icon 72x72                          (d) All of the these

2. When the publishing progress is finished; the _____ message box is displayed.

3. When the value in the _____ is set to 40%, you will notice that the opacity of the selected colors in the Stage is decreased.

4. _____ button is used to swap two symbols.

5. Android file (.apk) runs only on Android device. (T/F)

# EXERCISE

## Exercise 1

Create a Flash document and then create a certificate to publish this document. Next, publish this document to an android application.                          **(Expected time: 20 min)**

## Answers to Self-Evaluation Test

1. a, 2. Deployment, 3. Background, 4. Publish, 5. T

# Project 1

## Creating a Scrolling Background

### PROJECT DESCRIPTION

In this project, you will create a scrolling background animation. The final output of this project at frame **20** is shown in Figure P1-1.

**Figure P1-1**  *The output of the animation at frame 20*

Before you start the project, you need to download the *prj1_flash_cc.zip* file from *www.cadcim.com*. The path of the file is as follows:

> *Textbooks > Animation and Visual Effects > Flash > The Adobe Flash Professional CC: A Tutorial Approach*

Next, extract the contents of the zip file to *\Documents\Flash_Projects*.

## Creating a New Flash Document

In this section, you will specify the frame format settings.

1.  Choose **File > New** from the menubar; the **New Document** dialog box is displayed.

2.  In the **New Document** dialog box, choose **ActionScript 3.0** from the **General** tab. Next, choose the **OK** button; a new Flash document is displayed.

## Creating Reference of the Stage

In this section, you will use the rulers to create a reference of the stage.

1.  Choose **View > Rulers** from the menubar; the rulers are displayed in the Scene area.

2.  Drag the cursor from the Rulers bar to the Stage to create guides. Next, position the guides, as shown in Figure P1-2.

***Figure P1-2***  *The guides placed around the Stage*

## Creating the Road

In this section, you will create the road.

1.  Choose **Zoom Tool** from the **Tools** panel. Next, press and hold the ALT key and click on the center of the Stage and zoom it out to 50%. Alternatively, enter **50** in the Zoom edit box located at the extreme right of the Scene area and press the ENTER key.

2.  Choose **Rectangle Tool** from the **Tools** panel; the tool properties are displayed in the **Properties** panel.

3.  In the **Fill and Stroke** area of the **Properties** panel, choose the **Stroke color** swatch; a flyout is displayed. In this flyout, make sure **#000000** is entered in the Hex edit box and press the ENTER key.

4.  Choose the **Fill color** swatch; a flyout is displayed. Next, enter **#999999** in the Hex edit box and press the ENTER key.

5.  Create a rectangle in the Stage, refer to Figure P1-3.

6.  Choose **Selection Tool** from the **Tools** panel and double-click on the rectangle in the Stage; the fill and the stroke of the rectangle area are selected in the Stage and the **Shape** properties are displayed in the **Properties** panel. Make sure that the **Lock width and height values together** button is in the off mode ( 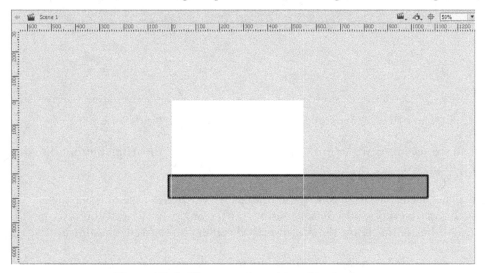 ).

7.  In the **Position and Size** area of the **Properties** panel, set the value of **W** to **1084** and **H** to **91**; the rectangle is resized according to the specified values. Next, set the value of **X** to **-14** and **Y** to **307**; the rectangle is positioned in the Stage, as shown in Figure P1-3.

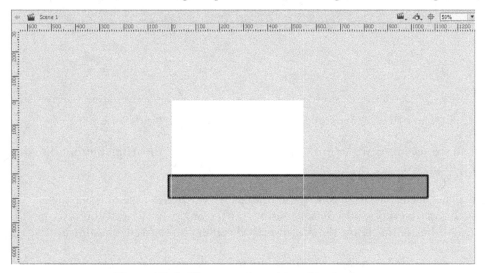

***Figure P1-3*** *The rectangle positioned in the Stage*

8.  Choose **Rectangle Tool** from the **Tools** panel; the tool properties are displayed in the **Properties** panel.

9.  In the **Fill and Stroke** area of the **Properties** panel, choose the **Stroke color** swatch; a flyout is displayed. In this flyout, choose the No Color button.

10. Choose the **Fill color** swatch; a flyout is displayed. Next, enter **#FFFFFF** in the Hex edit box and press the ENTER key.

11. Create a rectangle in the Pasteboard.

12. Choose **Selection Tool** from the **Tools** panel and select the rectangle in the Pasteboard; the **Shape** properties are displayed in the **Properties** panel.

13. In the **Position and Size** area of the **Properties** panel, set the value of **W** to **125** and **H** to **14**.

14. Create six copies of the rectangle in the Pasteboard using the ALT key, as shown in Figure P1-4.

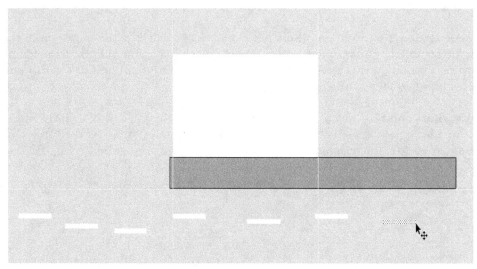

*Figure P1-4  Six copies of the rectangle created in the Pasteboard*

15. Select all the seven rectangles in the Pasteboard and choose the **Align** button; the **Align** panel is displayed.

16. In this panel, clear the **Align to stage** check box. In the **Space** area of this panel, choose the **Space evenly horizontally** button; the rectangles are placed equidistant from each other. Next, choose the **Align vertical center** button from the **Align** area.

17. Place the cursor on a rectangle and drag the rectangles and place them at the center of the rectangle already positioned in the Stage, refer to Figure P1-5.

18. Marquee select all the elements in the Stage (Layer 1). Next, press the F8 key; the **Convert to Symbol** dialog box is displayed.

19. In this dialog box, type **road_gr** in the **Name** text box and select **Graphic** in the **Type** drop-down list and also make sure the **Registration** is set to top left. Next, choose the **OK** button; the selected elements are converted into a graphic symbol and a graphic instance is created in the Stage.

*Figure P1-5* *The rectangles positioned on the other rectangle*

20. Rename **Layer 1** to **Road**.

## Importing the Buildings
In this section, you will import the buildings.

1.  Choose the **New Layer** button in the **Timeline** panel; a new layer is created. Rename this layer to **Buildings_1** and select it.

2.  Choose **File > Import > Import to Stage** from the menubar; the **Import** dialog box is displayed. In this dialog box, browse to **Documents > Flash_Projects > prj1_flash_cc > Resources > build.png**. Next, choose the **Open** button from this dialog box; the **build.png** file is displayed on the Stage, refer to Figure P1-6.

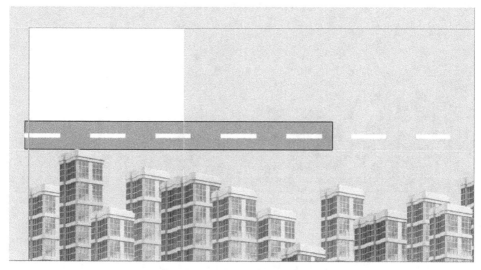

*Figure P1-6* *The build.png file displayed in the Stage*

3.  Select the **build.png** in the Stage. In the **Position and Size** area of the **Properties** panel, set the value of **W** to **760** and **H** to **309**; the buildings are resized according to the specified values, as shown in Figure P1-7.

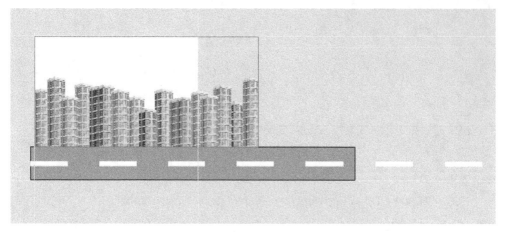

*Figure P1-7  The buildings resized in the stage*

4.  Lock the **Road** layer using the **Lock or Unlock All Layers** button of this layer.

5.  Select the **Buildings_1** layer in the **Timeline** panel; buildings are selected in the Stage.

6.  Press the F8 key; the **Convert to Symbol** dialog box is displayed. In the **Name** text box, type **buildings_near** and make sure **Graphic** from the **Type** drop-down list is selected. Next, choose the **OK** button; a graphic instance named *buildings_near* is placed in the Stage and its symbol is saved in the **Library** panel.

7.  In the **Timeline** panel, drag the **Buildings_1** layer and place it below the **Road** layer. Next, align the *buildings_near* instance behind *road_gr* instance in the Stage, refer to Figure P1-8.

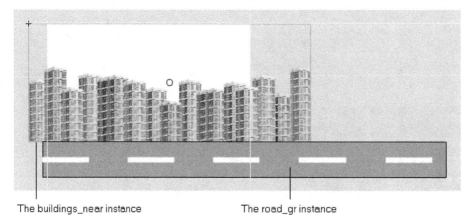

The buildings_near instance                    The road_gr instance

*Figure P1-8  The buildings_near instance positioned
and aligned behind the road_gr instance*

8.  In the **Timeline** panel, choose the **New Layer** button; a new layer is created. Rename this layer to **Buildings_2**. Next, select the **Buildings_2** layer.

9.  Choose **Rectangle Tool** from the **Tools** panel; the tool properties are displayed in the **Properties** panel.

10. In the **Fill and Stroke** area of the **Properties** panel, choose the **Fill color** swatch; a flyout is displayed. In this flyout, enter **#000000** in the Hex edit box and press the ENTER Key.

11. Choose the **Stroke color** swatch; a flyout is displayed. In this flyout, enter **#000000** in the Hex edit box and press the ENTER Key.

12. In the **Fill and Stroke** area of the **Properties** panel, make sure the value of **Stroke** is set to **1**.

13. Create a rectangle in the Pasteboard. Next, choose **Selection Tool** from the **Tools** panel and then double-click on the rectangle to select its fill and stroke.

14. In the **Position and Size** area of the **Properties** panel, set the value of **W** to **70** and **H** to **214**.

15. Choose **Rectangle Tool** from the **Tools** panel. In the **Fill and Stroke** area of the **Properties** panel, choose the **Fill color** swatch; a flyout is displayed. In this flyout, enter **#FFFF00** in the Hex edit box and press the ENTER Key. Next, choose the **Stroke color** swatch; a flyout is displayed. In this flyout, enter **#999999** in the Hex edit box and press the ENTER Key.

16. Create a rectangle in the Pasteboard. Next, select the rectangle along with its fill and stroke using **Selection Tool**.

17. In the **Position and Size** area of the **Properties** panel, set the value of **W** to **9** and **H** to **12**.

18. Create three copies of the rectangle using the ALT key. Next, choose **Selection Tool** from the **Tools** panel and select the four small rectangles and place them on the rectangle, refer to Figure P1-9.

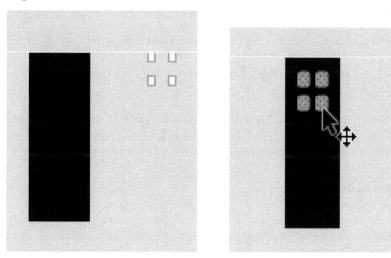

***Figure P1-9*** *Placing the smaller rectangles on the larger one*

19. Marquee select the large rectangle and press CTRL+G; all the rectangles are grouped.

20. Make sure the group in the Pasteboard is selected; the **Group** properties are displayed in the **Properties** panel.

21. In the **Position and Size** area of the **Properties** panel, set the value of **X** to **131** and **Y** to **91**; the group is positioned in the Stage.

22. Create eight copies of the group using the ALT key and place them randomly in the Stage, refer to Figure P1-10.

23. In the **Timeline** panel, move the **Buildings_2** layer below the **Buildings_1** layer; the group is placed behind the *buildings_near* instance in the Stage, as shown in Figure P1-10.

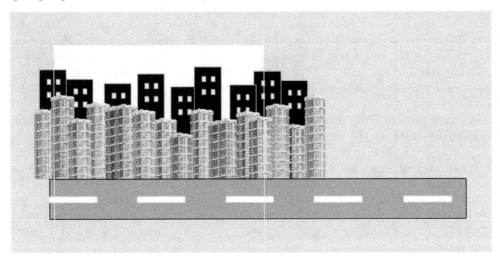

**Figure P1-10** *The group placed behind the buildings_near instance in the Stage*

24. Make sure the **Buildings_2** layer is selected in the **Timeline** panel.

25. Choose **Modify > Convert to Symbol** from the menubar; the **Convert to Symbol** dialog box is displayed.

26. In this dialog box, type **buildings_far** in the **Name** text box and make sure **Graphic** in the **Type** drop-down list is selected. Next, choose the **OK** button; all elements in this layer are converted into a symbol named as *buildings_far* and its instance is placed in the Stage.

## Importing the Trees

In this section, you will import the trees.

1. In the **Timeline** panel, choose the **New Layer** button; a new layer is created. Rename this layer to **Trees** and select it.

2. Choose **File > Import > Import** to Stage from the menubar; the **Import** dialog box is displayed. In this dialog box, browse to **Documents > Flash_Projects > prj1_flash_cc > Resources > tree.png**. Next, choose the **Open** button from this dialog box; the **tree.png** file is displayed on the Stage, refer to Figure P1-11.

*Figure P1-11* *The tree.png file displayed on the Stage*

3. Select the **tree.png** in the Stage. In the **Position and Size** area of the **Properties** panel, set the value of **X** to **10** and **Y** to **193** and also, set the value of **W** to **50** and **H** to **130**; the buildings are positioned and resized according to the specified values.

4. Place the **Trees** layer below the **Road** layer in the **Timeline** panel, refer to Figure P1-12.

5. Make sure the **tree.png** is selected in the Stage. Create four copies of the trees and align them, as shown in Figure P1-12.

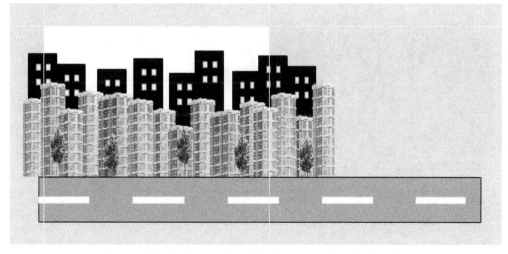

*Figure P1-12* *Four copies of the trees created and aligned*

6.   Select the **Trees** layer in the **Timeline** panel; all trees are selected in the Stage.

7.   Choose **Modify > Convert to Symbol** from the menubar; the **Convert to Symbol** dialog box is displayed.

8.   In this dialog box, type **Trees** in the **Name** text box and make sure **Graphic** in the **Type** drop-down list is selected. Next, choose the **OK** button; all the elements in this layer are converted into a symbol named *Trees* and its instance is placed in the Stage.

## Creating the Sky

In this section, you will create the sky.

1.   In the **Timeline** panel, choose the **New Layer** button; a new layer is created. Rename it to **Sky**. Place this layer below the **Buildings_2** layer.

2.   Make sure that the **Sky** layer is selected in the **Timeline** panel. Choose **Rectangle Tool** from the **Tools** panel and create a rectangle in the Pasteboard.

3.   Select the stroke of the rectangle and press the DELETE key.

4.   Select the fill of the rectangle and choose the **Fill color** swatch in the **Fill and Stroke** area of the **Properties** panel; a flyout is displayed. In this flyout, enter **#19597B** in the Hex edit box and press the ENTER key.

5.   Choose the **Align** button; the **Align** panel is displayed. In this panel, select the **Align to stage** check box. In the **Match Size** area of the panel, choose the **Match width and height** button; the dimensions of the rectangle change exactly as that of the Stage.

6.   In the **Align** area of the panel, choose the **Align horizontal center** and then the **Align vertical center** button; the rectangle is positioned exactly in the Stage, refer to Figure P1-13.

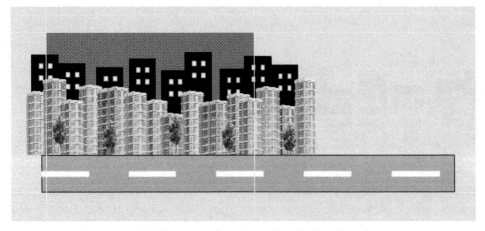

*Figure P1-13  The rectangle positioned and aligned in the Stage*

## Creating the Moon

In this section, you will create the moon.

1. In the **Timeline** panel, choose the **New Layer** button; a new layer is created. Rename this layer to **Moon**.

2. Make sure the **Moon** layer is above the **Sky** layer and then select it.

3. Choose **Oval Tool** from the **Tools** panel.

4. In the **Fill and Stroke** area of the **Properties** panel, choose the **Stroke color** swatch; a flyout is displayed. In this flyout, choose the No Color button.

5. Choose the **Fill color** swatch; a flyout is displayed. In this flyout, enter **#FFFFFF** in the Hex edit box and press the ENTER key.

6. Create a circle in the Pasteboard.

7. Marquee select one fourth fill of the circle using the **Selection Tool** and press the DELETE key. Next, drag the outline of the fill inward to create the shape of the moon, as shown in Figure P1-14.

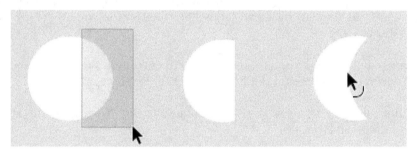

***Figure P1-14*** *Creating the moon*

8. Convert the moon shape into a graphic symbol with the name **moon_gr**.

9. Make sure the *moon_gr* instance is selected in the Stage; the instance properties are displayed in the **Properties** panel. In the **Position and Size** area of the panel, set the value of **W** to **43** and **H** to **72** and also set the value of **X** to **120** and **Y** to **6**; the *moon_gr* instance is positioned in the Stage, refer to Figure P1-15.

10. Save the Flash document with the name **Proj1**.

*Figure P1-15* *Positioning the moon_gr instance*

## Importing the Car Movie Clip Symbol

In this section, you will import the car movie clip symbol.

1.  Choose **File > Open** from the menubar; the **Open** dialog box is displayed.

2.  In this dialog box, browse to the location **Documents > Flash_projects > c04_tut >
    c04_tut_04 > c04_tut_04_start.fla**. Next, choose the **Open** button; the *c04_tut_04_start.fla*
    document is displayed.

3.  In the **Library** panel of this document, choose the **Pin current library** button and return
    to the *Proj1* document by choosing the **Proj1** tab above the Scene area.

4.  In the **Timeline** panel, create a new layer and rename it to **Car**. Next, select this layer and
    place it above the **Road** layer.

5.  From the **Library** panel, drag the *car* movie clip symbol to the Pasteboard; an instance of
    this symbol is created.

6.  Choose the **Pin current library** button to unpin the library. Place the *car* instance on the
    *road_gr* instance in the Stage, refer to Figure P1-16.

*Figure P1-16* *The car instance placed on the road_gr instance*

## Creating Parallax

In this section, you will create a parallax.

1.  In the **Timeline** panel, select frame **50** of the **Car** layer. Press and hold the SHIFT key and select frame **50** of the **Sky** layer; the 50th frame of all the layers between the **Car** layer and the **Sky** layer are selected. Now, press the F6 key to insert keyframes at frame 50 of the selected layers, refer to Figure P1-17.

***Figure P1-17*** *Inserting keyframes at frame 50 of all the layers*

2.  Select the **Road** layer and make sure that the Playhead is placed on frame **50**.

3.  Unlock the **Road** layer using the **Lock or Unlock All Layers** button of this layer. Next, select the *road_gr* instance in the Stage.

4.  In the **Position and Size** area of the **Properties** panel, set the value of **X** to -65.

5.  Select the *Trees* instance in the Stage and make sure that the Playhead is on frame **50**.

6.  In the **Position and Size** area of the **Properties** panel, set the value of **X** to **-172**.

7.  Select the *buildings_near* instance in the Stage and make sure that the Playhead is on frame **50**. In the **Position and Size** area of the **Properties** panel, set the value of **X** to **-188**.

8.  Select the *buildings_far* instance in the Stage. In the **Position and Size** area of the **Properties** panel, set the value of **X** to **-265**.

9.  Lock the **Buildings_1** layer using the **Lock or Unlock All Layers** button of this layer.

10. Select the *moon_gr* instance in the Stage. In the **Position and Size** area of the **Properties** panel, set the value of **X** to **-151**.

11. Place the Playhead on frame **1** and select the *car* instance in the Stage. In the **Position and Size** area of the **Properties** panel, set the value of **X** to **-34**.

12. Place the Playhead on frame **50** and select the *car* instance in the Stage. In the **Position and Size** area of the **Properties** panel, set the value of **X** to **744**.

13. Select frame **20** of all the layers excluding the **Sky** layer and right-click on it; a flyout is displayed. In this flyout, choose **Create Classic Tween**.

14. Save the flash file with the name *prj1* at the location *Documents/Flash_Projects/prj1_flash_cc*.

15. Press CTRL+ENTER to view the final output of the tutorial. You can also view the final rendered file of the project by downloading the file *prj1_flash_cc_rndr.zip* from *www.cadcim.com*. The path of the file is mentioned at the beginning of the project.

# Project 2

# Creating Interactive Navigation

## PROJECT DESCRIPTION

In this project, you will create a main SWF file and add movie clip symbols to it. Then, you will create another four SWF files with the names, *national_end, international_end, packages_end,* and *services_end*. In these files, you will add text, hyperlink text, bitmaps, and symbols. Finally, you will add ActionScript to the main SWF file for the movie clip symbols in it. These movie clips will be used to load the above mentioned four external SWF files during runtime. Figure P2-1 shows the main SWF file.

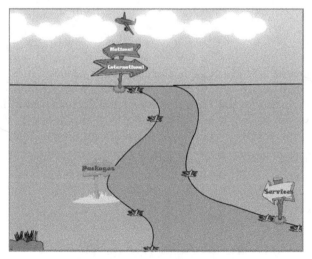

***Figure P2-1***   *The main SWF file*

Before you start the project, you need to download the *prj2_flash_cc.zip* file from *www.cadcim.com*.

The path of the file is as follows: *Textbooks > Animation and Visual Effects > Flash > The Adobe Flash Professional CC: A Tutorial Approach*

Next, extract the contents of the downloaded zip file to *\Documents\Flash_Projects*.

## Adding Elements to the Main Flash Document

In this section, you will add four instances of the movie clip to the Stage of the *proj2_main* Flash document. Using these movie clip instances, you will import four runtime SWF files.

1. Choose **File > Open** from the menubar; the **Open** dialog box is displayed.

2. Browse to **Documents > Flash_Projects > prj2_flash_cc> proj2_main.fla** in the dialog box. Next, choose the **Open** button from the dialog box; the Flash document is opened, as shown in Figure P2-2.

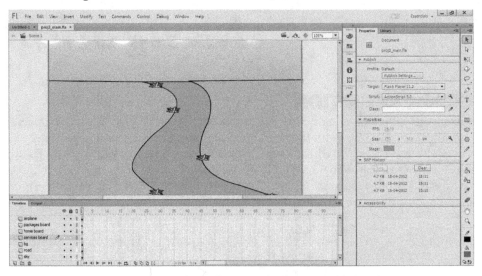

*Figure P2-2   The proj2_main.fla document displayed*

3. In the **Timeline** panel, choose the **Lock or Unlock All Layers** button in the Timeline Header; all the layers are locked, refer to Figure P2-3. Next, choose the **Lock or Unlock All Layers** button in the **services board** layer to unlock it, refer to Figure P2-4.

*Figure P2-3  Locking all layers by choosing the **Lock or Unlock All Layers** button in the Timeline Header*

**Figure P2-4** *Unlocking the **services board** layer by choosing the **Lock or Unlock All Layers** button*

4. Make sure that the **services board** layer is selected in the **Timeline** panel. Next, drag the *services* movie clip symbol from the **Library** panel to the Stage; its instance is displayed in the Stage and its properties are displayed in the **Properties** panel.

5. In the **Properties** panel, type **services_mc** in the **Instance name** text box. In the **Position and Size** area of the **Properties** panel, set the value of **X** to **686** and **Y** to **474** and press the ENTER key; the instance is positioned in the Stage, refer to Figure P2-5.

**Figure P2-5** *The services_mc instance positioned in the Stage*

6. Lock the **services board** layer and unlock the **packages board** layer, as discussed earlier.

7. Make sure the **packages board** layer is selected in the **Timeline** panel. Next, drag the *packages* movie clip symbol to the Stage; its instance is displayed in the Stage and its properties are displayed in the **Properties** panel.

8. In the **Properties** panel, type **packages_mc** in the **Instance name** text box. In the **Position and Size** area of the **Properties** panel, set the value of **X** to **222** and **Y** to **426** and press the ENTER key; the instance is positioned in the Stage, refer to Figure P2-6.

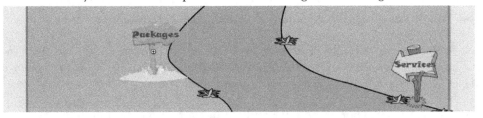

**Figure P2-6** *The packages_mc instance positioned in the Stage*

9. Lock the **packages board** layer and unlock the **inter/nat board** layer. Make sure the **inter/nat board** layer is selected in the **Timeline** panel. Next, drag the *international* movie clip symbol from the **Library** panel to the Stage; its instance is displayed in the Stage.

10. In the **Properties** panel, type **international_mc** in the **Instance name** text box. In the **Position and Size** area of the **Properties** panel, set the value of **X** to **286** and **Y** to **167** and press the ENTER key; the instance is positioned in the Stage, refer to Figure P2-7.

11. Drag the *national* movie clip symbol from the **Library** panel to the Stage. In the **Properties** panel, type **national_mc** in the **Instance name** text box. In the **Position and Size** area of the **Properties** panel, set the value of **X** to **302** and **Y** to **106** and press the ENTER key; the instance is positioned in the Stage, refer to Figure P2-7.

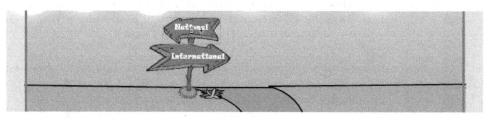

*Figure P2-7   The international_mc and national_mc instances positioned in the Stage*

12. Choose **File > Save As** from the menubar; the **Save As** dialog box is displayed. In this dialog box, browse to **Documents > Flash_Projects > prj2_flash_cc**. In the **File name** text box, type **proj2_main_end** and then choose the **Save** button; the Flash document is saved.

13. Press CTRL+ENTER to publish a SWF file. Next, close this document.

    Next, you will create *international_end* Flash document which will be loaded when the *international_mc* instance is clicked.

## Adding Text and Bitmaps to the International Document

In this section, you will add text and bitmaps to the *international_start* Flash document. You will also hyperlink the text. Finally, you will save this document with the name *international_end*.

1. Choose **File > Open** from the menubar; the **Open** dialog box is displayed.

2. Browse to **Documents > Flash_Projects > prj2_flash_cc > international_start.fla** in the dialog box. Next, choose the **Open** button from the dialog box; the Flash document is displayed, as shown in Figure P2-8.

3. In the **Timeline** panel, choose the **Lock and Unlock All Layers** button in the Timeline Header; the **clouds** and **text container** layers are locked.

4. In the **Timeline** panel, make sure the **text container** layer is selected and choose the **New Layer** button; a new layer is created above the **text container** layer. Rename it to **text** and select it.

5. Choose **Text Tool** from the **Tools** panel; the tool properties are displayed in the **Properties** panel. In the **Properties** panel, make sure the **Static Text** from the **Text type** drop-down list is selected.

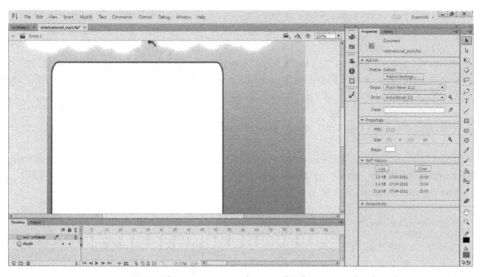

**Figure P2-8** *The international_start.fla document displayed*

6. In the **Character** area of the **Properties** panel, make sure **Arial** from the **Family** drop-down list is selected and select **Bold** from the **Style** drop-down list. Next, make sure the value of **Size** is set to **22**.

7. In the **Character** area of the **Properties** panel, choose the swatch right to **Color**; a flyout is displayed. In this flyout, enter **#3887FF** in the Hex edit box and press the ENTER key.

8. Drag the cursor in the Stage; a text box is displayed. In this text box, type the text as shown in Figure P2-9.

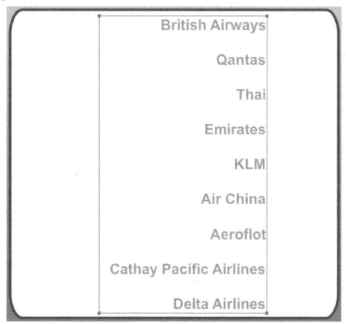

**Figure P2-9** *The text written in the text box in the text layer*

9.  Press CTRL + A; all text in the Static text box is selected. Next, in the **Paragraph** area of the **Properties** panel, choose the **Align left** button corresponding to the **Format** option.

10. Choose **Selection Tool** from the **Tools** panel and select the text box in the Stage. In the **Position and Size** area of the **Properties** panel, set the value of **X** to **39** and **Y** to **120** and press the ENTER key; the Static text box is positioned in the Stage.

11. Double-click on the text box and select **British Airways**, as shown in Figure P2-10.

12. Expand the **Options** area in the **Properties** panel and type **http://www.britishairways.com/ travel/dhome/public/en_gb** in the **Link** text box and press the ENTER key, refer to Figure P2-11; the hyperlink is added to the selected text.

*Figure P2-10  Selecting the British Airways text*

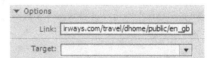

*Figure P2-11  The link in the Link text box*

13. Similarly, refer to Step 11 to add hyperlink to the other text, such as Qantas, Thai, and so on. Table P2-1 shows the text and their links.

14. In the **Timeline** panel, choose the **New Layer** button; a new layer is created. Rename it to **images** and select it.

15. In the **Library** panel, drag the *British Airways* bitmap to the Stage. In the **Position and Size** area of the **Properties** panel, set the value of **X** to **517** and **Y** to **79** and press the ENTER key; the bitmap is positioned in the Stage.

*Table P2-1  The texts and their links*

| Text | Link |
|------|------|
| Qantas | http://www.qantas.com.au/travel/airlines/home/in/en |
| Thai | http://www.thaiairways.com/ |
| Emirates | http://www.emirates.com/ |
| KLM | http://www.klm.com/ |
| Air China | http://www.airchinagroup.com/en/index.shtml |
| Aeroflot | http://www.aeroflot.com/cms/en |
| Cathay Pacific Airlines | http://www.cathaypacific.com/cpa/en_INTL/homepage |
| Delta Airlines | http://www.delta.com/ |

16. Similarly, position other bitmaps in the Stage, refer to Step 15. Table P2-2 displays the bitmaps and their positional values. Figure P2-12 displays all the bitmaps positioned in the Stage.

**Table P2-2**  *The bitmaps and their positional values*

| Bitmap | X value | Y value |
|---|---|---|
| Thai | 591 | 159 |
| Cathay Pacific | 517 | 208 |
| Qatar | 592 | 291 |
| Klm | 515 | 339 |
| Aeroflot | 571 | 436 |
| Emirates | 517 | 482 |

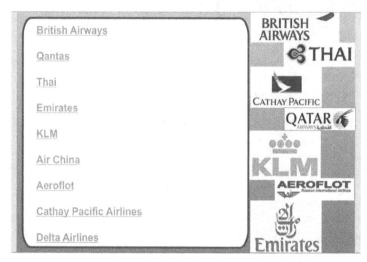

**Figure P2-12**  *The bitmaps positioned in the Stage*

17. Choose **File > Save As** from the menubar; the **Save As** dialog box is displayed. In this dialog box, browse to the location **Documents > Flash_Projects > prj2_flash_cc**. In the **File name** text box, type **international_end** and then choose the **Save** button; the Flash document is saved.

18. Press CTRL+ENTER to publish a SWF file. Next, close this document.

    Next, you will create *packages_end* Flash document which will be loaded when the *packages_mc* instance is clicked.

## Adding Button Instances to the Packages Flash Document
In this section, you will add elements to the *packages_start* Flash document.

1. Choose **File > Open** from the menubar; the **Open** dialog box is displayed.

2. Browse to **Documents > Flash_Projects > prj2_flash_cc > packages_start.fla** in the dialog box. Next, choose the **Open** button from the dialog box; the Flash document is displayed, as shown in P2-13.

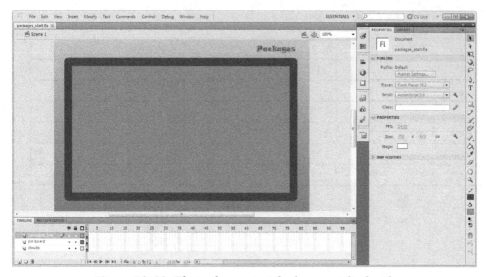

*Figure P2-13*  *The packages_start.fla document displayed*

3.  In the **Timeline** panel, choose the **Lock and Unlock All Layers** button in the Timeline Header to lock the existing layers.

4.  In the **Timeline** panel, choose the **New Layer** button to create a new layer above the **packages_text**. Rename this layer to **packages** and select it.

5.  In the **Library** panel, expand the **Buttons** folder and drag the *deal_btn* symbol to the Stage; its instance is created in the Stage and its properties are displayed in the **Properties** panel. Next, position it in the Stage using the **Selection Tool**, as shown in Figure P2-14.

6.  Similarly, position other button symbols from the **Buttons** folder in the Stage. Figure P2-15 displays all the buttons positioned in the Stage.

*Figure P2-14*  *Positioning the deal_btn instance*

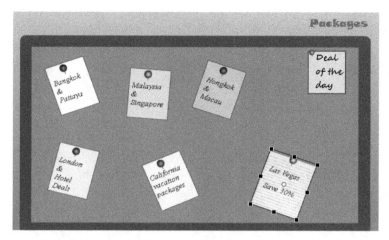

**Figure P2-15**  *Positioning other button instances*

7.  Choose **File > Save As** from the menubar; the **Save As** dialog box is displayed. In this dialog box, browse to **Documents > Flash_Projects > prj2_flash_cc**. In the **File name** text box, type **packages_end** and then choose the **Save** button; the Flash document is saved.

8.  Press CTRL+ENTER to publish a SWF file. Next, close this document.

    Next, you will create *services_end* Flash document which will be loaded when the *services_mc* instance is clicked.

## Adding Elements to the Services Flash Document

In this section, you will add elements to the *services_start* Flash document.

1.  Choose **File > Open** from the menubar; the **Open** dialog box is displayed.

2.  In this dialog box, browse to **Documents > Flash_Projects > prj2_flash_cc > services_start.fla**. Next, choose the **Open** button; the Flash document is displayed, as shown in Figure P2-16.

3.  In the **Timeline** panel, select the **buttons** layer, if it is not already selected. From the **Library** panel, drag the *hotels_btn* to the Stage; its instance is created in the Stage and the instance properties are displayed in the **Properties** panel.

4.  In the **Position and Size** area of the **Properties** panel, set the value of **X** to **99** and **Y** to **142** and the ENTER key; the instance of the *hotels_btn* button symbol is positioned in the Stage.

5.  Double-click on the *hotels_btn* in the Stage to display the symbol-editing mode, refer to Figure P2-17.

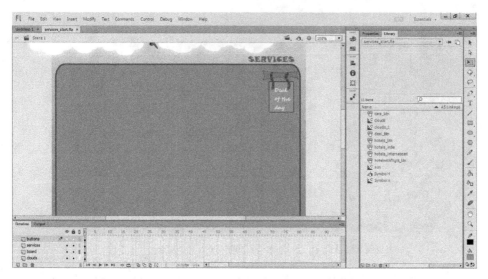

***Figure P2-16*** *The services_start.fla document displayed*

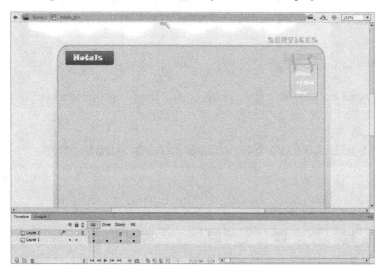

***Figure P2-17*** *The symbol-editing mode of hotels_btn displayed in the Scene area*

6.  In the **Timeline** panel, make sure **Layer 2** is selected and then choose the **New Layer** button; **Layer 3** is created.

7.  In **Layer 3**, select the **Over** frame and press the F7 key to insert a blank keyframe. Similarly, insert a blank keyframe on the **Down** and **Hit** frames, respectively.

8.  Select the **Over** frame. Next, choose **Text Tool** from the **Tools** panel; the tool properties are displayed in the **Properties** panel.

9.  In the **Character** area of the **Properties** panel, select **Snap ITC** from the **Family** drop-down list and make sure the value of **Size** is set to **22**. Next, choose the **Color** swatch; a flyout is displayed. In this flyout, enter **#00FFFF** in the Hex edit box and press the ENTER key.

10. Now, drag the cursor in the Stage to create a text box. In this text box, type the text as shown in Figure P2-18.

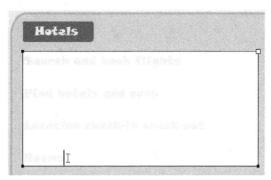

***Figure P2-18*** *The text in the **Over** frame of hotels_btn instance*

11. Choose **Selection Tool** from the **Tools** panel.

12. In the **Position and Size** area of the **Properties** panel, set the value of **X** to **-66** and **Y** to **35** to position the text box.

13. Click on **Scene 1** to return to the main Timeline.

14. In the **Timeline** panel, select the buttons layer, if it is not already selected. From the **Library** panel, drag the *hotelwithflight_btn* to the Stage; its instance is created in the Stage and its properties are displayed in the **Properties** panel.

15. In the **Position and Size** area of the **Properties** panel, set the value of **X** to **246** and **Y** to **142** and press the ENTER key; the instance of the *hotelwithflight_btn* button symbol is positioned in the Stage.

16. Double-click on the *hotelwithflight_btn* in the Stage to display the symbol-editing mode. In the **Timeline** panel, select **Layer 2** and then choose the **New Layer** button; **Layer 3** is created.

17. In **Layer 3**, select the **Over** frame and press the F7 key to insert a blank keyframe. Similarly, insert a blank keyframe on both the **Down** and **Hit** frames.

18. Select the **Over** frame. Next, choose **Text Tool** from the **Tools** panel; the tool properties are displayed in the **Properties** panel.

19. In the **Character** area of the **Properties** panel, make sure **Snap ITC** is selected in the **Family** drop-down list, and the value of **Size** is set to **22**. Next, choose the **Color** swatch; a flyout is displayed. In this flyout, make sure **#00FFFF** is entered in the Hex edit box.

20. Now, drag the cursor in the Stage to create a text box. In this text box, type the text as shown in Figure P2-19.

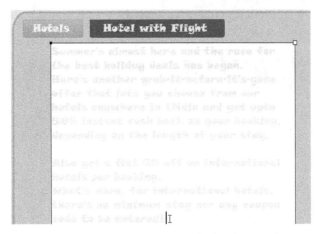

*Figure P2-19* *The text in the **Over** frame of the hotelwithflight_btn instance*

21. Choose **Selection Tool** from the **Tools** panel.

22. In the **Position and Size** area of the **Properties** panel, set the value of **X** to **-203** and **Y** to **33** to position the text box.

23. Click on **Scene 1** to return to the main Timeline.

24. From the **Library** panel, drag the *cars_btn* to the Stage; its instance is created in the Stage and its properties are displayed in the **Properties** panel.

25. In the **Position and Size** area of the **Properties** panel, set the value of **X** to **551** and **Y** to **142** and press the ENTER key; the instance of *cars_btn* button symbol is positioned in the Stage.

26. Double-click on the *cars_btn* in the Stage to invoke the symbol-editing mode. In the **Timeline** panel, make sure **Layer 2** is selected and then choose the **New Layer** button; **Layer 3** is created.

27. In **Layer 3**, select **Over** frame and press the F7 key to insert a blank keyframe. Similarly, insert a blank keyframe on both the **Down** and **Hit** frames.

28. Select the **Over** frame. Next, choose **Text Tool** from the **Tools** panel; the tool properties are displayed in the **Properties** panel.

29. In the **Character** area of the **Properties** panel, make sure **Snap ITC** from the **Family** drop-down list is selected and also, make sure the value of **Size** is set to **22**. Next, choose the **Color** swatch; a flyout is displayed. In this flyout, make sure **#00FFFF** is entered in the Hex edit box.

30. Now, drag the cursor in the Stage to create a text box. In this text box, type the text as shown in Figure P2-20.

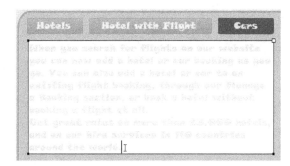

**Figure P2-20**  *The text in the* **Over** *frame of hotelwithflight_btn instance*

31. Choose **Selection Tool** from the **Tools** panel.

32. In the **Position and Size** area of the **Properties** panel, set the value of **X** to **-519** and **Y** to **36** to position the text box.

33. Click on **Scene 1** to return to the main Timeline.

34. Choose **File > Save As** from the menubar; the **Save As** dialog box is displayed. In this dialog box, browse to **Documents > Flash_Projects > prj2_flash_cc**. In the **File name** text box, type **services_end** and then choose the **Save** button; the Flash document is saved.

35. Press CTRL+ENTER to publish a SWF file. Next, close this document.

Next, you will create *national_end* Flash document which will be loaded when the *national_mc* instance is clicked.

## Adding Text and Bitmaps to the National Flash Document

In the section, you will add elements to the *national_start* Flash document.

1. Choose **File > Open** from the menubar; the **Open** dialog box is displayed.

2. In this dialog box, choose **Documents > Flash_Projects > prj2_flash_cc > national_start. fla**. Next, choose the **Open** button; the Flash document is displayed, as shown in P2-21.

3. In the **Timeline** panel, choose the **Lock and Unlock All Layers** button in the Timeline Header; all layers are locked. Unlock the **Text** layer and select it.

4. Choose **Text Tool** from the **Tools** panel; the tool properties are displayed in the **Properties** panel.

5. In the **Character** area of the **Properties** panel, select **Arial** from the **Family** drop-down list and **Bold** from the **Style** drop-down list. Next, make sure the value of **Size** is set to **22**.

6. In the **Character** area of the **Properties** panel, choose the swatch on the right to **Color**; a flyout is displayed. In this flyout, enter **#3887FF** in the Hex edit box and press the ENTER key.

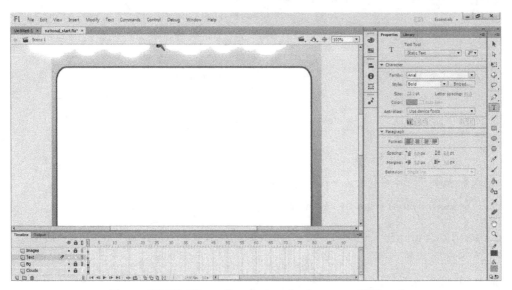

***Figure P2-21*** *The national_start.fla document displayed*

7. Drag the cursor in the Stage; a text box is displayed. In this text box, type the text, as shown in Figure P2-22.

JET AIRWAYS

INDIAN AIRLINES

AIR-INDIA

Paramount Airways

DECCAN Airlines

KINGFISHER AIRLINES

spiceJet

Indigo Airlines

***Figure P2-22*** *The text written in the **Text** layer*

8. In the **Timeline** panel, lock the **Text** layer. Next, unlock the **Images** layer and select it.

9. Drag the *images_gr* graphic symbol from the **Library** panel to the Stage; an instance of *images_gr* is created in the Stage and its properties are displayed in the **Properties** panel.

10. In the **Position and Size** area of the **Properties** panel, set the value of **X** to **573** and **Y** to **313** and press the ENTER key; the instance is positioned in the Stage, refer to Figure P2-23.

11. Choose **File > Save As** from the menubar; the **Save As** dialog box is displayed. In this dialog box, browse to **Documents > Flash_Projects > prj2_flash_cc**. In the **File name** text box, type **national_end** and then choose the **Save** button; the Flash document is saved.

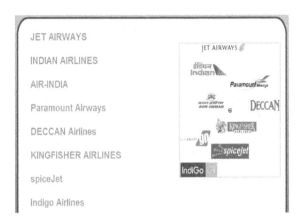

***Figure P2-23***  *The images_gr instance positioned in the Stage*

12. Press CTRL+ENTER to publish a SWF file. Next, close this document.

## Loading the External SWF Files

In this section, you will add the ActionScript code to the proj2_main_end Flash document to load four external SWF files using the movie clip instances.

1. Choose **File > Open** from the menubar; the **Open** dialog box is displayed.

2. In this dialog box, browse to **Documents > Flash_Projects > prj2_flash_cc > proj2_main_end.fla**. Next, choose the **Open** button from the dialog box; the Flash document is displayed.

3. In the **Timeline** panel, select the **outline** layer and then choose the **New Layer** button; a new layer is created. Rename the new layer to **actions**.

4. Select frame **1** in the **actions** layer and press the F9 key; the **Actions** panel is displayed. In this panel, type the following script:

```
var magLoader:Loader=new Loader ();
services_mc.addEventListener(MouseEvent.CLICK, page1);
function page1(myevent:MouseEvent):void{
var myURL:URLRequest=new URLRequest("services_end.swf")
magLoader.load(myURL);
addChild(magLoader);
}
packages_mc.addEventListener(MouseEvent.CLICK, page2);
function page2(myevent:MouseEvent):void{
var myURL:URLRequest=new URLRequest("packages_end.swf")
magLoader.load(myURL);
addChild(magLoader);
}
national_mc.addEventListener(MouseEvent.CLICK, page3);
```

```
function page3(myevent:MouseEvent):void{
var myURL:URLRequest=new URLRequest("national_end.swf")
magLoader.load(myURL);
addChild(magLoader);
}
international_mc.addEventListener(MouseEvent.CLICK, page4);
function page4(myevent:MouseEvent):void{
var myURL:URLRequest=new URLRequest("international_end.swf")
magLoader.load(myURL);
addChild(magLoader);
}
magLoader.addEventListener(MouseEvent.CLICK, removecontent);
function removecontent(myevent:MouseEvent):void {
removeChild(magLoader);
services_mc.gotoAndPlay(1);
packages_mc.gotoAndPlay(1);
national_mc.gotoAndPlay(1);
international_mc.gotoAndPlay(1);
}
```

5.   Press CTRL+S to save the script.

6.   Press CTRL+ENTER; the preview window is displayed. In this window, click on any movie clip instance to play the corresponding SWF file.

# Index

# Other Publications by CADCIM Technologies

The following is the list of some of the publications by CADCIM Technologies. Please visit www.cadcim.com for the complete listing.

## Autodesk 3ds Max Design Textbooks
- Autodesk 3ds Max Design 2014: A Tutorial Approach
- Autodesk 3ds Max Design 2013: A Tutorial Approach
- Autodesk 3ds Max Design 2012: A Tutorial Approach

## Autodesk 3ds Max Textbooks
- Autodesk 3ds Max 2014: A Comprehensive Guide
- Autodesk 3ds Max 2013: A Comprehensive Guide
- Autodesk 3ds Max 2012: A Comprehensive Guide

## Maya Textbooks
- Autodesk Maya 2014: A Comprehensive Guide
- Autodesk Maya 2013: A Comprehensive Guide
- Autodesk Maya 2012: A Comprehensive Guide

## Fusion Textbook
- The eyeon Fusion 6.3: A Tutorial Approach

## Flash Textbook
- Adobe Flash Professional CS6: A Tutorial Approach

## Premiere Textbook
- Adobe Premiere Professional CS6: A Tutorial Approach

## CINEMA 4D Textbooks
- MAXON CINEMA 4D Studio R15: A Tutorial Approach
- MAXON CINEMA 4D Studio R14: A Tutorial Approach

## ZBrush Textbook
- Pixologic ZBrush 4R6: A Comprehensive Guide

## NukeX Textbook
- The Foundry NukeX 7 for Compositors

## AutoCAD Textbook
- AutoCAD 2014: A Problem Solving Approach

## SolidWorks Textbooks
- SolidWorks 2014 for Designers
- SolidWorks 2014: A Tutorial Approach

## Autodesk Inventor Textbooks
• Autodesk Inventor 2014 for Designers
• Autodesk Inventor 2013 for Designers

## Solid Edge Textbooks
• Solid Edge ST6 for Designers
• Solid Edge ST5 for Designers

## NX Textbooks
• NX 8.5 for Designers
• NX 8 for Designers

## EdgeCAM Textbooks
• EdgeCAM 11.0 for Manufacturers
• EdgeCAM 10.0 for Manufacturers

## CATIA Textbooks
• CATIA V5-6R2013 for Designers
• CATIA V5-6R2012 for Designers

## Pro/ENGINEER / Creo Parametric Textbooks
• Creo Parametric 2.0 for Designers
• Creo Parametric 1.0 for Designers
• Pro/ENGINEER Wildfire 5.0 for Designers

## Creo Direct Textbook
• Creo Direct 2.0 and Beyond for Designers

## Autodesk Alias Textbook
• Learning Autodesk Alias Design 2012

## ANSYS Textbooks
• ANSYS Workbench 14.0: A Tutorial Approach
• ANSYS 11.0 for Designers

## Customizing AutoCAD Textbook
• Customizing AutoCAD 2013

## AutoCAD LT Textbooks
• AutoCAD LT 2014 for Designers
• AutoCAD LT 2013 for Designers

## AutoCAD Plant 3D Textbook
• AutoCAD Plant 3D 2014 for Designers

## AutoCAD Electrical Textbooks
- AutoCAD Electrical 2014 for Electrical Control Designers
- AutoCAD Electrical 2013 for Electrical Control Designers

## Autodesk Revit Architecture Textbooks
- Autodesk Revit Architecture 2014 for Architects and Designers
- Autodesk Revit Architecture 2013 for Architects and Designers

## Autodesk Revit Structure Textbooks
- Exploring Autodesk Revit Structure 2014
- Exploring Autodesk Revit Structure 2013

## AutoCAD Civil 3D Textbooks
- Exploring AutoCAD Civil 3D 2014 for Engineers
- Exploring AutoCAD Civil 3D 2013 for Engineers

## AutoCAD Map 3D Textbooks
- Exploring AutoCAD Map 3D 2014
- Exploring AutoCAD Map 3D 2013

## Paper Craft Book
- Constructing 3-Dimensional Models: A Paper-Craft Workbook

## Computer Programming Textbooks
- Learning Oracle 11g
- Learning ASP.NET AJAX
- Learning Java Programming
- Learning Visual Basic.NET 2008
- Learning C++ Programming Concepts
- Learning VB.NET Programming Concepts

## AutoCAD Textbooks Authored by Prof. Sham Tickoo and Published by Autodesk Press

- AutoCAD: A Problem-Solving Approach: 2013 and Beyond
- AutoCAD 2012: A Problem-Solving Approach

## Textbooks Authored by CADCIM Technologies and Published by Other Publishers

## 3D Studio MAX and VIZ Textbooks
- Learning 3DS Max: A Tutorial Approach, Release 4
  Goodheart-Wilcox Publishers (USA)
- Learning 3D Studio VIZ: A Tutorial Approach
  Goodheart-Wilcox Publishers (USA)

## CADCIM Technologies Textbooks Translated in Other Languages

### SolidWorks Textbooks
- SolidWorks 2008 for Designers (Serbian Edition)
  Mikro Knjiga Publishing Company, Serbia
- SolidWorks 2006 for Designers (Russian Edition)
  Piter Publishing Press, Russia

### NX Textbook
- NX 6 for Designers (Korean Edition)
  Onsolutions, South Korea

### Pro/ENGINEER Textbook
- Pro/ENGINEER Wildfire 4.0 for Designers (Korean Edition)
  HongReung Science Publishing Company, South Korea

### Autodesk 3ds Max Textbook
- 3ds Max 2008: A Comprehensive Guide (Serbian Edition)
  Mikro Knjiga Publishing Company, Serbia

### AutoCAD Textbooks
- AutoCAD 2006 (Russian Edition)
  Piter Publishing Press, Russia
- AutoCAD 2005 (Russian Edition)
  Piter Publishing Press, Russia
- AutoCAD 2000 Fondamenti (Italian Edition)

### Coming Soon from CADCIM Technologies
- Adobe Premiere Pro CC: A Tutorial Approach
- NX 9.0 for Designers
- Autodesk Simulation Mechanical 2014 for Designers
- NX Nastran 9.0 for Designers
- Autodesk Revit MEP 2015: A Tutorial Approach
- AutoCAD 2015: A Problem Solving Approach
- Autodesk Inventor 2015 for Designers
- Exploring AutoCAD Civil 3D 2015 for Engineers
- Exploring Autodesk Navisworks 2015
- Autodesk Revit Architecture 2015 for Architects and Designers

### Online Training Program Offered by CADCIM Technologies
CADCIM Technologies provides effective and affordable virtual online training on various software packages including computer programming languages, Computer Aided Design and Manufacturing (CAD/CAM), animation, architecture, and GIS. The training will be delivered 'live' via Internet at any time, any place, and at any pace to individuals as well as the students of colleges, universities, and CAD/CAM training centers. For more information, please visit the following link: *http://www.cadcim.com*

www.ingramcontent.com/pod-product-compliance
Lightning Source LLC
LaVergne TN
LVHW062303060326
832902LV00013B/2025